LIVE
& PROSPER.

LIVE LONG & PROSPER!

Invest in Your Happiness, Health, and Wealth for Retirement and Beyond

STEVE VERNON

John Wiley & Sons, Inc.

Published by John Wiley & Sons, Inc., Hoboken, New Jersey.
Published simultaneously in Canada.

For general information on our other products and services, or technical support, please contact our Customer Care Department within the United States at 800-762-2974, outside the United States at 317-572-3993 or fax 317-572-4002.

Wiley also publishes its books in a variety of electronic formats. Some content that appears in print may not be available in electronic books.

For more information about Wiley products, visit our web site at www.wiley.com.

Library of Congress Cataloging-in-Publication Data:
Vernon, Steven G., 1953-
    Live long and prosper! : invest in your happiness, health, and wealth for retirement and beyond / Steven Vernon.
        p. cm.
Includes index.
    ISBN 0-471-68344-2 (pbk.)
    1. Retirement—United States—Planning.   I. Title.
HQ1063.2.U6V47 2005
646.7'9—dc22   2004022894

Printed in the United States of America.

10 9 8 7 6 5 4 3 2 1

To all my friends, colleagues, and family who helped me with this book. Your support was essential, and confirms for the thousandth time that we are all one.

And to those of us who spend a good part of rest-of-life *using our skills, life experience, and passion to help make this Earth a better place.*

CONTENTS

ACKNOWLEDGMENTS

Many people helped tremendously with this book.

First, I'd like to thank Melinda Grubbauer and David Hoak, who read the drafts of the entire book, spent countless hours discussing the topics with me, and served as my muses and supporters throughout the project.

Marie Curran was tireless and patient with lots of logistical and administrative support.

Linda Eckholm, Jim Isbell, and Ron Littler also read most of the book drafts and provided great comments and support.

I have a great marketing and publicity team from Watson Wyatt to help get out the message—Gretchen Broderson, Ed Emerman, David Popper, and Katherine Shain.

Many people reviewed parts of the book, provided quality control on certain aspects, pointed me to key research, or spent time discussing these topics and providing ideas and inspiration. Here they are, in alphabetical order: Sue and Roger Bell, Gretchen Broderson, Kyle Brown, Joe D'Anna, Cary Franklin, David Friend, Gary Gausman, Carl Hess, Karen Holt, David and Laleh Lourie, Gail McKee, Gail Meyers, Janemarie Mulvey, Alicia Munnell, Michael Orszag, Neil Ronco, Syl Schieber, Patti Smith, Ed Spangler, Martha Spano, John Steinbrunner, Marilyn Venegas, and Arlene Weissman.

Adam Levine did a wonderful job preparing the asset/liability models in Chapter 10. Wayne Pages prepared the graphs in

Chapter 11. Amy Zahler helped with the Social Security calculations in Chapter 14. I'm grateful to Charlie Commander for donating his creative "Retiree Savings Menu" in Chapter 20, and "You Bet Your Life" quiz in Chapter 15. Chris Wisdom generated various actuarial factors that appear in Chapter 19.

Erica Curtis and Renee John of Watson Wyatt's library tracked down many research articles for me.

I'd like to acknowledge the hundreds of Watson Wyatt associates who sent me e-mails for case studies on health and working during their later years, and sent me their good wishes and support.

I'd like to thank Eric Lofgren, Gene Wickes, and Larry DiFiore, who allowed me the time from my day job to write.

Sandra Pope made a crucial suggestion to help me find my voice for this book.

I've had the benefit of hanging around great examples of successful agers—friends and family who continue to be active in their *rest-of-life*. This includes my father who pole-vaulted and skied until 80, my mother who has been the loving matriarch of the family and also skied late in life, and my Aunt Mimi Vernon who continues to amaze our family with her volunteer work and words of wisdom.

And last but not least, I'd like to thank my editor at John Wiley & Sons, Debra Englander, for publishing the book and providing key guidance along the way. I can't imagine a more supportive and collaborative editor. She also assembled a great team—Greg Friedman, assistant editor; Kim Craven, marketing; and Todd Tedesco, production.

LIVE LONG
& PROSPER!

INTRODUCTION

"Hey, Steve—How much is *enough*? How much money do I need to retire?"

I frequently get asked this question, once word gets out at parties, family gatherings, and social occasions that I am a consulting actuary[1] who works with retirement plans. Finally, this actuary is the life of the party!

How much is enough to retire comfortably and not run out of money in one's later years?

During my thirties, my answer was:

"I dunno—I've been wondering about that myself."

I jeopardized my status as the life of the party.

In my forties, I started answering in actuarial mumbo jumbo, talking about life expectancies, Social Security, anticipated retirement ages, and returns on various classes of investments. I

---

[1]Actuaries are professionals who measure the risks of important but unpredictable life events—risks such as death, serious illness, accidents, and outliving your money during retirement (living too long is considered a risk!). We design financial programs to mitigate these risks, such as life insurance, medical insurance, pension plans, and 401(k) plans. As part of our training, we study the mathematical chances of these life events happening, along with the types of investments and financial products and services that will protect individuals from the adverse consequences of these events. We've been called the "architects of financial security."

1

received blank stares, and lost what was left of my party animal status.

Now that I'm in my third quarter of life, I've been giving this question some serious thought. I've come to realize that my old ways of thinking about retirement are out of touch with the new realities of working and living in our later years. We baby boomers need a new model of living the rest of our lives—a model for the twenty-first century. This book shares what I've learned so far. I don't have all the answers, but I've developed some interesting and effective ways of thinking about our later years.

In the 1800s, when people worked until they died, working seemed like the best alternative. Actually, the model of retirement from the nineteenth century was quite simple:

Retirement = Death

In the 1900s, a new model emerged that was just as simple:

Retirement = Not working

In the twenty-first century, we have options that our ancestors didn't have. We will have a long period of life after our children are gone, and after we have devoted substantial energy to developing our careers. We could easily live into our late eighties, nineties, or even to 100—and be vigorous, healthy, and productive for most of these years. To be happy and healthy for such a long period, we will need fairly robust reasons for living. We should think about these reasons *before* asking the "how much is enough?" question.

As a result, my new response to the "How much is enough?" question is a challenge:

Enough for what?

To continue leading our current lives? Or enough for a life that we might find more healthy, meaningful, and fulfilling?

This is a different way to think about retirement. Traditional retirement strategies talk about duplicating the same standard of living we had while we were working.

Now I ask these big questions:

- What do we really want to do?

- What do we value?

- What has meaning for us?

- What is really interesting?

- Where would we like to live?

- Who do we want to be with?

- Who do we want to be?

I call these the WAI/WSID questions—"Who am I/what should I do?"

The WAI/WSID questions perplex many people. They've baffled me! Often the responses are something like this:

- "I haven't thought very much about it until now. I've just worked and raised a family."

- "I've thought about it, but nothing grabs my imagination."

- "Travel."

- "Do more golf, sewing, bridge, exercise, jogging, seeing friends and family, and so on."

- "Anything but work."

This last response hits the spot for many people.

Getting to the Bottom of Things

We want to be happier, we want to find meaning in our lives, and we've become tired of working. There are a variety of good reasons.

- We're bored with our work.

- We're physically worn out.

- We can't/don't want to keep up with the quickening pace of change in our jobs.

- We want more time to pursue our interests.

- We want to live a more meaningful life.

In short, we spend way too much time working much too hard at a job we're bored with, we're physically and mentally worn out, and retirement is the all-powerful cure that will make our life wonderfully happy!

Unfortunately, stopping work won't necessarily make us happy. Not being unhappy does not equal being happy. If I've been beating my head against a wall for 20 years and it hurts, when I stop, I feel good. *Real good.* For a while. Then, when the memory of the pain starts to fade, I ask myself:

"Is this all there is to life? Not beating my head against a wall?"

The mistake most of us are making is that we are equating retirement with happiness. So my intent is to be more conscious about what will really make me happy for the rest of my life.

Now I'm asking myself (and others who ask me the "enough" question) to spend some time thinking about the WAI/WSID questions.

Some people actually have answers, because they've been thinking and fantasizing about it for years. If that's true for you, great! Let's develop a plan to support this lifestyle.

Most of us don't have answers. Maybe we've never asked ourselves the WAI/WSID questions. Or maybe we've been asking the right questions, but haven't devised the answers. If that's you, let's go looking for the answers, and let's develop a plan to support this quest.

After years of thinking about it, I finally came to the conclusion that if I start by talking about money, I have it backwards.

We need to think about first the WAI/WSID questions, then health, and finally wealth—in that order! And we need to integrate them for an effective life plan.

Why integrate?

- Well, if I'm not living a meaningful, healthy life in my later years, then saving all that money during my working life was a waste.

- Not having enough money usually results in unhappiness, but if I really think about what will provide meaning in my life, enough might be less than I think. We'll come back to this line of thinking in a few chapters.

- People who are happy and have purpose in life are generally healthier than grumpy old men and women.

- If I'm not healthy, I'll spend my hard-earned savings on health care, and then I'll be broke and unhappy. I may not be well enough to do the things that provide meaning to me, or to work if I need the money.

- People who are flat broke are generally less healthy than those who have enough money.

- And so it goes.

So we need to make sure we're doing okay with our happiness, health, and wealth.

Why the emphasis on "enough"? It is my belief that we Americans have trouble distinguishing between enough and what we think we need. We end up acquiring more money and stuff than what is really necessary for a meaningful, happy life. This imbalance is the source of lots of problems, both for our own individual lives and collectively for the country as well.

So now I want to share my story with you—my search to figure out what I want to do with the rest of my life, and the plan I'm putting in place for myself. Like I said, I haven't got all the answers. But I've made enough progress to share my thoughts and process with you. You'll have plenty to think about, and you should be off to a good start with planning for the rest of your life.

My Story

I've been thinking about retirement since I was 22 years old. I was fresh out of college, and I had begun toiling in the cubicles as an actuarial analyst in the retirement practice of Coopers & Lybrand (now part of the accounting giant Pricewaterhouse Coopers).

Back then, retirement was an abstract concept for me. However, as my career progressed in my thirties, I became exposed to the people behind these abstractions. I began leading employee meetings to explain their retirement programs. I saw their struggles to understand a complex subject, but I also witnessed firsthand how emotional people became about retirement—particularly if they perceived a threat to it. It was almost as if they equated retirement to going to heaven, while they equated working in their later years to being damned to hell! As an actuary, I expressed this phenomenon mathematically:

$$\text{Retirement} = \text{Heaven} = \text{Happy!}$$

$$\text{Working forever} = \text{Burning in hell forever} = \text{Pretty damn mad!}$$

We'll return to these theories in a little bit.

Right after college graduation, I jumped on board life's train of responsibility. I had a mortgage at age 24, children at age 28. I studied hard to pass the actuarial exams, and by age 27, I had all the necessary actuarial pedigrees. During my thirties and forties, I raised a family, taking pride in being a good dad, and progressed nicely in my career.

I didn't give much thought to the WAI/WSID questions, because I thought the answers were to raise a family and succeed in my career. And actually, those were pretty good answers for that stage of my life, although they weren't complete. With the benefit of hindsight, I paid a price for not paying attention to all the WAI/WSID questions, but I have absolutely no regrets. I have memories and experiences that I will treasure all my life.

Somewhere in my mid-forties, the excitement of building a career started to wear thin. Repetition, boredom, the too-frequent absurdities of busyness in business, lack of time to do what really interested me, and mind-numbing traffic during rush hour—all took their toll.

My kids grew up and didn't place as many demands on my time (but demands on my wallet increased exponentially!). While they were in the house, their care and nurture were a primary source of meaning and purpose in my life. But now that they're gone, I've become aware of the need to fill this void—to again have important sources of meaning and purpose. So, the WAI/WSID questions began popping up. At first they were uncomfortable, so in good manly fashion I stuffed them away where they couldn't bother me. After all, Clint Eastwood would never have worried about the WAI/WSID questions! But as time went by, they kept getting in my face, refusing to go away.

I became increasingly aware of the deferred life I was leading. Interesting things were put off indefinitely into the future. So were the things that I should do to take care of myself, for both my physical and my emotional health. "I'll do that when I get some free time." I began to think that free time would not come until I retired.

Now, at age 50, retirement seems as remote as it did at age 22, due to the stock market collapse a few years ago, rising medical costs, and the decline of defined benefit and retiree medical plans that were formerly prevalent at large and medium-sized employers. But I still hunger for those golden years, whatever that means. And I know that if I continue working as I have since age 22, I'll die inside—a slow death like the proverbial frog in a boiling pot.

Do elements of this story sound familiar to you? I think I'm not alone!

How My Thinking Has Evolved

Now I'm a vice president with the influential human resources consulting firm, Watson Wyatt Worldwide. For nearly 30 years, I've helped large and medium-sized employers design, finance, administer, and communicate their retirement programs. During this period, I've seen a lot of changes—the invention of the 401(k) plan, widespread termination or reduction of defined benefit and retiree medical plans in the 1980s due to excessive regulation and increasing costs, the run-up of the stock market in the 1990s with resulting large surpluses in pension plans, and the swift deterioration of the financial strength of remaining plans in the early part of this century due to the severe stock market decline. As I write this, once again defined benefit and retiree medical plans are under attack, mainly because beleaguered employers can no longer afford them. And right now, I'm in the thick of helping my clients cope with this new tidal wave of events.

Throughout this period, I never stopped thinking about my own retirement. My book *Don't Work Forever! Simple Steps Baby Boomers Must Take to Ever Retire* (John Wiley & Sons, 1995) focused on the action steps we should take while we are working, so that eventually we'll have enough assets to retire.

I traveled around the country in 1995, 1996, and 1997 promoting *Don't Work Forever!*, appearing on TV and radio, in newspapers and magazines. I helped feed the popular belief that if you don't have a million bucks, you'll be eating dog food in your later years. The basic advice was work hard, save a lot, and invest in stocks "for the long run." The underlying premise was that not being able to retire was a fate worse than death. *Don't Work Forever!* had a good run, but now it's out of print (you can still find it at some used bookstores and Internet booksellers).

I gave a presentation on *Don't Work Forever!* to more than 150 different audiences around the country. I would always engage the audience right away by asking them the age at which they wanted to retire. The answers were always the same. It didn't matter where I was or the type of group I was addressing. Most people would say they would like to retire in their late fifties, and certainly no later than age 62, and many would answer, "Now!" I would conclude my opening remarks by saying, "There is no way this will happen, given how much people are saving. And when we all wake up to this, there will be millions and millions of grumpy old men and women!"

In some ways, this book takes the thinking in *Don't Work Forever!* to the next logical step. Now that I've followed my own advice and accumulated some assets, what next? Can I retire?

However, in some very important ways, my thinking has evolved. The main reason is that many of us aren't saving nearly enough. Many of us simply don't have the financial resources to retire— now, in 5 years, in 10 years, or even in 15 or 20 years.

With the possibility of living to our eighties, nineties, or beyond, full-time retirement in our fifties or sixties might not make sense for a number of reasons—emotionally, physically, and financially.

I have come to believe that the retirement industry creates a lot of unnecessary anxiety about saving for retirement. They tell us that retirement is the normal way to complete life, and that life is cheating us if we can't retire (and the earlier the better). Well-meaning experts tell us that we need to deny ourselves now and save every penny for retirement. If you don't do this, you get what you deserve (which means working during your later years, equivalent to "burning in hell").

Now, don't get me wrong. I think saving for retirement is an absolute necessity, and I will discuss it in more detail. However, there's an appropriate balance, and if we get too anxious about saving for retirement, we might eat dog food *before* retirement, just so we won't be eating dog food *after* retirement!

So here I'll share my own analyses, conclusions, and action steps to make the best of the rest of my life. I hope you will be helped by the story of an actuary who has spent a lot of time analyzing and thinking about retirement and the rest of life. My course of action will not be for everybody. However, I'm confident that the messages will connect with many of you, and I'm sure you will learn something along the way that will help you on your own path.

I plan to do well in the most important aspects of my life—financial, health, and happiness—without being so obsessive about perfection that I don't enjoy life. I also believe that half the battle is avoiding making big mistakes. In this book, I focus on simple, effective strategies that should work for most of us, for the things that we should really pay attention to. Also, I'll cover how to avoid the big mistakes that can set us back. I developed these strategies while trying to figure it out for myself; I share what I am doing to finance and support the life I want—for the rest of my life! I cover some variations—what I would do if my circumstances were different, and these circumstances are common.

However, I don't stop with providing just information, formulas, and strategies—these can take us only so far. Along the way, I also address the human and emotional side to making important decisions and changes in our lives.

As I mentioned before, I consult to large companies, helping them design, finance, administer, and communicate their retirement programs. Over the years, my clients have included Agilent, Charles Schwab, ChevronTexaco, Dole Food Company, Home Savings of America, Hughes Electronics, Lockheed Martin, City of Los Angeles, Northrop Grumman, Phillips Petroleum (now ConocoPhillips), RAND Corporation, Teledyne Technologies, and Times Mirror (publisher of the *Los Angeles Times*, now part of Tribune Company). Along the way, I've learned a lot about how retirement plans work, and how to make them work for people like us. And I've talked with lots of people about what retirement represents to us as individuals and for society.

There are many pieces to this puzzle that I've put together. My employer, Watson Wyatt Worldwide, is known for doing cutting-edge research on retirement issues and trends. I've also read other research on the later years in life, including the subjects of happiness, health, longevity, and wealth. I talked with many successful agers who made important changes in their lives, and along the way I will share their stories. For many years, I've dabbled and experimented in various health and transformative practices; my interest in these took off as the research for this book convinced me of their vital importance for enjoyment of our later years. This research, knowledge, and experience came together to form a picture of the rest of my life—and it's a pretty good picture! While the corroborating research and analyses appeal to the logical part of my brain, the picture feels right and makes intuitive sense as well.

Along the way, I repeatedly learned that nothing in life is certain. However, I'm confident that I'm doing all I can to survive this uncertainty and thrive—to make the best of the rest of my life. And I'm ready to share my insights and plans with you.

To sum up, this book discusses our finances in the context of the WAI/WSID questions and our health. Here we will *begin* exploring these issues, but by no means will we *finish* our inquiry in this book. I strongly encourage you to spend more time investigating your WAI/WSID issues, your health, and your wealth. Since we are talking about the rest of our lives, *a lot is at stake!* Along the way, I'll refer you to excellent resources that helped me with my inquiry.

Here Are the Main Messages

What people really want is to live the remainder of their lives with meaning, purpose, health, and happiness. We want things to go well for our loved ones, ourselves, and the world.

I believe that many middle-aged Americans have retirement as an important life's goal, but what they really want is a fulfilling and happy life. So, let's not wait for retirement to make this happen, particularly if we can't afford to retire for many years. We don't need to live deferred lives anymore. We shouldn't live lives that aren't sustainable indefinitely. If we're not fulfilled and happy, we shouldn't put up with it because we think that someday we will retire and that will make everything better.

The way we interact with the workplace has disconnected us in many ways from our spouses, family, friends, passions, and interests. What we really want is to *reconnect* with all that makes us human. Reconnect with taking care of ourselves, physically and emotionally. Reconnect with the land and the natural world. Reconnect with our curiosity and sense of adventure. Reconnect with our spirit. And we don't necessarily need full-time retirement to do this!

Many people make the mistake of retiring with insufficient assets, because they just can't wait any longer to reach for these goals. They feel something is missing in their lives. Unfortunately, a few years later they're broke and back at work. This book helps us determine realistically if we have the substantial financial resources that it takes to retire full-time.

But if we don't have a million bucks, no need for despair. Retiring full-time isn't the only way to enhance our lives, and in fact may not be the best way. We can restructure our work, and perhaps work a little less. We can improve our working situation if necessary, and begin reconnecting now. In fact, as you'll see in this book, I believe that *some* work may actually help achieve that meaningful, purposeful life *and* keep us in sound shape financially. We can build lives that are sustainable indefinitely. Someday we will retire full-time, but we'll have happier, healthier, and more meaningful lives in the meantime.

To reach these goals, I think we need to replace the word *retirement* with a new concept. *Retirement* has some connotions that are no longer healthy. The word gives images of retiring from life itself, into our final state before we die. The implication is that personal growth ends, and we are phasing down our life. This may sound harsh, but my observation is that for many people, retirement means "waiting to die." I'd rather replace the word *retirement* with the phrase *rest-of-life*. I'm planning for *rest-of-life*, not retirement. It may be more words, but it's the same number of syllables, so it's just as easy to think and say.

I advocate that we consciously *plan* for the many years that we have ahead of us. And our planning needs to go beyond finances to our health and happiness as well. We should continue to have personal growth and experiences, and not merely exist in some arrested state. Don't retreat from the world; instead, continue to remain actively engaged in life.

Actuaries constantly measure the mathematical chances of many types of life events, so here's one more actuarial secret. If we want to live a rich, full life, we will greatly increase the odds of this happening if we set our intent, plan for it, and then be open to learning from life's twists and turns. Picture a positive future for ourselves, and we'll find a way to get there.

We've all heard about the haves and the have-nots. As the next 50 years unfold, we'll see that these groups will mostly coincide with the "dids" and the "did-nots." Those who *did* prepare for a long, vital life will most likely *have* it!

What's Inside?

We'll build a new model for living our later years—a model for the twenty-first century, which we will compare and contrast with the old twentieth-century model. This book gives you an overall plan, a blueprint, to help you develop a model for living the rest of your life that might work best for you. However, you need to do your own work to make it happen for you, so I'll refer you to additional resources that have helped me. I've tried to strike a balance between giving you guidelines and insights to help you develop your own *rest-of-life* plan, and being prescriptive with specific action steps.

This book has four sections.

1. *Perspectives for* Rest-of-Life. The chapters in this section give us the information and insights to help us understand the underlying issues, which in turn will help us build realistic financial and lifestyle strategies. What should we do with the rest of our lives, and how does this vision integrate with our financial resources?

2. *Healthy Interest.* What can we do now to reduce the chances that we will have illnesses and accidents in our later years that could devastate us, both financially and emotionally? And if we do have such illnesses, how do we protect our-

selves financially? We'll discuss the idea that investments in our health are just as valuable as our investments in stocks and bonds.

3. *Money Matters.* How much should we withdraw from our 401(k) accounts and other investments, so that we don't run out of money before we die? How much should we save now so that eventually we can retire full-time? How should we invest these accounts? Do we need to work to supplement our income from investments, pensions, and Social Security? If yes, what should we look for? In short, how should we manage our time, income, and expenses in our later years to support a life that gives us meaning and happiness?

4. *Putting It All Together.* It's one thing to develop our lifestyle and financial plan, but it's another to actually put it into action. This might require making important changes in our lives, which are hard to make. Here we discuss how to make these important changes. We finish with a summary of the new model for living and working in the twenty-first century.

I need to make a confession. I got so excited about exploring how to invest in my *rest-of-life* that I got carried away. The first manuscript draft that I submitted to Wiley was way too long—I had too much good stuff. To make this book a reasonable length, we had to cut a lot of material. I struggled with choosing what to remove until I was inspired by the concept of "director's cuts" at the back of DVDs. So, I've posted additional material on my web site, www.restoflife.com.

I've kept in this book most of the new insights and special perspectives that I've gained. I moved to the web site some background and educational information on investing, 401(k) plans, Medicare, and a few other subjects. This information changes due to unfolding events and new legislation, so I can maintain up-to-date information on my web site.

Also, with some subjects I provide an overview in this book, while longer versions of these chapters are on the web site. I note these as I go.

One fascinating aspect of my quest was to talk with people who made important changes in their lives. Their stories gave me inspiration and confirmed many of the practices I recommend in this book. These accounts couldn't fit into this book, so I put them on the web site as well.

Finally, I continue to explore and learn about *rest-of-life* issues, and the world constantly changes. So, I'll post additional insights and updates as I go on my journey.

If you like what you read here and want more, visit the web site sometime!

Let's give it a go!

PERSPECTIVES FOR *REST-OF-LIFE*

Most excellent man, are you who are a citizen of Athens, the greatest of cities and the most famous for wisdom and power, not ashamed to care for the acquisition of wealth and for reputation and honor, when you neither care nor take thought for wisdom and truth and the perfection of your soul?

—Socrates

When writing this book, one thing led to another. Initially, I focused on the financial issues. How can I make my 401(k) balances last the rest of my life? How do I pay for medical expenses? I then started learning about how to take care of my physical health. This led me to the realization that if I did this, most likely I'd live a long time, increasing the need for financial resources that I can't outlive. As a result, I realized that I would need to work much longer than I previously had planned. This made me unhappy, but I remembered from my research on health that our emotional state affects our physical health. My unhappiness about working longer would affect my physical health, which would affect my financial health, and so on. Eventually, I came to the realization that I need to get all three things right—happiness, health, *and* wealth.

Some of you may want to get to the financial stuff right away. If you just can't wait to read about asset allocation, where to invest your money, Social Security, 401(k) plans, how much to save for a comfortable retirement, how much is enough, and so on, then there's nothing wrong with skipping ahead to Section III and reading it all the way through. In particular, Chapters 19 and 20 will be eye-openers for many people. They illustrate the significant financial resources that are necessary for a full-time retirement. They demonstrate why I say that many of us will need to work longer than we thought, and why we might want to consider phased retirement as an alternative future lifestyle that could be more feasible from a financial perspective. I'm confident that once you get through Chapters 19 and 20, you'll want to come back to this section of the book.

My goal is to show how it all hangs together—our happiness, health, and wealth. You can come to this realization in the order that best works for you. I wanted to start with happiness, so I set off on a quest to find what provides happiness and meaning during retirement.

I started reviewing the history of retirement. I quickly came to the perspective that retirement is a recent phenomenon in America, and is rare in other parts of the world. But countries with lots of retirees, like the United States, don't report any more happiness than countries with few retirees. This led me to realize that I should focus on happiness with the *rest-of-life*, not happiness with retirement.

So first we'll take a look at the history of retirement. Then we'll see how long we might live, which gives us motivation to consciously plan for a healthy, happy *rest-of-life* that most likely will last for 30 or 40 more years from our fifties and sixties, maybe even longer! Then we'll delve into research on happiness, both at work and with life in general. I was fascinated by this research, and I think you will be, too.

Before I went on this quest, all I had was *hope* that retirement would make my life better. I now realize that this vague hope is not a good strategy for making the best of the rest of my life. I need to be conscious of what I want for my *rest-of-life*, and be aware of the forces at play around me that might present obstacles. Now I feel much more confident in moving ahead with financial and health matters, being aware of the possible challenges, and having a plan that has a better chance of succeeding for happiness, health, *and* wealth.

I hope these insights give you the same confidence.

Trends—The Past and Future of Retirement

History is a vast early warning system.

—Norman Cousins

My clients pay me to keep track of economic, demographic, and political trends that affect their retirement programs. Some forward-thinking clients act in anticipation of these trends, while other clients react to them. Either way, these trends eventually make their way into the design of retirement programs, which in turn affects the retirement benefits that we will ultimately receive. As a result, our *rest-of-life* is significantly affected by these trends, and we will do well to understand them.

From the late 1980s until a few years ago, I had become increasingly worried, then depressed, as the trends steadily built to delaying retirement for our generation. My reactions during this period resembled the now-familiar five stages of grief, from Elisabeth Kübler-Ross' groundbreaking work on death and dying.

1. Denial—"That's just a blip—not to worry."

2. Anger—"This isn't fair!"

3. The most involved stage for me was bargaining—I spent 1993 and 1994 writing *Don't Work Forever!* "If only we work harder and save smarter, we can still retire early."

4. Next came depression —my friends jokingly renamed the book *Just Work Forever!*

5. Within the past few years, I finally got to acceptance. That's when I started writing *this* book.

Note that it took me more than 10 years to go through these stages!

Let's take a look at these trends that will influence how we live the rest of our lives. This will help you understand the reasons behind the strategies that I advocate in this book.

First, we'll look at the brief history of retirement—why it started in the first place, and its original purpose. Then we'll see how it has been transformed and has evolved through today, and the conscious and unconscious roles it plays in modern society. We'll forecast where the concept of retirement is going, in the context of the aging of the U.S. population, and the decline of traditional retirement income and retiree medical plans. We'll take a brief look at Social Security, and why I think cutbacks are inevitable. These programs enabled the early retirement of the previous generation, and they have contributed to our current expectations about retirement.

All of these trends point to the following conclusion: We'll experience later retirement than the previous generation, but in the process we will transform the workplace and the way we think about our later years.

Origins of Retirement

In most of the world today, humans still work as long as they are able—often right up until they die. Only the developed nations can afford to have a significant portion of their population not at work producing needed goods and services. Even in these nations, the widespread practice is less than 100 years old. Around the turn of the previous century (1900), Americans worked until about three years before they died.

Until the late 1800s, we were a nation of mostly self-employed farmers and merchants. Most people worked and lived in the same spot, and work was inseparable from life. The commute was nil, and people worked among their extended families and friends. It was natural that most people kept working their entire lives; for the majority, there was no such thing as full-time retirement. They might have slowed down somewhat in their later years, letting their children take over while they phased out. But they were still on the job, doing what they could and supplying their wisdom and experience. And if they didn't have enough money, they were supported by the younger members of their extended family.

Most Americans, being self-employed, were in control of their environment. They set their own pace, and chose what they wanted to do and how to spend their time—with healthy, direct consequences. If you magically transported an American citizen from 1900 to today, he or she would be bewildered if you raised modern issues such as work-induced stress and work/life balance. They may have lived harsh lives in the material sense, judging by today's standards, but there is little evidence of a pervasive unhappiness with life resulting from attitudes about work. I think one important reason is that they were in control of their environment, and they weren't disconnected from their family and friends.

During the late 1800s and early 1900s, our economy and workforce transformed dramatically. People moved off the farms, into the cities and factories. They moved away from where they grew up—away from their parents and extended families. They took jobs with corporations or governments, both of which started to grow quite large in their scope, influence, and power. These jobs were located away from their residences, so workers became disconnected from their families and friends.

Americans started working for someone else, taking direction for how and what they did and giving up control over their environment. Factory jobs were repetitious and physically demanding. Work became highly specialized, and nonpersonal efficiency became the trademark of successful corporations. The workweek was long, and work was dull for many people. Americans also became disconnected from their interests and passions. As a result, unhappiness and stress began to emerge as a workplace issue.

After a lifetime of work, people became worn out in their fifties and sixties, both physically and emotionally. In the first two decades of the 1900s, there were few retirement programs, and older workers didn't have the legal protection now available. They were no longer as productive as management needed, and older workers were often simply let go and discarded.

During this period, the birth rate started to decline in the United States, while at the same time people started living longer. The consequence was a rapid increase in the percentage of older citizens, and their issues began to gain the attention of government and business leaders.

In response to these issues, formal retirement programs emerged as a workforce management tool, to enable older workers to retire with dignity and to make room for more productive younger workers. Defined benefit pension plans, which provide workers a monthly retirement income for the rest of their lives, began appearing in the 1920s and 1930s. These plans designated age 65 as the normal retirement age, and in most cases the expectation was that workers would continue on the job until that age, and then retire full-time. Age 65 was selected primarily because people didn't live much longer than that. Pensions were meant to provide just a few years of retirement income.

Social Security was enacted in 1935, partly as a Depression-era means of boosting employment: Move older employees out of the workplace to make room for younger people who needed the work because they were raising families. An image emerged that older workers were less productive, and they should make way for younger, more productive workers.

The original intent of Social Security was to provide a floor of retirement income, at barely a subsistence level. Age 65 was again selected as the normal retirement age, for the reasons cited earlier and because age 65 had a certain "esthetic logic" to the staffers who developed the original design.

Over the years, Congress has expanded Social Security to beyond a subsistence level, and to provide medical insurance for older Americans. (Social Security and Medicare are discussed later in this chapter and in Chapters 8 and 14.)

Postwar Developments

The prevalence of defined benefit retirement plans expanded dramatically after World War II, and retirement was transformed significantly.

Unions pushed for enhanced features and increased retirement incomes. A 1949 report from the Steel Industry Board to the President of the United States contains a few sentences that reveal a lot about the thinking that still is influential to this day.

> The steel companies have, with some exceptions, overlooked the fact that the machines and plant on which the industry has prospered, and on which it must depend in the future, are not all made of metal or brick and mortar. They are also made of flesh and blood. And the human machines, like the inanimate machines, have a definite rate of depreciation.[1]

For the time, this expressed compassionate and humane thinking. However, it reveals two powerful assumptions from the mid twentieth century that simply are no longer appropriate in the twenty-first century.

These assumptions are:

1. That humans are like machines, which don't think on their own, don't have a personal sense of dignity and purpose, and don't have emotional needs. They just do the job they are directed to do, without thinking or reacting as human beings. This mind-set goes a long way to explaining the unhappiness that workers have when their employer ignores their sense of dignity and emotional needs. All of the recent research on employee satisfaction points to the importance of enabling employees to feel trusted and respected, giving them the information they need to succeed, and allowing them to grow.

2. That humans become outdated and worn out in their fifties and sixties, are no longer suitable for productive work, and need to be replaced by younger, more productive employees. Again, all of the recent research points to the ability to sustain performance well into a person's sixties and seventies.

However, these outdated assumptions have had a life in our collective mind-sets well beyond their usefulness, and only recently

---

[1]Steel Industry Board, *Report to the President of the United States on the Labor Dispute in the Basic Steel Industry*, September 10, 1949, p. 64.

have they begun to be replaced by more realistic assumptions for the twenty-first century.

In the postwar period, Congress gave generous tax incentives for employers to sponsor retirement plans, furthering the proliferation of employer-sponsored retirement plans. In the 1950s and 1960s, retirement programs became more popular at large and medium-sized employers.

In the 1960s and 1970s, American society, led by advertising from financial institutions such as banks and insurance companies, began promoting the concept of retirement as golden years. Retirement was transformed from a few years awaiting death with dignity, to an extended period where you finally could have the fun you deserved after a lifetime of hard work. As such, retirement became viewed as a right, an entitlement. We started believing that a lengthy retirement is the natural, inevitable culmination of life, and that life just isn't fair if you can't retire.

About this time, religion as an institution also began to decline in America. The cover of the April 8, 1966, issue of *Time* magazine asked, "Is God Dead?" Could it be that retirement replaced "going to heaven" as what we deserved after a life of being good? And not being able to retire became the equivalent of "going to hell"? I wonder if this is one subconscious way of thinking that causes so much emotion today about the subject of retirement.

In the 1960s and 1970s, large employers also began to offer medical insurance for the lifetimes of retirees. In 1966, Congress introduced Medicare, which provides medical insurance to citizens age 65 or older. Congress improved Social Security benefits several times during the 1960s and 1970s. Employers enhanced their defined benefit pension plans by offering generous benefits for employees who retired before age 65. Baby boomers, both men and now women, dramatically swelled the available workforce, adding more pressure to move out the older, supposedly less productive workers. Most older workers actually wanted more leisure time, so the interests of workers and employers coincided somewhat.

Let's look at some numbers that illustrate the growth of retirement programs during the postwar era. In 1950, about 10 percent of employees in the private sector participated in some type of retirement plan. These employees worked primarily at large corporations. This percentage grew to about 30 percent by 1965, and by 1980, more than 50 percent of private-sector employees participated in a retirement plan.

In the 1970s, 1980s, and 1990s, many employers offered special "early retirement windows," which gave special incentives for employees to retire early, before age 65. The goals were to reduce head count, remove older employees from the workforce, or both.

As a result of all of these enhanced benefits, older workers began leaving the workforce in droves in their early sixties or even late fifties. In 1900, 66 percent of all males age 60 and older worked. By 1970, this percentage declined to 40 percent, and by 1990 it declined further to 27 percent.

So far, we've briefly traced the emergence of retirement as a few years of dignity before death, which then evolved into an extended period of golden years. However, nothing remains constant—more change was in the works.

Developments to 2000

In the mid to late 1980s, new economic, demographic, and political forces began to impact retirement, starting another transformation that is still in play today.

Simply put, business got more competitive. American businesses are experiencing extreme cost pressures to operate more efficiently, both from abroad and here at home. Our capitalistic system is at work, as consumers are drawn to cheaper, better products. Many employers have their backs against a wall, and they have restructured their retirement programs in an effort to be more efficient and to better meet the perceived needs of their employees. In the process, many pension plans were cut back or eliminated.

At the same time, Congress began regulating pension plans to such an extreme that employers could no longer afford the costly regulations. In the early 1980s, 401(k) plans appeared on the scene. They became popular among younger workers, were much simpler to operate and understand, and often were less expensive than traditional retirement plans. This accelerated the movement away from defined benefit pension plans as employers' retirement vehicle of choice.

Let's look at a few statistics that illustrate this phenomenon. In 1983, the number of defined benefit pension plans in the United States peaked at 175,000. By 1998, this number had declined to 56,000, a drop of more than two-thirds. During the same period, the number of defined contribution plans such as 401(k) plans increased from 427,000 to 673,000. In 1983, there were roughly equal numbers of employees who participated in defined benefit and defined contribution plans. By 1998, over twice as many employees participated in defined contribution plans as defined benefit plans.

The implications of this shift on our financial security during retirement are tremendous. I'll briefly discuss this later in this chapter, and we'll go into more detail in Section Three.

Starting in the early 1990s, employers who sponsored medical plans for their retirees faced up to the significant costs of these programs, primarily due to stiffened accounting requirements and medical cost increases. As a result, employers started curtailing and terminating these programs, again with significant implications that we discuss in Section Two.

In the 1970s and 1980s, another important shift began to emerge, as our economy started changing from manufacturing to a service economy. Work became much less physically demanding. Even in manufacturing, automation continually replaced the physically demanding jobs. As a result, workers generally do not wear out physically, as they had in previous generations. We slowly began waking to the idea that older workers can still be productive and contribute to society.

Our Population Is Getting Older

Our country faces an unprecedented growth in the older population compared to the general population—we're in uncharted territory.

This trend is the result of declining birth rates and improving longevity. According to *The 2003 Aging Vulnerability Index* (produced jointly by Watson Wyatt Worldwide and the Center for Strategic and International Studies):

- In 2000, 16 percent of the population was age 60 or older. The report forecasts this percentage to increase to 26 percent by 2040.

- In 2000, there were 3.8 workers for every person age 60 and older. The report forecasts this number to decrease to 2.1 by 2040.

This latter statistic is thought provoking. When we retire full-time, we are no longer producers—we no longer contribute to delivering needed goods and services. However, retirees remain full-time consumers! So we will have fewer people producing the goods and services consumed by all of our citizens. How will our nation still produce collectively what we need? If we want to retire at the same ages as the previous generation, we must either become more efficient or consume less. However, there's another possibility—we'll all just work later so that we still have 3.8 workers for every person age 60 and older. The ultimate answer may lie somewhere between these possibilities!

The aging trend is affecting how employers think about older workers. Throughout the 1970s and 1980s, the mind-set of corporate America was that there was an endless supply of baby boomers who could take the place of older, supposedly less productive and more expensive workers. That mind-set is changing, since the generation of workers immediately following the baby boom generation is smaller—there is not an endless supply of younger workers anymore.

Employers are gradually awakening to the implications of needing older workers, and are offering nonsalary rewards such as benefits, flexible work schedules, respectful and safe working environments, and meaningful work. As a result, we'll see a shift in how employers treat their older workers, all for the good!

Another effect of the aging of our population is the emergence in the 1960s and 1970s of research and advocacy groups for older citizens, most notably AARP (formerly the American Association of Retired Persons). These groups began to lobby for improved benefits and conditions for older Americans, and today they are one of the most powerful and influential lobbying forces. They funded research that demonstrated that older workers could continue productivity into their sixties and seventies. Some older workers began demanding their right to continue working, and the advocacy groups helped promote their cause.

Social Security and Medicare will also be impacted by the aging of America. With fewer workers to pay taxes and more people who want to collect benefits, it's not a pretty picture. It is likely that either benefits will be reduced or Social Security taxes will be increased, or some combination of the two will be done. This won't be popular for our politicians, and the advocacy groups will resist fiercely. However, change is inevitable, and many experts have told us that our demography is our destiny. We'll look more closely at Social Security benefits in Chapter 14, and Medicare benefits in Chapter 8.

What's next? Some medical researchers believe that it is possible to live until 100 and beyond, but only if we consciously adopt a lifestyle that supports and enables this extended life. And for most of these years, they claim we will be vigorous, healthy, and productive. This research has fascinating implications for the concept of retirement and our *rest-of-life*. (Chapter 7 reviews some of this research and the implications for our lifestyles.)

We're Working Harder

On average, Americans now work longer hours than workers in most other industrialized nations. The United States recently surpassed Japan, which previously was the epitome of people who worked too hard. It's common for many people to work 50+ hours per week.

Do this for a few decades, and it's no wonder we want to retire! However, let's not throw out the baby with the bathwater. It's not *working* that is causing the problem—it's working *too much* that's the problem. It's enlightening to look at the employment practices in Europe. Employees there typically have much longer vacations than Americans, and it's clear they value their leisure time.

We're Saving Less

We've just seen that many employers are reducing their retirement and retiree medical plans, and we've mentioned the possibility of future reductions in Social Security benefits. The logical response to these cutbacks should be for us to increase our savings rates to make up for the cutbacks. Instead, Americans have steadily decreased their savings.

Let's look at an analysis of data from the U.S. Department of Commerce, Bureau of Economic Analysis, National Income and Product Accounts, prepared by Syl Schieber, Watson Wyatt's director of research. This analysis shows that collectively Americans saved about 7 percent to 8 percent of their pay from the 1950s to the 1980s. The savings rate started to decline in the 1990s, and today we save about half as much, under 4 percent of our pay. As I'll show you in subsequent chapters, saving about 4 percent of our pay is simply not enough to fund a comfortable retirement in our sixties.

Why don't we save as much? I'm convinced that collectively we succumb to the power of our consumer culture. Sophisticated advertising persuades us to spend our money today, and credit card companies are eager to provide us the convenience of easy money. We accumulate debts instead of financial assets. We're spending for today, and borrowing from the future—our future!

What are the consequences of not saving enough? Most of us won't have the financial resources to retire in our fifties or sixties.

Sobering Reality for the Average American

A number of surveys show that about three-fourths of Americans won't receive any pension from a traditional defined benefit plan, and that they will rely exclusively on Social Security and investment accounts like 401(k) plans.

The average 401(k) account balance for people in their fifties and sixties hovers around $100,000, depending on the survey. In Chapter 10, I'll show that if we're in our sixties, we should withdraw no more than 5 percent of our account balance in a year, to make sure we don't outlive our money and to leave a reserve for future inflation. Multiply this average account balance, $100,000, by 5 percent, and we get an annual income of $5,000 per year. Can you live on this amount? I can't.

Social Security doesn't start until age 62 at the earliest, as we'll see in Chapter 14. The average Social Security benefit income for somebody retiring at age 62 in 2004 is about $12,000 per year. Adding the two together gives us an annual income

(Continued)

of about $17,000 per year. Can you live on this amount? Most of us can't. However, if we've paid off our mortgage and we keep our expenses really low, we may be tempted. Let me dash cold water on this idea.

In Chapter 8, I show that retiree medical expenses, including premiums and out-of-pocket costs, can amount to more than $7,000 for the average 65-year-old. So we're left with $10,000 per year for everything else.

Before we get too depressed, let me say that these statistics are for the *average* American. I'll show you how to beat the averages. Also, I'll make the case that full-time retirement may not be the best route to *rest-of-life* nirvana.

If this doesn't convince you, skip to the examples in Chapter 19. There I show how much income can be generated by our 401(k) plans in a variety of situations, using techniques that I describe in Section Three. In most of these cases, I assume 401(k) balances that are larger than the average of $100,000. The people in these examples need to work part-time until their late sixties or early seventies.

We're on Our Own

The shift from defined benefit to defined contribution retirement plans means that most of us will be on our own for investing our assets in our later years, and making them last the rest of our lives. If we make a mistake, we'll run out of money before we die. This is a huge challenge for most of us, and one big reason why I wrote this book.

With defined benefit plans, the plan sponsor assumes the risk for us living too long. The plan pays our monthly retirement income for the rest of our lives, no matter how long. Our finances and our life goals coincide—the longer we live, the more money we receive. We can't outlive our resources.

With defined contribution plans, such as 401(k) plans, we simply get a lump sum of money when we retire. We need to make this last the rest of our lives. This puts us at odds with our life goals. If we live too long, we might run out of money. From a financial risk perspective, it's better to die young if we have only a defined contribution plan!

Earlier I discussed the decline of retiree medical plans sponsored by employers. Again, I conclude we are on our own for financing our health care. We are certainly on our own until age 65, when Medicare kicks in. Even then, Medicare pays for only a little more than half of our medical bills. And if Medicare becomes unaffordable and Congress reduces benefits, we'll need to fill in the gap.

What Happens When We All Sell Our Stocks (and Houses)?

Here's another concern I have. Many of us have been steadily buying stocks for the past 10 to 20 years, usually through mutual funds in our 401(k) plans. We saw a long bull market from the early 1980s through 2000. In spite of the recent decline in the stock market, the collective value of stocks remains at historically high levels, compared to their earnings (this is the price-earnings (P/E) ratio, which is one measure of whether the price of a stock is reasonable).

There are many reasons why stocks appreciated during the 1980s and 1990s, including growth in profits, improvement in productivity, and the decline of interest rates from historically high levels. A few experts believe that another reason for this run-up was that baby boomers and employers bought stocks to finance our retirement, and the law of supply and demand drove up the prices of stocks. If the prices went up when we were all buying stocks, what will happen if we stop buying stocks when we retire, and start selling them to finance our retirement? I'm worried that the law of supply and demand will continue to work, but unfortunately we'll be on the wrong side of this law.

I have the same concern with housing. What happens if we all start selling those large homes in the suburbs, once the kids have moved out?

Many people are planning to sell their stocks and homes in the future at prices higher than today, and use the profits to finance their retirement. I'm worried that this strategy might backfire, and that these profits might evaporate by the time we retire.

While I'm talking about investments, yields on bonds and stock dividends are near all-time lows. So we can't count on income from our investments to bail us out if the appreciation we expect doesn't materialize.

These are some of my concerns about the commonly accepted wisdom regarding investment strategies. Section III goes into further detail.

Fear and Anxiety from the Retirement Industry

Here's an example from a mutual fund newsletter that creates anxiety about investing for retirement. They discuss a hypothetical investor named Dave, age 40, who has already saved $150,000 for retirement. (This makes Dave far better off than the average 40-year old.) Dave's current annual salary is $90,000, and he figures that he needs a retirement income of 70 percent of his salary to be comfortable. In today's dollars, that would be $64,000 per year.

Dave considers inflation and the expected earnings on his retirement savings. He assumes that when he retires, he'll have no other income sources outside his own savings—no employer pension or Social Security benefits—and that he will live until age 90. He determines that he needs to save 14 percent of his pay, or $13,000 in today's dollars, *so that he can retire at age 67.*

Dave is probably very frustrated! It's very hard to save 14 percent of pay, although not impossible. Dave will need to sacrifice to reach this goal. And all this so he can retire at age 67!

I disagree with some assumptions that Dave makes:

- No Social Security benefits? When the baby boomers all join AARP, Social Security won't go away.

- Dave hasn't considered part-time work to supplement his investments.

- He hasn't considered reducing his expenses. His current level of expenses is substantially higher than an average single person in the United States.

Finally, if Dave takes care of his health, he might live past age 90, so he should plan accordingly.

I'd rather see Dave make a more realistic calculation of his required savings amount, and factor in some Social Security benefits. This would bring his saving amount down to about 10 percent of pay, which is more manageable. And if his employer provides a matching contribution in his 401(k) plan, that further reduces his required savings amount.

Better yet, see if it's possible to find an employer that sponsors a defined benefit pension plan. Dave still has 15 to 25 more good working years—plenty of time to earn a substantial lifetime income in a defined benefit plan.

We'll go into more detail on saving for retirement in later chapters, and we'll review some realistic examples. But don't get me wrong about saving! If Dave can save 14 percent of pay and enjoy his life now, great! However, I'm worried that most people will throw up their hands and do nothing. They simply won't save the amounts advocated by well-meaning people in the retirement industry.

Where Are We Today?

Let's review the key points:

- Employers have cut back their defined benefit and retiree medical plans to respond to cost pressures and excessive regulation.

- We are not saving enough to fund retirement in our late fifties or early sixties.

- We've suffered a setback with the recent declines in the stock market, and I'm concerned that future returns might be meager, due to the law of supply and demand for our investments. Ditto for our homes.

- Dividends and interest from stock and bond investments are near all-time lows as I write this book.

- Many of us have worked hard for decades, are tired, and want to get off the merry-go-round of work.

- The population is aging, resulting in fewer young workers and an ample supply of older workers.

- It's inevitable that Social Security and Medicare benefits will be reduced in some way, to respond to the large number of baby boomers who will be retiring in 10 to 20 years.

- We're living longer. If we believe and follow the latest research on longevity, we might live vigorous, healthy lives well into our nineties and beyond, further taxing our financial resources. Even if we have the resources to retire in our fifties, should we? If we did, we might spend more of our life retired than working. This improvement in longevity is one important reason to re-think the concept of retirement.

- Slowly but steadily, our society is accepting the image of older workers as productive and able to make a contribution to society.

To summarize, there's something wrong with the picture we have in our minds for living the rest of our lives. We say that we want to retire in our late fifties or early sixties, but the financial resources just aren't there. Employers will need us anyway, so they will make it attractive for us to work. This is why I conclude that we will retire later than the previous generation. However, I believe that delayed retirement won't be the hell that we might think, and in fact it might be healthy.

Unfortunately, many of us don't take a realistic look at our circumstances and plan accordingly. Instead, we plan by looking around. We look at the retirement of our parents and older relatives. They seemed to do okay, so we should also. Unfortunately, we're missing something crucial—the generous retirement benefits that the prior generation had.

"If we take a late retirement and an early death, we'll just squeak by."

Accepting these new circumstances is the first step to a more realistic action plan. Instead of planning by looking around, let's plan by assessing the situation, and let's take advantage of the solutions that are realistic and most effective for us. Let's consciously envision, create, and plan a positive future for ourselves.

WRAP-UP

Many of us will need a different type of retirement. Instead of full-time retirement in our fifties or sixties, we might have a two-stage retirement. Stage 1 might still be in our fifties and sixties, but we'll need some work to support us. However, now we work on our terms—terms that suit our stage of life.

We'll want part-time work, giving us more time to reconnect. We want to be respected for who we are and what we know. We want a friendly working environment. We'll want more than just money—we'll want social connections and meaningful work. We'll look more for inner accomplishments instead of endlessly chasing promotions and more money.

Stage 2 of our retirement may come in our late sixties, mid-seventies, or even later—here's the full-time retirement of the previous generation. By now we will have built enough financial resources for full-time retirement, if we plan accordingly.

At every age, the baby boom generation has changed our society, and our later years won't be any different. We'll redefine retirement to be actively engaged in the *rest-of-life*.

Let me end with a thought challenge for you.

How would you feel about retirement if you really enjoyed your entire life situation, including work? You enjoy the work itself, the working environment, and the number of hours you work relative to your hours of free time.

Sit with this challenge for awhile, and really imagine that this is true. Imagine a satisfying balance of work and other pursuits. For the days that you work, you wake up looking forward to going to work. If this could describe your life, would you want to retire full-time?

Is this possible? I believe the answer is yes, and we'll revisit this idea in later chapters.

How Long Will We Live?

Science works with the concepts of averages which are far too general to do justice to the subjective variety of an individual life.

—Carl Jung, in *Memories, Dreams, Reflections*

A few years ago, the actuarial world eagerly awaited the introduction of the RP-2000. Was this the latest turbocharged sports car? No, it was a new mortality table, based on the latest research, reflecting improvements in longevity and giving insights into differences in longevity among various classifications of individuals.

Understanding how long we will live is crucial to the topic of how we live and finance the rest of our lives. For most of us, the answer is "a long time," so *a lot is at stake*. In this chapter we will see what insights we might gain from something as mundane and dry as mortality tables.

Predicting Average Life Expectancy

In much of our work, actuaries predict how long we will live— *on average*. For example, Table 2.1 shows what the RP-2000 predicts for the remaining years of life for healthy[1] Americans—*on*

---

[1]For the RP-2000 mortality study, "healthy" means not collecting some type of support under a program of disability.

TABLE 2.1   Remaining Average Years of Life

Our Current Age	Females	Males
50	34.1 years	31.3 years
55	29.4	26.7
60	24.9	22.2
65	20.6	18.1
70	16.7	14.4
75	13.2	11.1

average. This study reconfirms what we have known for a long time—that women live longer than men *on average.* We don't exactly know why, although we don't lack for theories—differences in styles of working and living, differences in emotional attitudes, differences in underlying physiological constitution, and so on.

One way to restate the same information is to show the average age at death (see Table 2.2).

This shows another interesting phenomenon—if you survive five more years, your average age at death gets pushed back. For example, if you are a female currently age 65, your average age at death is 85.6 years. However, if you make it to age 70, your average age at death is now 86.7 years. These are averages, so we calculate the average age at death for a 65-year-old by including people who die between 65 and 70, as well as people who die at all future ages. However, once you're age 70, we don't include the

TABLE 2.2   Average Age at Death

Our Current Age	Females	Males
50	84.1 years	81.3 years
55	84.4	81.7
60	84.9	82.2
65	85.6	83.1
70	86.7	84.4
75	88.2	86.1

people who died between age 65 and 70, so the average age at death gets older.

If we are trying to make our 401(k) balances last for the rest of our lives, the target keeps getting pushed back if we survive.

In the Introduction, I suggest that some of us might be living deferred lives. Ask yourself this question:

How much of my average remaining life do I want to put into the "deferred" category and how much in the "having a meaningful life" category?

To drive the point home and give it a sense of urgency, I borrowed a trick from an interesting book, *Your Money or Your Life* (Penguin USA, 1999) by Joe Dominguez and Vicki Robin. Let's restate the previous life expectancy table in hours, as shown in Table 2.3.

TABLE 2.3   Average Remaining Hours of Life

Our Current Age	Females	Males
50	298,716 hours	274,188 hours
55	257,544	233,892
60	218,124	194,472
65	180,456	158,556
70	146,292	126,144
75	115,632	97,236

How many of these hours should be in the "deferred" category? Think about it.

Dangers of Planning for the Average

Some people will live longer than the averages, and some people will live less. Let's take a look at the potential variation in longevity for *individuals*, and what might cause this variation.

Consider that healthy 55-year-old woman. *On average*, the RP-2000 data in Tables 2.1 and 2.2 predicts that she will live another 29.4 years, to age 84.4. But now let's take a look at the possible variance predicted by RP-2000.

Out of 100 women currently age 55:

Two will die before age 60.

Three will live to age 60, but die before age 65.

Six will live to age 65, but die before age 70.

Nine will live to age 70, but die before age 75.

Thirteen will live to age 75, but die before age 80.

Seventeen will live to age 80, but die before age 85.

Twenty will live to age 85, but die before age 90.

Seventeen will live to age 90, but die before age 95.

Nine will live to age 95, but die before age 100.

Three will live to age 100, but die before age 105.

One will live to age 105, but die before age 110.

Note there is a large difference between the *average* life span and the *maximum potential* life span, which appears to be between ages 110 and 120.

The RP-2000 data predicts that out of 100 women who make it to age 55, 30 will live to be age 90 or older—well beyond their average age at death of 84.4 years. That means their odds of living to age 90 are 30 percent—almost one out of three! Who will these women be?

The RP-2000 data also predicts that 20 women will die before age 75—well before the average age at death. These odds are one out of five. Who will these women be?

Let's do the same thing for that healthy 55-year-old man. *On average*, the RP-2000 table predicts that he will live another 26.7 years, to age 81.7. But now let's take a look at the possible variance predicted by RP-2000.

Out of 100 men currently age 55:

Two will die before age 60.

Four will live to age 60, but die before age 65.

Seven will live to age 65, but die before age 70.

Eleven will live to age 70, but die before age 75.

Sixteen will live to age 75, but die before age 80.

Twenty-one will live to age 80, but die before age 85.

Twenty will live to age 85, but die before age 90.

Thirteen will live to age 90, but die before age 95.

Five will live to age 95, but die before age 100.

One will live to age 100, but die before age 105.

The RP-2000 table predicts that none will live beyond age 105 (sorry, guys).

The RP-2000 data predicts that out of 100 men who make it to age 55, 19 will live to be age 90 or older, well beyond their average age at death of 81.7. That means our odds of living to age 90 are 19 percent—almost one out of five! The RP-2000 data also predicts that 24 men will die before age 75, well before the average age at death. These odds are nearly one out of four.

If I repeat the process for different current ages, the picture will be the same—lots of people living well beyond their average life expectancies, and vice versa.

Common and Not-So-Common Knowledge

Many studies confirm what is now common knowledge: People who exercise, don't smoke, don't abuse alcohol, and aren't overweight will live on average longer than people who don't exercise, smoke, abuse alcohol, and are overweight. While there are other factors that affect longevity, most studies show these are the four most significant predictors of longevity. Note that these are lifestyle choices.

In addition, I found many studies that reveal interesting, not-so-common knowledge. For example, a fair amount of research demonstrates statistically significant correlations between our social contacts and improved health and longevity. Such contacts include marriage, close friends and relatives, church membership, and belonging to special interest groups. Even more fascinating is research that correlates improved health and longevity with the *perception* of our social environment as supportive and caring. This shows something that I consistently encountered in my quest—that our attitudes, intentions, and perceptions are as important to our health and financial well-being as investments in stocks and bonds, and medical insurance coverage.

In a few paragraphs, I'll discuss other surprising research that gives us insight into living a long, healthy life. But first, let's address a common misperception.

Is Longevity in Our Genes?

There's a common belief that longevity comes from our genes. We hear about the "Winston Churchill effect"—he smoked, drank, and was overweight, but lived a long life. We also hear about supposedly healthy people who suddenly die young. The research is showing that the gene factor doesn't dictate our longevity fate. Instead, there's a complex interaction between our DNA and our lifestyle choices.

A good metaphor for the interaction between genes and lifestyle is an evening of poker or bridge. Our genes represent the card hands that we're dealt over the evening, and how we play our cards represents our lifestyle choices. We can't do anything about the longevity hands that we get, but we can influence how we play. In poker or bridge, by the time the evening is over, most of the outcome is influenced by how well we play. Occasionally we get nights of good or bad luck, just like a few people get a great set or a poor set of genes. However, most of the time we're dealt an average set of hands, and most of us get an average set of genes. It's how we play that makes the difference.

If we choose to live a healthy lifestyle, the odds are in our favor that we will outlive our average life expectancy. Some researchers believe we can live to 100 and beyond. Chapter 7 covers what living a healthy lifestyle means and reviews more of the research that connects increased longevity with our lifestyle choices.

The actuarial study that produced the RP-2000 tables had two interesting results that aren't so well known, but are relevant to our inquiry.

Interesting Result #1: Do We Live Longer If We Work?

The RP-2000 task force studied the mortality rates separately for men between ages 50 and 70 who worked and those who didn't work. Disabled men were excluded from both groups. The death rates for men who didn't work were about *twice*, more or less, the rates of men who worked. Stated in reverse, if I work between ages 50 and 70, I am half as likely to die in a given year compared to if I don't work. This effect is also there for women, although it is much less pronounced than for men.

Is this causation or correlation?

- *The causation theory:* If you work, you have purpose in life, which helps you be healthier and live longer.

- *The correlation theory:* Healthier people are more likely to work, and people who are unhealthy are less likely to work.

Can We Resolve the Causation versus Correlation Controversy?

The biggest obstacle to finding a conclusive resolution to the "causation versus correlation" controversy is that it is impractical to construct an experiment in the normal scientific way. It would be difficult to take one group of people and make them golf, knit, or sit around all day, watching TV and eating bonbons, while another group goes to work, and then wait 20 years to measure the difference in mortality rates. However, we have done this with man's best friend!

Here's where the Dog Aging and Cognition Project comes in. This is a joint effort of the University of Toronto and the University of California. They have been completing longitudinal studies[2] of the effects of environment and nutrition on successful aging in beagles. The theory is that dogs can be good proxies for humans in studying the reasons why people might live longer and be healthier. The researchers took different groups of older beagles. One group was confined to a dog pen and didn't have much activity (for our purposes, we can say that they retired). Another group was allowed to roam in fields (we might say they kept working). The researchers

---

[2]A longitudinal study looks at two or more different groups of subjects, and attempts to identify factors that can be associated with their development over time.

also varied the diets of the different groups of dogs. Guess what? The active beagles had less cognition impairment and lived longer than the retired dogs. The enriched diet helped even more (we'll come back to nutrition in Section Two). This is probably the closest we will come to solid scientific evidence on the side of the causation theory, but critics will argue that humans are different from dogs.

Is there any evidence that applies to humans? I persisted in looking for evidence, and eventually I got lucky. Watson Wyatt's research librarians, Erica Curtis and Renee John, began uncovering research that hit the mark. They found a number of studies that correlate paid work or volunteering with improved health and longevity, but these studies didn't address the causation versus correlation issue. However, a recent study, reported in the December 2002 *Journal of Health and Social Behavior*,[3] did give us some tantalizing insights. They conducted a longitudinal study of older people, and classified people into different groups by their health status at the beginning of the study. Then they tracked each group's health and longevity for periods of two years, five years, and seven years. They found that within each group, the people who worked or volunteered had significantly better health and longevity after the various periods than people who didn't work or volunteer. The study's authors are planning additional research to gain additional insights, but perhaps this is as good as it gets for now.

Later chapters review other significant longitudinal studies that tracked groups of people over long periods of time and noted characteristics common to successful agers versus nonsuccessful agers. These studies support the causation theory, and provide additional interesting insights into our inquiry as well.

Here's my take on the causation versus correlation controversy. Keeping active and engaged with life will help us stay healthy and happy, and we will live longer than if we withdraw from life. Working is just one way to keep active, but there are other ways as well. Volunteering, interesting hobbies, providing emotional support to family and friends—these can all give us purpose and meaning.

---

[3]"Individual Consequences of Volunteer and Paid Work in Old Age: Health and Mortality," by Ming-Ching Luoh and A. Regula Herzog, *Journal of Health and Social Behavior* 43 (December 2002).

Interesting Result #2: Do We Live Longer If We Have More Money?

The second interesting finding in the RP-2000 study is that death rates among pensioners varied by the amount of pension. Men receiving small monthly pensions were more than one and a half times more likely to die in a given year than men with large monthly pensions. The effect was present for women, but also less pronounced. (For this purpose, a small pension was $500 per month or lower, and a large pension was $1,200 per month or higher. This just includes the person's pension from prior employment—most of these people had additional income from Social Security).

Other studies confirm this finding. The reasons seem to be obvious—if we have the means to take care of ourselves, we are more likely to be healthy and happy.

Let's think about this a little. Adjusted for inflation to the year 2004, the large pension comes to about $1,500 per month. If we add typical Social Security benefits, the total monthly income might amount to $2,500 to $3,500 per month. This is much less than the wages that most Americans live on, so we're not talking about lots of money. Obtaining a monthly income of $1,500 per month from our retirement savings and working a little shouldn't be too hard. We explore this way of thinking in great detail in Section Three.

So here, at least, is one way to define "enough" retirement income: enough to enjoy the most favorable longevity experience. While this is by no means the only consideration, it does give us one way to look at how much is enough.

WRAP-UP

If we lead a healthy lifestyle in all respects, it's entirely possible that we could live to age 90 or more. In fact, it's my own goal to have a healthy, vital life until age 100. After all, the maximum natural human life span seems to be about age 110 or 120, so why not aim for 100? If we adopt a healthy lifestyle, we should *plan* to live this long. Later chapters discuss the financial implications for our retirement savings and medical expenses.

Working in our later years might actually be a good thing, for our financial, physical, and emotional well-being. While money can't buy us love or happiness, having *just enough* money might be one way to increase our odds of living a long life.

These ideas lead to a big WAI/WSID challenge:

How would we feel about stopping working now if we believe that we will live vigorous, healthy, productive lives until our late eighties, nineties, or even to 100? How would we feel about the next 20 years if we have 30 or 40 more good years ahead of us?

What Do We Really Want?

Only a life lived for others is the life worthwhile.

—Albert Einstein

Most of us really want to live the rest of our lives with meaning, purpose, health, and happiness. We want things to go well for our loved ones, ourselves, and the world. We want to realize our full potential as human beings. This is the way I think, and I suspect I have lots of company.

I know these statements might sound lofty, noble, and idealistic. But we're talking about the rest of our lives, so *a lot is at stake.* There's only one person who should judge if these are worthwhile life goals—each one of us! We don't need approval from our parents or anybody else, so why the hell not?

We have the benefit of substantial research that focuses on what makes people happy. Let me elaborate on what most researchers mean by happiness. We're not talking about temporary pleasures from a delicious meal, a good movie, a great vacation, or buying some nice clothes. These provide pleasure, for sure, but the good feelings quickly fade, and they aren't the source of lasting satisfaction with life. Most of the research on happiness focuses on the traits and experiences of people who are truly satisfied with the meaning and purpose in their lives. It is this definition of happiness that I use in this book.

So here we'll look at this research, and the guidance it can give us on living the rest of our lives. I'll show how pursuit of our goals is inseparable from our finances, and why we need a lifestyle plan that integrates happiness, health, and wealth.

I draw from the following sources, which I highly recommend for further reading.

- *Authentic Happiness* (Free Press, 2002) by Martin Seligman, Ph.D., who is a former president of the American Psychological Association. This book translates the latest research on happiness and Positive Psychology into a practical guide for living.

- *Aging Well* (Little, Brown, 2003) by George E. Vaillant, M.D. This book summarizes three longitudinal studies that traced groups of people from adolescence through old age to death. It identifies traits of people who have aged successfully compared to those who haven't.

- *Successful Aging* (Dell, 1999) by John W. Rowe, M.D., and Robert L. Kahn, Ph.D. They summarize a comprehensive study of aging by the MacArthur Foundation.

Here I summarize the key findings from these books that will help us in our quest, and their relevance to our financial resources in our later years. Then, I review interesting research and stories of centenarians—they have a lot to teach us. Near the end of the chapter, I also discuss a surprising and possibly controversial source of insight—the substantial findings and research that is emerging on near-death experiences. The implications for how we live the remainder of our lives can be mind-boggling!

But first, let's get one question out of the way.

Does Money Buy Happiness?

I started with this question, because of the obvious link to our finances. I did the easiest form of research—I typed in the words "happiness" and "money" into the Google search engine, and waited for wisdom from the Great Oracle (my pet name for the Internet). I quickly found dozens of articles summarizing opinions and research. While there are arguments on either side of this question, my take from this research is that not having enough money to meet our basic living needs can cause unhappiness, but acquiring more money than *just* enough does not significantly increase our happiness. Of course, the $64,000 question is *how much is enough?*

Here are a few interesting factoids from my Internet research:

- People from the *Forbes* list who had assets exceeding $100 million reported only slightly more happiness than the average American (www.newscientist.com).

- People who had sudden inheritances or won the lottery reported an immediate increase in happiness, but after six months to a year they were soon reporting about the same amount of happiness as before their windfall (www.newscientist.com). This finding is confirmed by other research.

Martin Seligman's book summarizes some fascinating research that correlates happiness with the overall wealth of a nation.

Researchers asked the following simple question of thousands of people from 29 nations around the world:

On a scale of 1 (dissatisfied) to 10 (satisfied), how satisfied are you with your life as a whole these days?

Here are some interesting contrasts, from page 52 of Seligman's book:

- Chile scored 7.55 on the 1 to 10 happiness scale, while the United States scored 7.73. Yet the purchasing power of Chile's citizens is only 35 percent of U.S. citizens' purchasing power.

- Five countries topped the United States in reported happiness (Netherlands, Ireland, Canada, Denmark, and Switzerland). All have lower purchasing power than the United States; the lowest of the five is Ireland, with just 52 percent of the U.S. purchasing power.

- Perhaps the most astonishing result was China, with a reported happiness scale of 7.29, yet its citizens have only 9 percent of the purchasing power of the United States.

On page 53 of *Authentic Happiness*, Seligman says:

Overall national purchasing power and average life satisfaction go strongly in the same general direction. Once the gross national product exceeds $8,000 per person, however, the correlation disappears, and added wealth brings no further life satisfaction.

George Vaillant also weighs in on the subject of money in *Aging Well*.

As will be demonstrated again and again, money has relatively little to do with successful aging. . . .

As you get older, you need people, not dollars and cents.

Here are some conclusions I made for the purposes of our quest.

- If I need to work during my later years to get enough income, I'll do it without frustration or feeling cheated out of life. I'd rather work to have enough money than not have enough and be unhappy.

- However, the trick is to figure how much is *just* enough, because once I have that much, I might have better things to do with my time than make more money.

Now that we've addressed money and happiness, let's look at what really does cause people to be happy. We'll review the three books mentioned earlier.

What Can We Learn from Positive Psychology?

This is a term coined by psychologists for applying the emerging research on happiness. Most of the psychological and psychiatric research over the past few centuries has concentrated on what can go wrong—on diseases and dysfunction. This has definitely been worthwhile; nobody would argue about whether alleviating pain and suffering is a noble goal. However, absence of pain and suffering does not equal happiness, so the pursuit of happiness is the focus of Positive Psychology.

In *Authentic Happiness*,[1] Martin Seligman distinguishes between the *pleasurable life*, the *good life*, and the *meaningful life*.

---

[1]Reprinted and edited with the permission of The Free Press, a Division of Simon & Schuster Adult Publishing Group, from *Authentic Happiness: Using the New Positive Psychology to Realize Your Potential for Lasting Fulfillment*, by Martin Seligman. Copyright © 2002 by Martin Seligman. All rights reserved.

The *pleasurable life* can mean a great vacation, nice clothes, interesting hobbies, or a good movie. While nobody says these are bad, they aren't the complete answer for an authentically happy life. The good feelings from these activities are temporary.

The *good life* consists of identifying and applying our signature strengths—permanent traits that are deeply characteristic of us— to the main realms of our lives: work, love, and raising children. Seligman believes that "the highest success in living and the deepest emotional satisfaction comes from building and using your signature strengths." His book identifies 24 possible signature strengths. It has exercises for identifying our signature strengths, and his web site has a more extensive survey (www.authentichappiness.org).

Seligman goes on to describe the *meaningful life* as beyond the good life.

> I am not sophomoric enough to put forward a complete theory of meaning, but I do know that it consists in attachment to something larger, and the larger the entity to which you can attach yourself, the more meaning in your life.

The *pleasurable life* (golf, hobbies, travel, etc.) dominates much of the advertising and popular cultural images of retirement. Why? Because this involves spending money, while the good life and meaningful life often involve little or no spending. Also, it's harder to portray the *good life* and *meaningful life* in 30-second commercials. There are a few images of the *good life* in our popular culture—time with family—but I haven't seen *any* images on the *meaningful life*.

I believe that a lot of us get caught in a trap regarding the *pleasurable life*. We work hard, with long hours preventing us from doing what really satisfies us. So, to reward ourselves, we buy the *pleasurable life*—a nice car, an expensive vacation, nice clothes, nights out on the town. After all, we deserve it, right?

Consumer advertising aggressively promotes this way of thinking. If you examine most commercials, they very cleverly associate buying their products with human needs—needs such as wanting to be happy, being attractive to the opposite sex, staying healthy, connecting with other people, and bonding with family. While these are legitimate human needs, very often buying these products is *not* the best way to satisfy these needs. We're going to the wrong source. However, the advertising is very sophisticated and seductive—often using research on the best ways to convince us to part with our money.

So we end up spending our hard-earned money to buy things that we hope will satisfy our very natural needs, but really don't give us true life satisfaction. However, we pay a steep price. We must continue working to replace the money we just spent, and we don't save very much for our later years.

We compound the mistake when we analyze how much money we should have when we retire, and we factor in money that we need to buy all this stuff. This can result in overestimating the amount of financial resources we need to retire. The financial institutions also feed this way of thinking. Their advertising persuades us to want our justly earned golden years, when we can travel, play golf, dine out, and buy nice things for our grandchildren, all using the money we have invested with their institutions. The activities for the *good life* and *meaningful life* might not involve as much money—one reason for not seeing them in the advertisements on saving for the golden years.

Don't get me wrong. We do need reputable financial institutions for our investments, which are necessary for retirement. However, let's not allow their advertising to define our perceived needs and drive our behavior. Actually, the behavior it often drives is postponing retirement due to all of the anxiety and fear of not having enough money.

We can align nicely the *good life* and the *meaningful life* with our opening statement: We want things to go well for our loved ones, ourselves, and the world.

I'll be living the *good life* if I identify and apply my signature strengths to my work, my loved ones, and my personal growth. Use my experience and skills to help my family and friends, to help things go well with them. Find work that aligns with my values, and do the best job I can. Always look for ways to grow and learn new things.

If I apply these strengths to some entity or cause that is bigger than my immediate surroundings, I'll be living the *meaningful life*. Use my experience and skills to help make the world a better place. Return to the idealism of our youth from the 1960s and 1970s, but use the wisdom gained by living the intervening 30+ years.

To sum up: I want a healthy balance between spending for today and saving for tomorrow. And I'll have a healthy balance between living the *pleasurable life*, the *good life*, and the *meaningful life*.

Now let's turn to the longitudinal studies that are summarized in *Aging Well*.

What Can We Learn from Harvard?

A longitudinal study takes a group of individuals and follows them over the course of their lives, to gain insights into various factors such as health, happiness, and career progress. The concept is similar to time-lapse photography of blooming flowers. In the case of *Aging Well*, researchers studied three different groups of individuals—a group of male Harvard students, a group of inner-city males in Boston, and a group of female students from Stanford University.

This quote from the book's jacket describes the study.

> Harvard Medical School has spent more than fifty years studying the basic elements of adult development, looking at life choices, health, and happiness in hundreds of individuals. Now, for the first time ever, the results of this unprecedented study are being made public, and they reveal an extraordinary set of conclusions about how men and women can lead a happier, more fulfilling, healthier life—into their sixties, seventies, eighties, and beyond.

George Vaillant, M.D., is the director of the study, and he has fascinating conclusions on the factors that determine people who age successfully.

One key to successful aging he identifies is Generativity—taking care of the next generation: "The old are put on earth to nurture the young."

Of course, for many of us this involves caring for immediate and extended family members, but Generativity need not be confined to family. Any activity that helps younger people will count. He discusses many case studies that provide evidence for his claim—examples of people who are happy and healthy and do a good job with Generativity, and examples of people who are not happy, are lonely, and don't have any contact with younger generations.

He also advises older people to be the Keeper of the Meaning. Here's a quick summary (his excellent chapter on the subject goes into detail). Keeper of the Meaning is passing along our wisdom and experience from our life experiences. Keeper of the Meaning is about justice, as distinguished from Generativity, which is about love and care. Again, he has a number of case studies showing people who do a good job with Keeper of the Meaning.

Another key to successful aging he calls "Integrity: Death Be Not Proud." Maintain a healthy understanding of our physical limitations as we age. Be realistic and don't push the limits, but don't underestimate ourselves, either. Defy old age in a healthy way by continuing to be as vigorous and active as possible. Again, he has many examples of people who continue to be quite active in pursuing their interests in ways that are appropriate for their ages.

Let me repeat a consistent theme: Generativity, Keeper of the Meaning, and Integrity do not involve lots of money. And working, whether full-time or part-time, will not get in the way. In fact, working might give us an opportunity to practice Generativity and Keeper of the Meaning in the workplace, and help keep us fit and active.

George Vaillant goes on to identify four basic activities that make retirement rewarding:

1. Replace workmates with another social network. "In meeting such needs, grandchildren often work spectacularly well." However, having an extended group of friends with common interests also works quite well.

2. Rediscover how to play. "Competitive play—social bridge, cribbage, shuffleboard—lets one make new friends."

3. Follow our creativity. When we're raising a family and earning a living, we can't always be creative. Our later years provide this opportunity.

4. Continue lifelong learning.

To wrap up this section, here is some wise advice from *Aging Well*:

Before and after age 50, cultivate the richest social network you possibly can. Your life will be better for it.

Let's look at another comprehensive study of aging for more insight.

What Can We Learn from the MacArthur Foundation?

In 1984, the John D. and Catherine T. MacArthur Foundation initiated a multidisciplinary project to investigate successful aging. They assembled a group of 16 scientists drawn from biology, neuroscience, neuropsychology, epidemiology, sociology, genetics, psychology, neurology, physiology, and geriatric medicine. The study, which was actually a set of dozens of individual research projects, took more than 10 years to complete. The resulting book, *Successful Aging*,[2] has very interesting insights, some of which we'll share here.

The study identifies three components of successful aging:

1. Avoiding disease.

2. Maintaining high cognitive and physical function.

3. Engagement with life.

These are somewhat hierarchical. Avoiding disease enables us to maintain high cognitive and physical function, which in turn enables us to be engaged with life. It is the combination of the three that defines successful aging. The first two components—avoiding disease and maintaining high cognitive and physical function—are covered later in Section Two on health.

Engagement with life has two important factors:

1. Relating to others.

2. Productivity.

The study links social supports not only to happiness, but to health and longevity as well.

> The linking of social relationships to longevity, the discovery that social support lies at the core of those relationships, and the special role of social support in aging have been gradually, but unmistakably, demonstrated.

---

[2]From *Successful Aging* by John Wallis Rowe and Robert L. Kahn, copyright © 1998 by John Wallis Rowe, M.D., and Robert L. Kahn, Ph.D. Used by permission of Pantheon Books, a division of Random House, Inc.

The study goes on to identify various types of support: confiding, reassuring, providing sick care, expressing respect or affection, and talking about health or about problems. The authors use the metaphor of a "convoy of support"—a close group of friends and family to provide love, support, and companionship, and the more diverse, the better.

At the risk of sounding like a broken record, none of this requires lots of money.

On the subject of productivity, the study describes in detail how people can remain productive well into their seventies and eighties.

The book cites some interesting views from people age 60 and over:

- Nine out of 10 agreed with the statement "After a life of work and service, retirement and leisure are well deserved."

- Almost 9 out of 10 agreed with the statement "A person should continue to work as long as he or she is able."

- Eight out of 10 agreed with the statement "Life is not worth living if one cannot contribute to the well-being of others."

Although the first statement might seem to disagree with the other two statements, together these statements make a powerful case for part-time work or volunteering, with plenty of time for leisure.

What Can We Learn from the Centenarians?

People aged 100 and over are the fastest growing age segment in the United States. In 1990, more than 37,000 Americans had reached age 100 or older. By 2000, that number most likely exceeded 100,000, and by 2050 it is projected to exceed 1 million.

These remarkable people haven't gone unnoticed by scientists, physicians, and authors. A number of books describe various studies, surveys, and interviews of centenarians, and a consistent picture is emerging of what makes these people tick, and tick, and tick. . . .

In a preview of what's to come in this book, if we want to live to 100, we should eat lots of fruits and vegetables, hold off on fatty foods, exercise, not smoke, drink alcohol in moderation, and wear seat belts.

But there's much more. The centenarians have an optimistic attitude about life, slough off stress, and are very much engaged with life. Many work and volunteer late in life and are very active with family and friends. They are curious about anything and everything, continue learning, and very much live in the present. The successful centenarians aren't much different from you or me, other than they are much older.

In particular, I enjoyed the following books, which I highly recommend.

- *Living to 100: Lessons in Living to Your Maximum Potential at Any Age* (Basic Books, 1999), by Thomas T. Perls and Margery Hutter Silver. This book describes the New England Centenarian Study, where a group of Harvard researchers studied the mental, physical, and emotional health of all centenarians in a specified area of New England.

- *If I Live to Be 100: Lessons from the Centenarians* (Crown Publishers, 2002), by Neenah Ellis, provides intimate portraits of a handful of remarkable people across the country.

- *Centenarians: The Bonus Years* (Health Press, 1995), by Lynn Peters Adler, describes her surveys of more than 400 centenarians, and a series of interviews with a smaller group.

The preceding paragraphs dryly distill much of the advice from these books. However, this doesn't do justice to their stories. You've got to read them to be inspired, for them to come alive in your imagination. They provide a compelling picture of potential for us in 40 to 50 years. In addition to hearing *how* they lived to be 100, I learned *why* they wanted to live to 100. They had powerful reasons for getting up each morning. They just kept on living, and their positive intent helped keep them ticking.

Now, let's turn to the most surprising and potentially controversial source of insight on living a meaningful life.

What Can We Learn from Research on Near-Death Experiences?

The pages that follow have the potential to be the most controversial in this book. Please bear with me for a while. The implications of this research could well have a profound influence on the

WAI/WSID questions, and how we live and finance the rest of our lives. I really benefited by keeping an open mind on this research, so I kept this material in the book to let you decide for yourself.

Why are we exploring dying in a book on retirement and living the rest of our lives? Well, dying is the way we conclude a successful retirement!

What happens when we die? This question has haunted religious leaders, philosophers, scientists, and ordinary folks like you and me since the dawn of human consciousness. In the late twentieth century, however, findings of scientific inquiry began converging with traditional religious beliefs, as medical technology has brought people back from the brink of death and they have lived to tell their tales. As these findings become widespread, there could be a significant shift in commonly held beliefs in Western society.

Near-death experiences (NDEs) are situations where a person is dead by clinical standards but revives, often as a result of the latest in medical technology, and reports experiences that cannot be explained by commonly accepted science. For example, they may accurately describe conversations among relatives in the waiting room while they are in surgery in the operating room. Other consistent features of many reported NDEs are out-of-body experiences, conversations with dead friends and relatives, instantaneous life reviews, and encounters with religious figures or beings of light.

Documented NDEs are a phenomenon of twentieth- and twenty-first-century medical technology. We are now able to revive people from severe accidents or sudden illnesses. Before, these people would have had death experiences, not near-death experiences, and they wouldn't have lived to tell their stories. Interest in this subject started with physicians whose patients had NDEs and told their stories. At first, these stories seemed incredible and were dismissed, but when these experiences were repeated by many patients and their stories had many elements of consistency, inquisitive physicians started their investigations.

While there are many possible explanations for such experiences, NDE researchers contend that the events are evidence that there is more to us than our physical bodies—our consciousness that can understand events, have experiences, and survive our physical death.

After becoming aware of the NDE phenomenon, I became hungry for more information. I quickly ran across the pioneering work on the subject, *Life after Life* (HarperSanFrancisco, 2nd Ed., 2001) by Dr. Raymond Moody, M.D., Ph.D. It is a short but fascinating book, and I recommend it to anybody who is interested in the subject.

Dr. Moody interviewed many patients who had NDEs, and found certain similarities in their stories. He was able to pick out 15 elements that occurred frequently in the narratives he collected. Not all of the interviewees had identical experiences, and many of them had only a handful of the 15 elements he was able to identify. When he reviewed the mass of evidence, he was able to construct a theoretically ideal or complete experience that incorporates all of the common elements. The central part of this complete experience is consciousness that is not connected with the physical body, and an awareness that survives physical death.

His book goes on to relate experiences with his patients that form the basis for this composite experience. Patients described events and details during their near deaths that normally they would need to be present to witness. Often these events took place away from the operating room where their physical bodies lay, and were validated by witnesses. Somehow their consciousness was able to sense these events and remember them, without being present in their physical bodies. These patients came from all walks of life, were of all ages, and held all types of religious beliefs. Often they were afraid to discuss their stories for fear that people would think they were crazy. There is no possible explanation for these events with conventional science; one important theme that the book advocates is to be open to alternative experiences and points of view. The impact on the lives of people who have had NDEs has been profound.

The research on NDEs represents a significant convergence of science and religion, and has the potential to transform how we live our later years. This area is gaining more acceptance, as respected institutions such as the University of Connecticut, University of Virginia, and British Royal College of Psychiatrists have duplicated and added to Dr. Moody's findings.

The fact that respected medical doctors, scientists, and institutions have taken these phenomena seriously has made a tremendous impression on my thinking about my *rest-of-life*. My reaction is that the conventional image of retirement—the golden years of R&R—feels trivial and less relevant. Again, this is consistent with Dr. Seligman's statement that the *pleasurable life* is not the source of life's satisfaction. I'm drawn to the main message—that the purpose of life is love and knowledge, serving others, and expressing kindness, support, and love to my family and friends.

What are the implications for the rest of our lives?

- I don't need huge amounts of money to seek what has meaning for me.

- Helping and serving others is a good way to have meaning in my life, and again this need not be expensive. In fact, if I do this through paid work, even if the pay is modest, I'm that much better off.

- I'd rather have growth and learning experiences than material things.

- There is no need to spend huge amounts of money staving off death. I'll lead as healthy a life as possible, but I'll be at peace when my time comes. I'd rather die six months earlier, with family and friends around me, than spend gobs of money hooked up to machines, only to die all alone in some institution.

- It takes the pressure off of retirement as my golden years—as the just reward for working hard and saving all my life. I don't need a great finish to life, as it appears there is a transition instead of a finish. This lets me relax and just go on living and learning from my life's experiences for the rest of my life.

For me, believing in an afterlife, or not believing in an afterlife, is a matter of faith. Neither point of view has been proven conclusively, and probably never will (at least not in our lifetimes!). So why not choose the belief that removes fear, is reassuring, lets me relax, and basically has a happy ending?

However, if you don't believe these stories, the basic conclusions for how we live the rest of our lives don't change. In fact, they become more important. Because if it really is "game over" when we die, then wouldn't we want a happy, meaningful, healthy life for as long as possible? That's what this book is about!

This subject really intrigued me, and I did a fair amount of research on it. For a lengthier review of NDEs and the impact on our *rest-of-life*, please see my web site www.restoflife.com.

WRAP-UP

Our challenge is defining how much money we need for our basic needs, and securing this support for our lifetime. This might involve some paid work during our later years. But don't get me wrong—I'm not advocating working like a dog until we die! We need a healthy balance of work and the pursuit of meaning and happiness. Once we secure enough financial support, we can turn our time and energy into pursuing what really makes us happy.

Since we might need to work during our later years for financial support, the next chapter discusses how we can make work be a meaningful and joyful experience.

I'll end with a few more thought challenges.

What has meaning for me?

Can I make progress toward getting this now, instead of waiting for retirement?

How would I live the rest of my life if I didn't fear death?

What, Me Work?

All work and no play makes Jack a dull boy.

—Proverb

n Chapter 2, I make the case that I might live for a long time if
I take care of myself, to my mid-eighties, early nineties, or even
to 100.

In Chapter 1, I make the case that for much of this time, I
might need to work, due to inadequate financial resources for
full retirement.

These realizations greatly heightened the urgency to find meaning and purpose in my work and life *now*, and to stop leading a
deferred life.

Here's a suggestion for this moment. After you read to the end
of this suggestion, put the book down. Sit in a quiet place and
make sure you have no distractions. Breathe in and out slowly and
comfortably for several breaths to relax your mind. Picture yourself doing something you really enjoy—a hobby, a sport, any activity where time flies by. Imagine you're having a lot of fun, and you
wish you could do this indefinitely. However, after awhile you remember that you must now go back to work. In fact, you recall
that you just learned you must work for a long time, well into your
seventies, due to your meager financial resources. Picture yourself
now working for 20 more years. Let this belief sit with you for

awhile—don't dismiss it easily as just an exercise of your imagination. Truly believe this is your life's situation.

Now put the book down for at least five minutes and pay attention to what you think and feel.

Are you back? How do you feel? Was your reaction: "Oh boy, I love my work and I get to keep doing it for 20+ years!"?

If this is you, then skip this chapter. In fact, you may be wasting your time with this book!

Or did you feel trapped, angry, stifled, or depressed? Did you have a sense that life is unfair? Then read on. If you had a strong reaction, write your feelings down and save them for later. You might need them in the future for motivation.

I did have a strong reaction to this exercise. I felt exhausted and defeated. I just couldn't see myself working in my current circumstances for that long. After awhile, though, I relaxed, took a few deep breaths, settled down, and felt a surge of energy to *do something*.

And I'm not alone. It's common knowledge in my business that dissatisfaction in work is prevalent in the United States. Depending on which survey you read, half of American workers or more are dissatisfied at work, unhappy with their jobs.

Many surveys identify a number of possible reasons for this dissatisfaction: Inadequate compensation. Boredom. Poor workplace conditions. Lack of recognition. A feeling that work has little meaning or purpose. Lack of respect. Lack of control over one's life. Maybe even injustice in the workplace. Clearly, something is missing!

No wonder we say we want to retire in our late fifties or early sixties!

Now don't get me wrong. My current work is satisfying and enjoyable, and Watson Wyatt treats me just fine. However, I've been doing this work for 30 years, and can't see myself doing it for another 20 years.

So, I set off on a quest to see how I can make work satisfying, meaningful, and even joyous—not just tolerable—for the rest of my life. I want all of my life circumstances to be sustainable indefinitely, so I'm not waiting for some future external event such as retirement to make my life better. As we shall see, work satisfaction is a very important component of overall life satisfaction. In this book I make a case for working longer than we had originally planned, to improve our financial situation and to help us lead a healthy, engaged life. So I need to balance the desire to retire with the need to continue working.

Let's start with an important aspect of working during our later years and a major theme in this book: phased retirement. I didn't have to go far—a study conducted by my employer gives us some interesting insights.

What Can We Learn from Watson Wyatt Worldwide?

In late 2003, a research team led by a friend of mine, Janemarie Mulvey, commissioned a telephone survey[1] of 1,000 people between the ages of 50 and 70. The goal was to learn about phased retirement from the perspective of people who were actually in a program where older people work less than a full schedule. (Starting the receipt of retirement benefits may or may not be part of a phased retirement program.)

The survey found that nearly two-thirds of workers over age 50 hope to scale back their hours or work in a more flexible working environment before retiring full-time. However, a challenge is that only about 40 percent of their employers currently allow phased retirement. The survey showed that one-third of older workers will leave their current employers earlier than they would if the employer provided the opportunity for phased retirement. So currently, there is a disconnect between older workers' desires and employers' phased retirement programs. However, as I mentioned in the first chapter, our population is aging, and employers will need older workers. Phased retirement will be a wave of the future to meet the needs of both employees and their employers.

The survey identified three main categories of phasers (no, this isn't the weapon of choice in *Star Trek*). The first and most prominent are "planned phasers"—about 57 percent of the survey group. Planned phasers deliberately and voluntarily chose phased retirement because they wanted more time for nonwork activities.

The second group (about 32 percent of the total) are those who

---

[1]Reprinted with permission from *Phased Retirement: Aligning Employer Programs with Worker Preferences, 2004 Survey Report.* © 2004 Watson Wyatt Worldwide. For more information, visit www.watsonwyatt.com.

retired fully from their career job but later reentered the work-force. Either they didn't have enough money or they missed work-ing. While the report calls these people "unplanned phasers," I like to say that they had a "near-retirement experience (NRE)"!

For both groups, shorter and more flexible hours were the most often reported reasons for phased retirement. Other reasons in-cluded eligibility for early retirement, family reasons, too much stress, or just being unhappy with their career job.

The third category of phasers are those whose career job was eliminated. The survey called them "forced phasers," and they comprised about 10 percent of the survey group.

One clear result from the survey was that phasers had a higher income than people who fully retired. Yet extra income was not al-ways the most important reason why people chose to work. Among the planned phasers, the most common reason for working was the "enjoyment of working," cited by 40 percent. Only 27 per-cent of this group said they needed the income, while 15 percent said they needed access to medical benefits. Planned phasers were also the happiest and most productive in the survey group.

Motivation for working was almost the opposite for the un-planned phasers—more people in this group cited extra income as more important than enjoyment of working.

When we asked current workers what was the most important reason they would choose phased retirement, the most often cho-sen answers were:

- 25 percent wanted to work part-time.

- 23 percent wanted more flexible hours.

- 22 percent wanted to do something completely different.

Here's another reason why phased retirement might be a good idea. It's a safer strategy than immediately shifting from full-time work to retiring full-time. If we retire full-time and are out of the workforce for several years, it's hard to get back in. There are a number of reasons: Our skills might become out-of-date, our work habits may slip or we might have a bigger hurdle convincing po-tential employers that we are serious about coming back to work. Phased retirement lets us try out retirement without disconnecting totally—with respect to both our finances and our psyches. If we really like our time off and have the financial resources, we can go to the next step. If we aren't happy with our partial retirement, we can ramp back up to full-time work. Initially I'll think of phased retirement as a test-drive, but ultimately it could be a way of life for a significant part of my *rest-of-life*.

The survey report shows that this is an emerging phenomenon, even if employers need to make progress in this area. If your employer doesn't offer such a program, I suggest you diplomatically inquire about it, and give them a copy of our research report titled *Phased Retirement: Aligning Employer Programs with Worker Preferences—2004 Survey Report* (go to www.watsonwyatt.com).

Actually, there's an important precedent for phased retirement. Working mothers have helped pave the way for people who want to work less than a full schedule, yet still stay meaningfully engaged in the workplace. So I have hope that employers will adapt to older workers, just as they have adapted to working mothers.

The happiest working mothers I know have a balanced attitude about their roles as a mother and as an employee. Both are important, and somehow they manage to avoid sacrificing one for the other. Easier said than done, but I think this is a lesson for those of us who want to be planned phasers. We'll need to strike a healthy balance between work and activities outside of work. Many of us have put career advancement first for a long time, and we'll need to ease these ambitions somewhat to realize a more balanced lifestyle.

Let's now examine how to strike this balance. How can we make work a meaningful part of our lives? We'll gain some valuable insights from a surprising source.

What Can We Learn from the Dalai Lama?

In 1998, Howard Cutler, M.D., transformed a series of interviews with the Dalai Lama into the best-selling *The Art of Happiness: A Handbook for Living* (Riverhead Books, 1998). In 2003, they teamed up again to produce *The Art of Happiness at Work* (Riverhead Books, 2003).[2] I heartily recommend both books, although all the quotes here are from their second book.

---

[2]From *The Art of Happiness at Work* by the Dalai Lama and Howard Cutler, copyright © 2003 by His Holiness the Dalai Lama and Howard Cutler, M.D. Used by permission of Riverhead Books, an imprint of Penguin Group (USA) Inc.

The beginning of their second book summarizes significant insights from their first book.

Happiness can be achieved through the systematic training of our hearts and minds, through reshaping our attitudes and outlook.

Happiness is determined more by the state of one's mind than by one's external conditions, circumstances, or events—at least once one's basic survival needs are met.

This latter quote should sound familiar to us by now!

Like Martin Seligman, the Dalai Lama distinguishes between two types of human satisfaction: pleasure and happiness.

Pleasure can certainly provide a temporary kind of happiness and engender intense emotional states. He explained that pleasure arises on the basis of sensory experiences, but since it depends on external conditions, it is an unreliable source of happiness.

He pointed out "True happiness relates more to the mind and heart. Happiness that depends mainly on physical pleasure is unstable; one day it's there, the next day it may not be." To the Dalai Lama, true happiness is associated with a sense of meaning, and arises on the basis of deliberately cultivating certain attitudes and outlooks.

He makes the case that we can find this at work.

I think it is important to remember that in all human activities, whether it is work or some other activity, the main purpose should be to benefit human beings. Now, what is it that we are seeking in our work, what is the purpose of work? Like any other human activity, we are seeking a sense of fulfillment and satisfaction and happiness.

The Dalai Lama has many insights on how one's attitude and outlook can address dissatisfaction with work. Here are a few that resonated with me.

Another way to build contentment, for example, is simply to reflect on how fortunate one is to have the work, how there are many people unable to get any kind of work.

And I think if we make a special effort to cultivate good relationships with people at work, get to know the other people, and bring our basic good human qualities to the workplace, that can make a tremendous difference.

But it shows how one person can influence another's attitude, which implies that even one person can make a big difference. One person can change the atmosphere of the workplace environment.

Here's a view I have on attitude. If I'm working too many hours and am worn out, it's difficult to change my attitude the way the Dalai Lama advocates. However, if I reduce my hours such that I have time for other activities, it's a lot easier to have patience and acceptance, and to take the initiative to make my workplace better.

The Dalai Lama talks about many aspects of balance.

To enjoy maximum work satisfaction and performance, workers must find a balance between two poles—with too much challenge on one end and not enough challenge on the other. With too much challenge, workers experience stress, strain, and deterioration of work performance. With too little challenge, workers become bored, which equally inhibits job satisfaction and hinders performance.

No matter how satisfying our work is, it is a mistake to rely on work as our only source of satisfaction.

If your basic outlook on life is, *Yes, money is important, but there are also other factors equally or probably more important for one's sense of well-being*, then I think you will lead a happier life.

The Dalai Lama and Dr. Cutler discuss a study by Dr. Amy Wrzesniewski, of New York University, that divides workers into three main categories:

The first group views work as just a job. For them, the primary focus is on the financial rewards that the work brings.

The second group of individuals views work as a career. Here, the primary focus is on advancement. Rather than financial motivation, these people are more motivated by prestige, social status, and the power that comes with titles and higher designations at work.

The final category is those who view their work as a calling. These individuals do the work for the sake of the work itself.

I was definitely in the second group in my thirties and forties, and maybe that was age-appropriate. However, now I want to be in this third group! I can get there by doing different work, but I can also get there by looking for and appreciating the meaning and contribution in my current work.

The Dalai Lama goes on to say there are many ways to seek a higher purpose, to contribute to society. It doesn't have to be grandly noble—we don't all need to emulate Mother Teresa.

> In the same way, there are many thousands of people who provide the food we eat, the clothes we wear.

> And also, they should recognize that by actively participating in this workforce, in some way they are acting out their role as a good citizen in their society, a productive member of society.

> That alone can be enough to give them a sense of purpose, a sense of calling.

At the end of the book, Dr. Cutler makes an insightful observation about the Dalai Lama.

> His personal life and work life were perfectly integrated—so fully integrated, in fact, that there was no separation between his "personal" life, "work" life, "spiritual" life, or "home" life.

For me, this describes the ideal way to live and work—*to be*—during our *rest-of-life*.

The workplace environment is very important to job satisfaction. If we are simply a means of production, a human machine, then we'll lose sight of many of our good values and characteristics. So now let's turn to research on effective work environments that will give us more insights.

What Else Can We Learn from Watson Wyatt Worldwide?

Our company's mission statement is to help our clients create financial value through people, and for people. As such, we are intensely interested in the characteristics of successful work environments.

The Human Capital Index and WorkUSA[3] are two of our most powerful research efforts. They identify and measure statistically significant links between superior people practices and higher shareholder return—win-win situations. Here are examples of these superior people practices at financially successful organizations:

- Pay and benefits are perceived to be fair and meet employees' needs. They are linked to the employer's success and business strategy.

- The company promotes the most competent employees, and helps poor performers improve.

- The company shows flexibility in work arrangements (phased retirement is an example).

- Trust in senior leadership is actively engendered.

- Managers demonstrate the company's values.

- The company culture encourages teamwork and cooperation.

- The company avoids using titles to designate status and authority, avoids varying perquisites by position, and avoids varying office space by position.

- The company shares business plans, goals, and information with employees.

- Employees at all levels give ideas and suggestions to senior management, and the company takes action on employee feedback.

- Employees know how to contribute to the success of their employers.

- Employees have the necessary things to properly do their jobs— helpers, information, supplies, equipment, and materials.

- The company encourages employees' growth and development.

---

[3]Reprinted with permission from *Human Capital Index: Human Capital as a Lead Indicator of Shareholder Value,* © 2002 Watson Wyatt Worldwide and from *WorkUSA 2002, Weathering the Storm: A Study of Employee Attitudes and Opinions,* © 2002 Watson Wyatt Worldwide. For more information, visit www.watsonwyatt.com.

- Employees are satisfied with the quality of the company's goods and services.

- The company treats employees and customers with respect and integrity.

For our purposes, we can use these findings to identify a work environment that best suits us, or to help create such an environment if we like our current job. If we must work for financial reasons, then hopefully we'll do it on our terms, and having a healthy work environment should be one of those terms. Fortunately, Watson Wyatt listens to its own advice, so I have most of these characteristics in my current situation. If and when I need to look for work elsewhere, I'll look for these characteristics during job interviews.

I am fascinated to note that the Human Capital Index and WorkUSA studies reinforce the themes expressed by the Dalai Lama. Fairness. Compassion. Integrity. Honesty. Open communication. Less reliance on external measures of success and more reliance on internal human values. Humans are not machines of production.

Is Work Toxic?

When I discuss the concept of working in our later years, some people have very negative reactions. They want to retire as soon as possible, and they really dislike their jobs. For some people, their work is toxic to their very being. Work can be a little toxic for some people and a lot toxic for others. There are several possible ways that work can be toxic:

- There's too much of it.

- It's the wrong type of work for us at this stage in life—either we are no longer capable of meeting the job requirements or the work conflicts with our values.

- The working environment might be unhealthy, either physically or emotionally, or too stressful.

So, in our quest for work in our later years, we'll need to be aware of reducing the potential for toxicity.

However, as mentioned in the Introduction, removing sources of unhappiness does not necessarily result in happiness. So, while reducing toxicity is one important goal, I'll also seek ways to make my work meaningful and productive, and align with my life's interests and goals.

What Can We Learn from Our Friends?

I've talked with a number of friends about the concept of a sustainable life, including liking our work situation sufficiently that we can continue it indefinitely. Most of my friends can't see themselves in their current situation in 5 or 10 years. However, a few of them have told me they can see themselves working 10 to 20 years from now. The natural question is "Why?" Here's what I've found.

- All have plenty of time to pursue interests outside of work. Either they are working no more than four days per week or they have very flexible schedules.

- Some are self-employed or run their own businesses. They answer only to their customers, and have a large degree of control over their work environment and how they spend their time.

- Others describe an open, supportive, friendly work environment.

- Some (a few doctors and teachers, for example) truly love their work and feel they are making a difference in the world.

- Most are satisfied with the amount of money they are making. They've matched their expenses to their income; they feel that they have enough.

It was encouraging to get firsthand confirmation of much of the research that I discuss here!

You might have some fun with this one, to see what you can learn. First, ask yourself, "Can I see myself working in my current situation 10 or 20 years from now?" Then ask your friends the same question. For those who say no, ask why not. For those who say yes, ask why. The answers should give you plenty to think about.

Follow My Bliss

This simply means that we are doing work that we love, that we would do for free if necessary. This is work that we were meant to do.

This reminds me of my wise Aunt Mimi. Over the years, I visited with her at various family gatherings and road trips. At every meeting, she asked me if I was doing my "life's work." In my twenties and thirties, I didn't have a good answer to the question, but I had this uneasy feeling that the answer might be no. I would think about this on my trip home, but then upon my return, the onslaught of family and career responsibilities required me to put these musings aside. However, in my forties, the uneasy feeling became certainty that the answer was no, and I set out on a journey to transform the answer into yes. As it turns out, I was closer to yes than I thought. Before finishing this story, let's explore this topic a little more.

Many of the thoughts and suggestions so far in this chapter help us transform our work situation from being unhappy to not being unhappy. Also, it's not like there is an all-or-nothing switch that makes us totally happy or completely unhappy with our work; the reality is often somewhere in between. For many of us, some elements of our work provide fulfillment and enjoyment, and other aspects produce frustration, boredom, or some other unpleasant emotion.

If we eliminate these frustrations, boredoms and other negative feelings, are we happy? Not necessarily—as we have discussed previously, not being unhappy is not the same as being happy with our work. For many of us, not being unhappy might be the best we can do. This might be okay if we have activities and passions outside of work to fulfill us, and we have enough spare time to pursue these activities. Achieving the state of not being unhappy enables us to keep working to bring in necessary money and remain active and engaged, which in turn helps us maintain our physical and emotional health in our later years. This is certainly better than being unhappy with work. I won't think that I've failed with my *rest-of-life* if I attain not being unhappy with work and I have lots of other things to give me meaning and purpose in life.

However, many of us want to be truly happy in our work. This is the ideal. For me, *rest-of-life* nirvana means loving my work *and* having enough time to pursue other activities that also give me meaning and purpose. One important purpose of this book is to address significant barriers to pursuing happiness at work in our later years; these barriers are having inadequate financial resources and the fear of high medical bills. These are the main subjects of the next two sections in this book. While we might not be able to remove these barriers completely, we can successfully deal with them so that we aren't paralyzed by fear. This gives us the freedom to pursue dreams!

That's when we come to the hard part. Often barriers are the excuses we tell ourselves as justification for not taking a leap. When we remove the fear of these barriers, we're faced with just ourselves—no more excuses! At this point, most of us need to summon the courage to leave our comfort zone to follow our bliss. For some of us, we know exactly what we want to do. We've been thinking about it for years and can't wait to start. Or we're already pretty close and just need to make a few adjustments. But many more of us might not know exactly what our bliss is, and we need to go on a journey to find out.

I can't tell you what your calling is, or give you a formula to find out. We need to have our own experience to find our way. Here I'll share a few thoughts that helped me get started.

- In our childhood, what did we want to be when we grew up? What were our dreams? To make this exercise work, we need to broaden our perspective and be a little flexible. Let me give an example. A lot of us wanted to be astronauts when we grew up, but now this might be a little impractical. However, when we think about it, what really appealed to us was the excitement of exploration, the sense of adventure, and learning new things. If we think of being an astronaut in these terms, the possibilities are limitless, and more realistic.

- Do we have activities where we lose track of time? Are we so focused in this work that hours go by without our noticing? This might be a clue to our bliss. Again, we might not be able to translate this literally into income-producing activities, but we can come close if we open our minds. Love to hike? Get a job with an organization that sells hiking equipment. Love photography? Work at a camera store and take paid assignments on the side. Love being with children? Teach, work at a day care center, or work in some role that supports these activities. Love helping ot ers heal? There are lots of possibilities here, given the aging of America.

- What are our favorites? Favorite subjects in school? Favorite tasks at work? Favorite people? They give us clues.

- Let death be an adviser. Before I die, I really want to . . . (Fill in the blank!)

- In our gut, is there work that we just know we were meant to do? Do we have a strong feeling or intuition about it?

After thinking about these questions, ask ourselves whether it is possible to rearrange our current working situation to do less of the annoying stuff and more of our blissful activities. In my situation, I enjoy writing, sharing what I know to help people, and speaking engagements. This led me to writing this book and my previous two books and to the resulting speaking opportunities. Some things just need to unfold over time, and we need the patience to let them happen.

While transforming from being unhappy to not being unhappy might be the best we can do, it might also be an intermediate step to finding our bliss. Once we are no longer preoccupied with being unhappy, we might notice new opportunities and be open to different possibilities. There's not one single way, and the path isn't always direct!

One last option: We might need to create our own jobs. Some of my friends who truly love their work are self-employed. This gives them the freedom to do what makes them happy; they don't need to do what somebody else wants them to do.

There are many advantages to seeking our bliss that are consistent with the themes in this book. We need to do a lot of thinking about who we are, what we like to do, what we have to offer the world, and what we want to accomplish on this earth. We need to be patient—sometimes the way is not as we originally expected, and it takes awhile to unfold in stages. It's not easy and will take some time, but it is well worth it!

At this point, we'll move on to other topics. I'll pick up where we just left off in Chapter 17, called "What, Me Work?—Revisited." That chapter shifts to the more practical aspects of working in our later years, including looking for work that is truly enjoyable and some practical aspects of self-employment.

By the way, "follow my bliss" is a colorful expression coined by

Joseph Campbell, and if you haven't had a chance to read his work, I highly recommend it.

The Power of Intent

When we set our intent to have fulfillment with our life's work, it happens.

Here's one example. Once my colleagues and I were bidding on some important work, but everybody told us that we had no chance of winning this work due to the circumstances. I disagreed, and we all set our intent to win the work. We went about discovering what it took to win, making the necessary contacts, being open to new opportunities as they unfolded, and not losing faith. We got lucky, although we thought that we made our own luck. Eventually we astonished everyone by winning the work.

What happened here? Was it perseverance? Positive attitude? Alertness to new opportunities? Networking, luck, self-fulfilling prophecies, or divine intervention? Call it what you like—it works!

Here's how we can use the power of intent to help us think about working during our *rest-of-life*.

I am doing my life's work.

I tell myself this is happening, in the present tense. I say it to myself when I look in the mirror in the morning. I repeat it at a quiet period during the day. I repeat it again when I encounter obstacles. I hold the intent after I've tried for what seems a long time and I'm ready to give up.

I am open to new ways of finding what I seek, or to unexpected doors that open. I believe it is happening!

Try it. You'll be surprised with the results.

WRAP-UP

While we might need the money from work to support ourselves in our later years, job satisfaction is not about money. We should make sure we make just enough money to meet our needs, but look for other things to provide satisfaction and happiness at work.

It's unlikely anyone will find a job or career that matches all the issues and factors discussed in this chapter. For most of us, the challenge is to find enough of these considerations to make us satisfied, without a feeling that we are compromising too much.

I'll end with another thought challenge.

How would we feel about working during our later years if we truly enjoyed our work, and had enough time for friends, family, and pursuing our interests?

Now we're finished with our exploration of the WAI/WSID issues. The next short chapter summarizes the first section of the book, and then we move on to the sections that address our health and finances.

What Should I Do?

It did not really matter what we expected from life, but rather what life expected from us. We needed to stop asking about the meaning of life, and instead to think of ourselves as those who were being questioned by life—daily and hourly.
—Viktor Frankl, in *Man's Search for Meaning*

This short chapter summarizes the section on perspectives for the rest of our lives. This is my foundation for my life's plan, so that I can move on to matters of health and wealth.

Here are my underlying assumptions.

- I'm on my own to make my financial resources last the rest of my life. Nobody else will take this responsibility.

- If I take care of my health, I make this problem more challenging, since I might live to my late eighties, nineties, or even to 100.

- As a result, most likely I'll need to work into my late sixties or early seventies to have enough money.

- Since I need to work for a long time, I'll improve my work situation *now* so that I can sustain my life indefinitely. This means being satisfied with all of my life's circumstances, including work.

This calls for a more healthy life balance between the periods of our lives that we spend working and not working. Many of us have bought into an unhealthy life plan. It goes something like this.

> Work really hard now, with the consequence that there isn't enough time to pursue our other life interests to our satisfaction, or to take care of ourselves physically or emotionally. We do this to ourselves so that later we can completely retire and not work at all. We think that life will get better when we retire, sometime in the future.

A more healthy life plan goes like this.

> Have a good balance now between time spent working and time spent not working. Continue this healthy balance for as long as I can, maybe into my seventies or beyond. I'll pursue what makes my life satisfying now, and take care of myself now, rather than defer these to a future date.

Here's a summary from Chapter 3 of the substantial body of research on happiness, and how it relates to our *rest-of-life*.

- Not having enough money can cause unhappiness, but after we meet our basic needs, other activities are more likely to make us happy.

- I won't be frustrated if I need to work during my later years to have enough money. Working might increase, not decrease, my happiness—as long as there is a healthy balance between time spent working and time spent not working.

- The cultural images of a life of leisure, traveling and playing golf, promote temporary pleasures but generally do not lead to lasting satisfaction.

- Using our strengths and lifetime experience in work, love, and family can lead to happiness and life satisfaction.

- Devoting ourselves to causes beyond our immediate surroundings, to help make the world a better place, provides meaning and purpose to our later years.

- Another key to successful aging is helping the next generation through our support, care, and sharing of our life's experiences.

- We also need a healthy understanding of our physical limitations: Don't overestimate our abilities, but don't underestimate them, either.

- Cultivating a broad network of friends, both for support and for rich human relationships, greatly increases the chances of successful aging.

- Remaining productive into our later years increases the chances that we will age successfully and be satisfied with life.

I'll strike a healthy balance between the *pleasurable life*, the *good life*, and the *meaningful life*. I know that focusing too much on the *pleasurable life* won't give me lasting satisfaction and meaning.

This doesn't require lots of money, just enough money to meet my basic living needs, plus a little margin for comfort. Then I can pursue other goals that give me health, happiness, meaning, and purpose.

What does *just enough* mean to me?

- I don't need the latest car, the biggest house with the finest decorations, and the very best clothes. I'll spend *just enough* to meet my basic living needs and be comfortable, but no more. Of course, what is *just enough* is a matter of personal taste, and everybody will have their own standards. However, by this age, I don't need to own things to impress others.

- Owning less stuff frees up my time and money, which I can use for more meaningful pursuits. For example, home and auto insurance will cost less. I don't need to spend as much time shopping, fixing, maintaining, and worrying.

- I'll spend just enough on food and dining out. This has a double payoff, as we will see, as it will also help me lead a healthier life.

- I'll focus my leisure time and vacations on learning experiences, rather than seeking luxury or exotic getaways. I'll make my home have enough comfort and beauty so that restful vacations can be spent at home—why spend money traveling to some beautiful spot just to lie around? I'll save the money for travel experiences that will have meaning and open me to new perspectives.

■ I'll make investments of time and money in my health. Over the long run, I'll spend less time and money, compared to letting my health slide and resorting to expensive medical fixes.

These are some of the main ideas. For my *rest-of-life*, I'll continue to look for ways to spend *just enough* for my basic living needs.

If I must work for financial support, the research summarized in Chapter 4 gives me hope that I can make my work situation a satisfying aspect of life. I'll look for reduced hours and flexible work schedules, so I have time to pursue other interests. I'll seek work that contributes to the overall good of society in some way. I'll use my skills and life's experience to help others. I will continue to look for personal growth through work. I'll look for a work environment that is healthy and successful for both my employer and myself. This environment has plenty of room for fairness, compassion, integrity, honesty, and open communication.

Finally, the fascinating research on near-death experiences, as summarized near the end of Chapter 3, lets me relax about the inevitable conclusion to my life. I'll take care of myself, and hopefully live a long, rich life, but I won't spend lots of money fighting the inevitable. I'll enjoy life for what it has to teach me, but I won't put pressure on myself to get the good life now because that's all I have. *Instead, it's all about love, learning, and service to others.*

I'll have a number of good things going in my life—love and family, friends, personal growth, productivity and creativity. I won't have just one or two sources of happiness—this would leave me too vulnerable to inevitable setbacks when the unexpected happens.

This vision makes for a pretty tall order! But I have lots of time to make it happen, so I'm going to relax and take it one step at a time. I know what to look for with several aspects of my life, but I don't need to do it all at once. And I know another thing: life will deal me unexpected blessings, setbacks, and opportunities. So I'll be flexible and go with the flow!

When I started this book, I focused just on the financial aspects of retirement. I had no idea I would go on such a fascinating journey to explore happiness, meaning, and purpose in life. However, I'm very glad I did. Without such an exploration, all I had was *hope* that retirement would make life better. But *hope* is not a strategy!

Now I feel much more confident in moving ahead with financial matters, knowing that I have a conscious, yet flexible, plan to support a life that I really want.

Let me wrap up by quoting Viktor Frankl again.

Man's search for meaning is the primary motivation in his life. . . .

Our later years give us the opportunity to search for our highest potential as human beings.

SECTION TWO

HEALTHY INTEREST

The rest of the world lives to eat, while I eat to live.

—Socrates

nvestments in our health have as much importance to our financial well-being as our investments in stocks and bonds. Hence the name of this section.

Being healthy is a very important part of enjoying our later years. It's also necessary to maintain our ability to work in case we need the money. Poor health can be a significant threat to our financial health. As a result, many of us have considerable anxiety about obtaining adequate medical insurance in our later years. Often this fear paralyzes us enough so that we may not live the life we want, for fear of jeopardizing our medical insurance. Are these fears justified?

I had the same fears, until I did the research and thinking for these chapters. Now I've concluded that these fears shouldn't prevent most of us from taking the steps we need for a fulfilling life. We can take charge of our health, rather than letting outside circumstances dictate our lives. In the next three chapters, I advocate that we keep a healthy fear of the potential for high medical bills, but that we channel this fear into taking the necessary steps to take charge of our health.

I believe that most of us can manage our health and protect our wealth, by adopting a healthy lifestyle and obtaining just enough medical insurance. I'll show you that it's not rocket science—most of us can access the knowledge and insurance products that will give us the protection we need.

My employer, Watson Wyatt Worldwide, helps large employers design, finance, administer, and communicate their group medical plans. Lately, our clients have experienced large cost increases with their group medical plans. As a result, we've focused on the best way to contain these cost increases over the long run—helping employees to adopt healthy lifestyles and become informed medical consumers. So part of my process was to consult with our health care and medical insurance experts on the issues in this section. I also spent a fair amount of time with some doctors to get their perspectives as well.

In the process, I ran across fascinating research that suggests if we take proper care of ourselves, we can have vital, productive lives well into our eighties, nineties, and even to 100 and beyond. This means I could live for 50 more years! Not only does this increase the challenge of making my 401(k) balances last for the rest of my life, but it significantly changes my outlook on living, working, and investing as well. This is one reason why I changed my thinking from retirement to *rest-of-life*.

Chapter 6—"Healthy Fear"—is intended to generate exactly that. We need a realistic picture that will motivate us to take action, but doesn't paralyze us. Chapter 7—"Take Care"—describes the action steps we need to do just that. How do we take care of ourselves so that we minimize the chances for high medical bills? Chapter 8—"Just in Case"—recommends that we obtain the right amount of medical insurance, at the right cost, so that we're protected financially just in case.

Let's go!

Healthy Fear

What we have today in the United States is not so much a
health-care system as a disease-cure system.

—Edward M. Kennedy.

ost of my life, I never worried too much about my weight. In my
twenties and thirties, I exercised a lot, and used that as an excuse
to eat anything I wanted. However, in my forties, I kept my eating
habits but not my exercise habits! I slowly expanded, until I was
25 pounds heavier than when I was in college.

This didn't seem too bad. When I checked the body mass index (BMI) tables, which show the ideal weight for a person's
height, I was over the ideal by 15 to 20 pounds. I consoled myself with the thought that these tables don't account for variations in bone and muscle density, and surely I have denser
bones and muscles than the average person! But it turns out it
was my brain that was dense!

Having good health is essential to enjoying my later years, as
well as maintaining my financial health. From my consulting to
larger employers, I know that employers of all kinds are terminating or cutting back their retiree medical plans, as costs have become unbearable. My company, Watson Wyatt, is no exception, as
we have significantly reduced the benefits from our retiree medical plan to contain costs to an affordable level. So I know firsthand
how this presents a challenge to our health and financial security

in retirement. In my case, the fear of high medical bills has made me very cautious about retiring anytime soon, so I was intensely interested to learn and think more about this topic.

Let's first talk about the healthy fear.

Many of us are on a collision course with the inevitable results of our unhealthy behaviors. If we don't do anything about it, we will crash and burn. But here's the optimistic spin: The train is moving slowly, and we have the time to grab the controls before it's too late. The bright side to our unhealthy behaviors, though, is that they may be one way to prevent the problem of outliving our 401(k) balances!

Over the years, I came to understand that most people don't make necessary changes in their lives until, well, you know. I knew this intellectually and was smug that I realized this, could analyze problems in my life, and take corrective action to avoid them. Then I had a series of humbling personal crises that taught me that I'm really no different from most people. However, after settling down from the shock of each experience (which took awhile), I felt a surge of energy to *do something about it*. I finally had the motivation to make changes that I knew in the back of my mind were necessary, but just couldn't seem to get around to.

So now I'm taking charge of my health, and I'm taking it very seriously. In this chapter, I'll tell you why this is so important. In the next chapter, I'll tell you what I am doing to take care of myself.

What's the Problem?

Actually, there are three problems.

1. My employer won't pay anymore.

2. My doctor isn't perfect.

3. I've been behaving badly.

First problem. My employer pays my medical plan costs, so I don't need to be responsible for my actions. The trouble is, my employer is coming under a lot of competitive cost pressures and medical costs are skyrocketing, so my employer can't afford it anymore. My employer is mad as hell and is not going to take it anymore!

Second problem. I can mess up (i.e., get sick from my lifestyle) but my doctor can always fix it and make it better with a magic pill, or for really serious stuff, magic surgery. The trouble is, I'm finding that my doctor isn't perfect. He's good at certain things, like diagnosing illnesses once my health has gone sour. And in many cases, the pharmaceutical and surgical interventions are necessary to recover. However, my doctor isn't much help with maintaining the optimum health that I need, or with helping me prevent serious illness.

Third problem. As a result of the first two problems, I've been living an unhealthy lifestyle. If my employer and doctor take care of me, why do I need to care? I'm free to have a bad diet, not bother with exercise, and not worry about too many toxins in our environment. Wrong! Our unhealthy lifestyle will eventually catch up to us.

Let me elaborate on all three points.

What's Happening with Employer-Sponsored Retiree Medical Plans?

Through the 1980s, most large employers sponsored some sort of medical coverage for their retirees. However, since the early 1990s, most companies have either eliminated retiree medical coverage or sharply reduced benefits.

In 2002, Watson Wyatt issued a report titled *Retiree Health Benefits: Time to Resuscitate?*[1] This report shows that in the year 2000, only 25 percent to 30 percent of people over age 65 have some employer-sponsored retiree medical benefits. The rest have only Medicare, or they buy supplemental insurance on their own. The report goes on to show that employers who haven't terminated their retiree medical plans have reduced benefits by:

- Reducing average premium contributions by employers.

- Imposing more stringent minimum service requirements.

- Tying the employer's portion of the retiree health benefit premium to the worker's length of service.

- Placing caps on the amount the company will pay.

---

[1]Reprinted with permission from *Retiree Health Benefits: Time to Resuscitate?* © 2002 Watson Wyatt Worldwide. For more information, visit www.watsonwyatt.com.

The report estimates that by the year 2031, the level of employer financial support will drop to less than 10 percent of total retiree medical expense.

The report goes on to look at typical costs for retiree medical benefits. In the year 2001, the average medical costs for retirees during the year were $5,645 for pre–age 65 retirees and $3,248 for post–age 65 retirees (the reason for the difference is Medicare, as we shall see in a bit). These costs include insurance premiums and direct out-of-pocket expenses, such as deductibles, co-payments, and services not covered by insurance. And medical costs continue to skyrocket.

However, here's an eye-opener: The report shows the present value of a retiree's lifetime medical costs. The present value is the estimated in-the-bank amount that it would take to pay for all our future medical expenses, not counting Medicare.

If we retire in the year 2011, these amounts are as follows:

- $158,000 if we retire at age 55.

- $122,000 if we retire at age 60.

- $87,000 if we retire at age 65.

The amounts are higher for earlier retirement ages because we will have a longer period of retirement if we retire early, and Medicare pays for a large portion of medical bills after age 65.

Keep in mind that these are savings that we need for medical expenses, over and above any investments we might have for retirement income. And if we're married, double these amounts!

Most of us simply won't have that kind of money.

Let me stress that these are *averages*. As we'll see, we have the power to beat these averages through our lifestyle choices. Speaking of averages, however, here's another scary statistic. We also have the potential to spend more than the averages; if we develop a serious chronic disease, we might spend $300,000 or more on medical bills over our lifetime. But more than 70 percent of chronic diseases are preventable, so we're back to leading a healthy lifestyle as the best way to protect ourselves financially.

These quotes from the Watson Wyatt study sum up the problem:

Our assessment of the future evolution of retiree health benefits in this country is relatively dire.

Retirees will have no choice but to assume greater responsibility in planning for medical costs in retirement, including consideration of increased personal savings and delayed retirement.

On that cheery note, let's go on to take a look at Medicare.

Medicare—the Good, Bad, and the Ugly

I'm very appreciative of the benefits provided by Medicare, but it's a mistake to think it will totally take care of me. Let's take a look.

The Good

The good news is that, once we reach age 65, Medicare pays for roughly half of our medical expenses.

I'll go into more detail on Medicare in Chapter 8, where we describe strategies for obtaining medical insurance.

The Bad

Medicare has some gaps in coverage, most notably long-term nursing care. With these expenses, Medicare pays for a good chunk immediately following a surgery or illness, but it doesn't pay much for long illnesses. Again, we'll go into more detail in Chapter 8.

And well-meaning experts tell us scary stories—that we have a one in three chance of being admitted to a nursing home, that nursing home expenses can cost over $50,000 per year, and that we should all buy their long-term care insurance policies (with high premiums). Actually, I don't buy these scary stories, and I'll tell you why in Chapter 8.

The Ugly

I'm very concerned that Medicare won't be able to keep its promises when the baby boom generation retires. And I'm not alone—many experts share this concern.

We pay for Social Security and Medicare through Federal Insurance Contributions Act (FICA) taxes. If you look at your pay stub, you'll see a deduction for Medicare taxes. Your employer pays an equal amount. However, the government is on the hook for paying the total bill—if our contributions and our employers' contributions fall short, the government pays the rest.

And that's the problem. The taxes that we and our employers pay aren't enough to fund future benefits. To compound the problem, the government isn't saving our taxes for the rainy day when we all retire—it's spending this money now on all the other things the government does. Basically we are relying on our children to pay an enormous amount for Medicare benefits when we retire, and I'm worried that they simply won't be able to afford it. In this case, one or more things must take place.

- Benefits must be reduced.
- FICA taxes must be increased.
- Additional revenues must come from the federal government.

How might benefits be reduced? In my opinion, the most likely way is to increase the eligibility age a few years beyond age 65.

And how might Congress increase taxes? While this might be necessary, tax increases haven't been too popular with politicians lately. I hope that eventually we—the citizens and the politicians who represent us—wake up to the fact that nothing is free. We get what we pay for. We will need to increase taxes to pay for Medicare benefits, and I'll gladly vote for the brave politician who is willing to demonstrate leadership on this issue.

We'll go into more detail on the financing problems with Social Security and Medicare in Chapter 14.

Why the Doctor Isn't Perfect

We behave as if the doctor can fix anything that is wrong with us. Just give me a pill. If it's really serious, then wouldn't surgery do the trick? Don't make me do something hard, like exercise or improve my diet.

We're finding that conventional medicine is really good with the following things.

- Diagnosis, often using very expensive equipment.
- Emergency interventions when things get really bad with illnesses or accidents. These interventions include surgeries, expensive prescriptions, and lengthy hospital stays.

However, evidence is emerging that even the expensive interventions aren't always the best way to cure or heal. One study identifies medical errors as the eighth leading cause of death in the United States—and many of these errors result from the interactions of prescription drugs.

Alternative medicine is a rapidly growing field that uses more natural and inexpensive methods of treating disease. And until recently, conventional medicine hasn't paid much attention to prevention or maintaining optimum health. This sounds harsh, but I'll say that there's not much money in prevention for the medical industry. In fact, if the entire country followed the advice of the next chapter, demand for medical services would plummet.

Fortunately, several physicians and researchers are interested in prevention and optimum health, and a cottage industry is emerging that will help us with these goals. Many excellent books, courses, therapies, and treatment centers can help us avoid illness and maintain optimum health. These are reviewed in the next chapter.

I've Been Behaving Badly

We Americans need to put labels on things, and medical problems are no exception. We're constantly seeing new terms for disorders that we never heard of before. A friend of mine has an interesting insight into our problem. His diagnosis is that many Americans have "lifestyle disorder"—we are literally killing ourselves.

Here's an analogy. This is like never changing the oil in our car, never taking it in for scheduled maintenance. When the inevitable happens—our car breaks down prematurely—we just expect to change the engine, or even get a new car. That's the way we are behaving with our health. The trouble is, we can't get a new body, and changing the parts is very disruptive and expensive.

We've all seen the statistics from the popular media. Depending on the article or news program, we hear that 50 percent, 60 percent, or 70 percent of Americans are overweight. The same percentages don't get enough exercise. Anywhere from one out of five to one out of three of us smoke or abuse alcohol.

Fortunately, we have the knowledge and tools to cure our lifestyle disorder. The hard part is the motivation and will. We shouldn't panic about the prospect of high medical bills—we can take action to significantly reduce the chances of catastrophic medical bills. Let's take a look.

What Are Our Odds of Incurring Expensive Medical Bills?

It's common knowledge in my business that only a small number of people incur high medical bills. One rule of thumb is that about 80 percent of the total medical bills in the country are incurred by about 20 percent of the people.

Let's look at one study that was published in the March/April 2001 issue of *Health Affairs*—"The Concentration of Health Care Expenditures, Revisited," by Marc L. Berk and Alan C. Monheit.[2] This study shows that:

- The sickest 10 percent of the population incurs 70 percent of total medical expenditures.

- The sickest 30 percent of the population incurs 90 percent of this total.

- The sickest 50 percent of the population incurs 97 percent of this total.

Turn these statistics around, and we conclude that the healthiest 50 percent of the population incurs only 3 percent of total medical bills in the country. In 1996, this healthiest group had medical expenses that averaged $122 per year, while the sickest 1 percent of the population had medical bills that averaged $56,459 per year.

This study shows that this phenomenon has remained remarkably steady throughout the 1970s, 1980s, and 1990s.

After I thought about these statistics, I came to the following conclusion.: *I want to be in the group that doesn't incur high medical bills!* (Hey, I'm pretty smart!)

When these statistics appear in the popular media or in advertisements from insurance companies on the wisdom of buying their medical or long-term care policies, they typically strike fear

[2]*Health Affairs*, by Marc Berk and Alan Moneit. Copyright 2001 by Project Hope. Reproduced with permission of Project Hope in the format Other Book via Copyright Clearance Center.

in the readers. We get the impression that the small group of people who incur high medical bills are selected randomly, by some cruel cosmic roll of the dice.

As we'll see, it isn't entirely random. Most of the people who incur the high medical bills have lifestyle disorder, which they can change. (Of course, a few people who incur high medical bills do lead healthy lifestyles and have indeed had bad luck with their health. However, this is a very small percentage of the total population.)

Using the statistics quoted previously, there's a 70 percent to 90 percent chance that I won't incur high medical bills. These are pretty good odds—70 percent is 7 out of 10, and 90 percent is 9 out of 10. And this is assuming it is random, which it isn't. By leading a healthy lifestyle, I can almost guarantee that I'll be in the healthiest 50 percent of the population (that's the top half) that incurs only 3 percent of the total medical bills (which averaged $122 per year in 1996). This gives me the hope that I can manage the fear of incurring high medical bills that could wipe out my retirement savings.

Let's go on to look at the most expensive conditions to treat, and see if we can reduce the odds of incurring these illnesses.

What Are the Most Expensive Conditions to Treat?

Let's take a look at a study commissioned by the Institute of Medicine, and published in the March/April 2003 issue of *Health Affairs*.[3] It was titled "Spending and Service Use among People with the Fifteen Most Costly Medical Conditions, 1997." These conditions are (first being most costly):

1. Heart disease
2. Cancer
3. Trauma
4. Mental disorders
5. Pulmonary conditions
6. Diabetes

---

[3]*Health Affairs*, by Joel W. Cohen and Nancy A. Krauss. Copyright 2003 by Project Hope. Reproduced with permission of Project Hope in the format Other Book via Copyright Clearance Center.

7. Hypertension

8. Cerebrovascular disease (e.g., stroke)

9. Osteoarthritis

10. Pneumonia

11. Back problems

12. Endocrine disorders

13. Skin disorders

14. Kidney disease

15. Infectious disease

The total medical bills for any of these conditions in a year can run from $20,000 to more than $50,000. If these are chronic conditions, then we might pay a lot more over our lifetime. Most of these conditions are partially or fully preventable. Let's take a look.

- Five of these conditions—heart disease, pulmonary conditions, hypertension, cerebrovascular disease, and back problems—can be prevented or mitigated through diet, exercise, and lifestyle corrections.

- While cancer can appear to strike randomly, a large portion of the medical expenses are attributable to lung cancer caused by smoking. Another large portion is attributable to diet and toxins in our environment.

- A large portion of trauma expenses is attributed to drunk driving, driving without seatbelts, recklessness in recreational activities, or accidents in the workplace where safety standards were not followed.

- Diabetes can be managed through early diagnosis and treatment.

- Much of the expenses to treat kidney disease are attributable to alcohol abuse.

- A large portion of expenses attributable to infectious diseases is for AIDS.

As you can see, prevention, early detection, and healthy lifestyle can greatly improve our chances of avoiding the physical and financial disruption caused by these ailments.

Let's dig deeper on the most expensive condition to treat—heart disease.

In 2003, the *Journal of the American Medical Association* published the findings of two sweeping studies that exploded the myth that heart attacks result from bad genes or bad luck. Northwestern University studied 400,000 people for over 30 years, and the Indiana Heart Physicians in Indianapolis studied roughly 120,000 heart patients who were taking part in 14 clinical trials of heart disease drugs. These studies indicate that up to 90 percent of heart disease patients have one or more of the following risk factors:

- Smoking

- Diabetes

- High cholesterol

- High blood pressure

Very few heart disease patients had none of these factors, which dispels common folklore that heart disease is in our genes or the result of bad luck, and is out of our control.

At the risk of repeating myself, these factors can all be mitigated or prevented through proper diet, exercise, treatment (in the case of diabetes), and lifestyle choices.

Now let's take a closer look at cancer, the second most expensive disease to treat.

Many people have the impression that cancer is a random stroke of fate—that there is little we can do to prevent it or mitigate its effects. Not true! Let's take a look at some statistics that demonstrate that we can dramatically reduce the odds of getting cancer. These statistics come from various sources—the American Cancer Society, the National Cancer Institute, and the National Institutes of Health.

- Smoking is directly linked to one out of three cancer deaths.

- A report titled *Food, Nutrition and the Prevention of Cancer: A Global Perspective* states that 30 percent to 40 percent of cancers are directly linked to dietary choices. Yet only about 23 percent of our population consumes the diet recommended by the study.[4]

---

[4]Reprinted with permission from the *American Institute for Cancer Research.*

- Only about 5 to 10 percent of cancers are clearly hereditary—of these, the effects can be reduced significantly by early detection.

- Seventy-seven percent of all cancer diagnoses are for people age 55 and older, so clearly we need to pay attention!

The National Cancer Institute reports the following incidences of different types of cancer diagnoses:

- Twenty-two percent are for female breast cancer.

- Seventeen percent are for prostate cancer.

- Eleven percent are for colon cancer.

- Ten percent are gynecologic, such as ovarian cancer.

- Seven percent are for other cancers involving the genital and urinary systems.

- Seven percent are hematologic (involving the blood, such as leukemia).

- Six percent are for melanoma.

- Four percent are for lung cancer.

- Sixteen percent are classified as other.

Not many of these cancers are primarily out of our control. Either most are preventable, such as lung cancer, or their effects are significantly mitigated by early detection. The top five, comprising two-thirds of all cancers, are clearly helped by early detection through periodic checkups.

Another study links obesity to increased risk of cancer. According to this study, approximately 20 percent of our population is classified as obese, using the body mass index, or BMI (we'll go into more detail in the next chapter). Obese men have a 52 percent higher chance of incurring cancer than men with normal weight; for women, the chances increase to 62 percent. Again, here's another factor that we can affect through our lifestyle.

Here's an encouraging quote from a report titled *Preventing and Controlling Cancer* from the Centers for Disease Control (CDC):

The number of new cancer cases can be reduced substantially, and many cancer deaths can be prevented. Healthier lifestyles can significantly reduce a person's risk for cancer—for example, avoiding tobacco use, increasing physical activity, improving nutrition, and avoiding sun exposure. Making cancer screening and information services available and accessible to all Americans is also essential for reducing the high rates of cancer and cancer deaths. Screening tests for breast, cervical, and colorectal cancers reduce the number of deaths from these diseases by finding them early, and when they are most treatable. Screening tests for cervical and colorectal cancers can actually prevent these cancers from developing by detecting treatable precancerous conditions.

So it's clear to me that I can greatly reduce the chances of getting cancer through my lifestyle. We'll go into more detail in the next chapter.

WRAP-UP

We all need a healthy fear of high medical bills to stimulate us to do something about avoiding them.

I'm convinced that we can beat the odds by adopting healthy lifestyles as the first line of defense against high medical bills.

One problem many of us have is time—or lack thereof. For many of us, it's all we can do to get through the day and deal with life's daily issues. We just don't seem to find the time or energy to improve our lifestyle. Here's another reason for phased retirement: It gives some extra time to take care of ourselves. One more thought: Spending the time now to take care of ourselves buys us more total "life time"—and with a higher quality as well. So investing time in our health will pay off over the long run.

Here's my strategy with respect to my health, as a result of my fear and encouragement:

- Most importantly, I'll take care of my own physical well-being, to prevent serious illnesses and maintain optimum health, so I can enjoy my later years. I will be part of the healthiest half of the population that incurs low medical bills.

- I'll make the necessary investments in my health—in terms of both time and money. One strategy is to buy a high-deductible health insurance policy, and take the savings in premiums to invest in my health. Also, if I cut back my working hours, I'll use some of the newly found time to take care of myself. How to do this is discussed in the next chapter.

■ Finally, I'll make sure I am covered by some kind of health insurance, in case I have a catastrophic illness, accident, or just bad luck. This can be from work, from a policy I buy on my own, or through Medicare once I reach age 65. Strategies for health insurance policies are discussed in Chapter 8.

I'll end with another thought challenge:

How do we feel about prevention and maintaining optimum health, if we believe that we are truly on the hook for paying our medical bills? Bills that could wipe out our retirement savings.

I'll end on an optimistic note. We have all the tools and information we need to handle these challenges. It's up to us to use them!

Take Care

One-fourth of what you eat keeps you alive. The other three-fourths keeps your doctor alive.
> —Saying, from hieroglyphics
> found in an ancient Egyptian tomb

'm now totally convinced that investing in my health is as important for my later years as investing in stocks and bonds. If I don't make these health investments, I might go broke paying medical bills, I might not be able to work part-time, and my later years might be miserable as well. If I make these investments, I'll save tremendous amounts of money—money that can be better spent enjoying life! Here I'll get more specific about what I mean by health investments.

I'm also convinced that the fear of high medical bills, and the resulting need for medical insurance, should not be an obstacle to living the life I want. We need to take necessary precautions, but let's take charge and not let outside factors dictate our lives.

Some of you (or your family members) might have serious pre-existing health conditions that require you to maintain medical insurance coverage with your current employer. This situation is discussed in the next chapter on medical insurance. In any case, the ideas suggested in this chapter will help mitigate the effects of serious illnesses, and hopefully will reduce your medical bills as well.

Taking Charge

The way I am taking charge is to take care of myself.

I now believe that I can live a rich, full life to my natural life-span *if* I take care of myself. I've now set this for one of my life's goals—to enhance my physical and emotional health such that I live a vital, productive life until 100! However, if I'm successful, I'll put strain on my financial resources. This will increase the challenge of making my 401(k) balance last the rest of my life. I'm up for this challenge, and I'll cover it in the next section.

Succeeding at my goal could also put a strain on the need for medical insurance. Note, however, that a medical insurance policy, by itself, won't do anything to optimize my health. It is just a piece of paper that promises to pay for some of the medical bills if I get sick. So insurance is *not* the answer to living a full, healthy life.

Unfortunately, the vast majority of Americans choose to ignore the keys to longevity, and are afflicted with lifestyle disorder. As a result we have a health care crisis with skyrocketing health care costs. I believe that this crisis is avoidable and reversible, and here I'll share how I plan to deal with it.

Some people define healthy as not being sick. For years, this is how Western medicine has defined health, and it has focused on fixing the body once things have gone wrong. I want a more robust definition. Sure, an important part of being healthy is to prevent and avoid illness and injury. However, I want to go beyond that to encompass a state of body and mind where I feel vital and energetic, and I have set the foundation for sustaining this feeling for the rest of my life. I also believe that mental and physical health are two sides to the same coin, since my state of mind often drives my state of body, and vice versa. So I'll pay attention to my mental and emotional health as well.

To strive for my preferred definition of health, I don't need to wait for dramatic discoveries or technological breakthroughs. I can access the necessary knowledge and methods myself. While it helps to get input and guidance from health professionals, they are merely resources in my goal to optimize my health. In the end, I am responsible for my own well-being, and I need to take responsibility for it. Nobody else cares about my health as much I do!

Modern Western medicine has been studying physical and mental health for a few hundred years, using the scientific method and modern technologies. And we've discovered much useful infor-mation in this way. However, other societies and cultures have been studying this subject for a lot longer, combining scientific ob-servation with trial and error, meditation, intuition, and other methods of discovery. For instance, the Chinese have been study-ing health and longevity for thousands of years. Modern medicine is beginning to confirm the validity of these practices that other cultures have accepted for centuries. As a result, there's a lot we can learn from around the world about health in our *rest-of-life*.

Here's one example. Twenty years ago, acupuncture was viewed in the West as an exotic treatment, only for people who were daring, desperate, a little weird, or all of these! Now Western medicine has confirmed that acupuncture works well for certain conditions, and it is reimbursed by many health insurance policies as an appropriate treatment. Many other alternative health prac-tices are emerging as well, and we will do well to pay attention.

First let's address an important question.

Genes or Lifestyle?

What causes people to live long, healthy lives—is it luck of the ge-netic draw, or is it lifestyle?

Lately, the lifestyle factor is gaining credence, and rightly so. After all, we can't choose our genes, but we can choose our lifestyle. How-ever, what I'm finding is that it isn't an either-or answer. Genes and lifestyle have a complex interaction. We can have a genetic disposi-tion toward certain diseases, which are then triggered by an un-healthy lifestyle. Often it takes many years of this lifestyle to eventually develop the disease. So, we might not prove that our lifestyle was unhealthy until we keel over from a heart attack in our seventies. This reinforces one theme that I advocate in many areas: Actions we take in our fifties and sixties will dramatically impact our enjoyment of life in our seventies, eighties, nineties, and beyond.

Here's an analogy that I'm keeping in mind for optimizing my health. I need an owner's manual for my body, which tells me the types of foods I should eat, the supplements I should take, the amount, and types of exercise that are appropriate, and the diagnos-tics I should have at various times in my life. All of these take into account the genetic predispositions that I inherited, as well as my stage of life. If I have a family history of cancer, then I should really pay attention to certain dietary practices, and perhaps get certain diagnostics more frequently than the average person. If I have a family history of heart disease, then reducing stress and cholesterol and getting the appropriate amount of exercise are critically important for me. We all have different body chemistry and metabolism that influence the types and amount of food we should eat.

Am I at Risk?

A useful new tool has emerged in the past few years, called "health risk assessments." These are typically online questionnaires that ask a bunch of questions about our circumstances and lifestyles. They summarize areas for improvement and sometimes point us in the right direction for additional information. Many large employers' medical plans offer health risk assessments. Really progressive employers might offer financial incentives for us to take action steps to improve our health. Needless to say, it's a good use of our time to complete a health risk assessment. There are several free versions online that are available to anybody; here are a few good ones:

- www.youfirst.com
- www.mayoclinic.com
- www.drweil.com
- www.prevention.com

Another interesting web site is sponsored by Northwestern Mutual Life Insurance Company at www.northwesternmutual.com /games/longevity. It asks a number of lifestyle questions, and then calculates our expected life span. It then encourages us to see how our expected life span would change, if we have different answers to the questions. It's a fun way to learn about the lifestyle factors that influences our longevity.

Provocative Implications of Longevity Research

My inquiry on health led to research by physicians on practical, natural steps that ordinary people can take to prolong life. According to this research, the magic "fountain of youth" is not in a remote and inaccessible spot. It's right in front of us with our lifestyle choices.

Roy Walford, M.D., was a professor of pathology at UCLA starting in 1966. He conducted years of research on the physiological process of aging and the connection between caloric restriction and longevity. He concluded that we can add years of healthy, vital living—possibly to a life span of 100 or more—if we substantially restrict our intake of calories. However, the restricted calories must be nutrient-rich. Two interesting books that describe the lifestyle he advocated are:

- *The Anti-Aging Plan* (Four Walls Eight Windows, 1995), in which Dr. Walford describes his research and the elements of a restricted diet. He includes recipes to help us on our way.

- *Beyond the 120-Year Diet* (Four Walls Eight Windows, 2000) , in which Dr. Walford describes the recommended diet and recipes, but goes beyond diet to describe a total lifestyle that is intended to add years of vitality to our life span.

Dr. Walford points to medical research that demonstrates that about 75 percent of the killer diseases for the Western world are due to lifestyle and environment, a large part of which is what we eat. He shows that only 10 to 20 percent of cancers are genetically determined; the rest are caused by our lifestyle. This is consistent with information introduced in Chapter 6. His books describe the action steps to help prevent these major killers: heart disease, cancer, hypertension and strokes, diabetes, osteoporosis, Alzheimer's disease, and Parkinson's disease. Note that these are also the most expensive to treat, so we would do well to take steps to prevent these diseases.

Although Dr. Walford recently passed away just shy of age 80, this unfortunate turn of events in no way invalidates his messages, which are aimed squarely at the diseases resulting from "lifestyle disorcer." He succumbed to amyotrophic lateral sclerosis, otherwise known as ALS or Lou Gehrig's disease, which is an inherited disorder. Using the metaphoric language from Chapter 2, he was dealt poor cards in the hand of life, and he might have passed away much sooner had he not played his cards so well with his life-extending techniques. In spite of our best efforts, nothing in life is certain!

Like Dr. Walford, James Williams, O.M.D., in his book *Prolonging Health: Mastering the 10 Factors of Longevity* (Hampton Roads Publishing Company, 2003) also summarizes the physiological process of aging and the results of extensive research on the subject. He offers more than 90 self-help tips, and argues that "there's no reason you can't live to well over 100 years—enjoying good health all the while."

The next book is a great example of serendipity. As I mention later when discussing housing, I have recently purchased my *rest-of-life* townhouse, for reasons I explain in Chapter 18. When the previous owners moved, they left some books in the house. One of them was *Brain Longevity* (Warner Books, 1997), by Dharma Singh Khalsa, M.D.

Dr. Khalsa makes the point that physical longevity might not be desirable if our brains and minds don't stay healthy as well. Many of the steps he recommends are the same as for physical health. He says that what's good for the heart is good for the brain as well.

Finally, I found that the Chinese have been studying longevity for thousands of years, and have incorporated their knowledge into a complete lifestyle that is consistent with this modern research. There's an excellent book on the subject for Westerners, titled *The Taoism of Health, Sex, and Longevity* (Simon & Schuster, 1989), by Daniel Reid.

The lifestyle changes all of these books advocate are the same as those needed to keep healthy and reduce our medical bills. So even if we don't live to 100, it's worth it to make these changes just to address our fear of high medical bills during our *rest-of-life*. However, if we do this, there's a good chance we might live into our nineties or even to 100, so I'm planning my financial strategies with this possibility in mind.

So What Should We Do?

I've done a fair amount of dabbling, reading, and research on self-care over the past several years, including taking many health risk assessments and paying attention to the suggested action steps. Based on my experience, here I suggest 15 practices of self-care. I don't pretend that these are the final words on the subject, but for me they're a good place to start. I intend to continue learning and trying new practices for the rest of my life, and I encourage you to do the same.

1. Adopt a nutrition regimen that is appropriate for our own circumstances. This includes a healthy diet, taking supple-

ments, and most importantly, eating the right *amount* of food.

2. Get regular exercise.

3. Don't smoke.

4. Don't abuse alcohol and other substances.

5. Get enough sleep (this can be influenced by our work lifestyles). Eight hours per night is a good place to start.

6. Drink enough water. Eighty ounces per day is a good place to start.

7. Get regular checkups, including the appropriate diagnostic tests for diseases that are common in older people, or that are important given our genetic dispositions.

8. As much as possible, utilize our bodies' natural ability to diagnose and heal. This includes being aware of circumstances when our bodies will heal themselves naturally, without intrusive and sometimes harmful interventions. It also means listening to and respecting the signals our bodies send to us that tell us something might be wrong.

9. Create a supportive health care team. Seek health care professionals who advocate self-healing as the first line of defense. And when we get sick, they will help us select among conventional and alternative medicines, whichever is most appropriate for the circumstances.

10. Be aware of and avoid toxins in our environment, which substantial research is linking to the incidence of various cancers.

11. Have a daily practice to calm our minds and reduce harmful stress, such as meditation, prayer, yoga, tai chi, or exercise.

12. Find ways to identify and work out life's stresses and problems, including therapy, employee assistance programs, group discussions, church resources, friends, or spiritual advisers.

13. Periodically take healing days, where we get body care treatments to help us stay in optimum health. Examples include massages, Jacuzzi or steam room visits, and healing treatments such as acupuncture, reiki, or healing touch.

14. Have purpose in life—strong reasons for getting up in the morning. Often this means connection to family and community or helping meet social needs.

15. Create a supportive lifestyle, which includes a healthy work/life balance, a supportive social network, and basic economic security. Have at least enough to meet basic living needs.

These practices are all designed to prevent, delay, and/or mitigate the chronic and debilitating ailments of old age, most notably heart disease, cancer, Alzheimer's, osteoporosis, and broken bones due to falls. These practices should significantly decrease the chances of depleting our retirement resources for expensive medical treatments and prescription drugs. A substantial amount of research suggests and supports these practices.

Collectively, how much money would our nation save if we adopted these principles? As Carl Sagan would say, "billions and billions!" And we would be a lot more healthy and happy!

In my original manuscript, this chapter was much longer. You can see this longer version on my web site, www.restoflife.com. I provide much more information about each of these 15 practices, including how-to details. Also, I summarize the research that supports and suggests these practices.

These are some resources that have helped me on my path to pursuing a healthy lifestyle. First, here are some good books on diet and nutrition:

- *Eating Well for Optimum Health,* by Andrew Weil, M.D. (Alfred A. Knopf, 2000). This book has good descriptions on the basics of nutrition, an overview on a healthy diet, and recipes to help us get started.

- *Vitality Foods for Health and Fitness*, by Pierre Jean Cousin and Kirsten Hartvig (Duncan Baird Publishers, 2002).

- *Food as Medicine: How to Use Diet, Vitamins, Juices, and Herbs for a Healthier, Happier and Longer Life*, by Darma Singh Khalsa, M.D. (Atria Books, 2003).

Here are some good books on the body's natural ability to heal:

- Dr. Andrew Weil's book *Health and Healing* (Houghton Mifflin, 1995) does a good job of explaining different types of healing practices, and when each might be most effective. It's a great way to learn about this subject, so I can have informed conversations with my health care team. Another good book by Dr. Weil is *Spontaneous Healing* (Ballantine Books, 1995).

- *Prescription for Nutritional Healing*, by James F. Balch, M.D., and Phyllis A. Balch, C.N.C. (Avery Publishing Group, 1997).

- *The Herbal Drugstore: The Best Natural Alternatives to Over-the-Counter and Prescription Medicines*, by Linda B. White, M.D., and Steven Foster (Rodale, 2000).

For more details on pursuing a healthy lifestyle for longevity and enjoyment of life, here are some books and web sites that have helped me, in addition to the books mentioned previously.

- Dr. Andrew Weil has a great web site (www.drweil.com), which has an excellent online tutorial called "My Optimum Health Plan," based on his book titled *8 Weeks to Optimum Health* (Alfred A. Knopf, 1997). I highly recommend this tutorial, as it gives week-to-week guidance which helps us break ingrained, unhealthy habits and replace them with a healthy lifestyle that integrates diet, nutrition, exercise, and emotional health.

- The Mayo Clinic web site at www.mayoclinic.com has a wealth of information and tools on health, including a health risk assessment.

- The National Institutes of Health have an excellent web site on exercise at www.nihseniorhealth.com.

WRAP-UP

I'm advocating nothing less than actively and consciously pursuing a healthy lifestyle as an important part of my way of life, for the rest of my life. This is simply who I am. It includes lifelong learning on health, and being open to new experiences that can enhance my well-being.

Let me finish by emphasizing that this chapter summarizes a *rest-of-life* quest. We can't possibly do everything at once. It took me several months to read the resources I list in this chapter, and I frequently revisit them for reference and to enhance my understanding. It took even longer to adopt some of the practices into my lifestyle, and I'm still working on several. However, we don't need to do everything at once. We have decades to put these practices into place. I started with the first four, which are the most important, and am taking my time with the rest. I don't expect to be perfect. I acknowledge that I need to change some deeply ingrained lifestyle habits, which can be hard to do. Chapter 21 has some strategies for making difficult changes in our lives. I'll just do my best, and focus on improvement over time.

I believe that most of us don't make significant changes in our lives, until we get a message that we can't ignore. We might know intellectually that we should make important changes, but we just can't seem to get around to them. Waiting until we get our own personal health message is not a good strategy. The message can kill us!

So part of my quest for motivation was to hear from other people who survived their own personal health message, made significant changes in their lifestyles, and are willing to share their stories with us. These stories were in my original manuscript, but I moved them to my web site to make this book a reasonable length. I got their messages! I'm not going to wait to get my own message, and I hope these stories do the same for you!

As a result of my inquiry, I now feel confident that I won't let the fear of high medical bills prevent me from making important changes in my life. I hope you feel the same way, too. Cheers!

Just in Case

Be prepared.
  —Boy Scout motto, from the founder Lord Baden-Powell

T he preceding chapter advocates taking care of ourselves as the first line of defense against high medical bills and to make sure we can enjoy life to its fullest. This chapter discusses the best ways to protect ourselves, including whether to buy long-term care insurance and how to buy medical services when we need them. This topic is the second part of my strategy that lets me move ahead with my *rest-of-life* without the fear of high medical bills holding me back.

There are three distinct sets of strategies: strategies for before age 65, strategies for after age 65 when I become eligible for Medicare, and strategies I'll use for the rest of my life, both before and after age 65.

Strategies before Age 65

- While I am working, either full-time or part-time, I'll try very hard to work for an employer that sponsors a group medical plan. I'll do this at least until age 65, when I become eligible for Medicare.

- In the next few years, I expect to take advantage of certain features in recent legislation (these changes affect employer-sponsored group medical plans before age 65). Specifically, if my employer offers a high-deductible medical plan together with a health spending account (HSA), most likely I'll sign up.

- If I retire full-time before age 65, or if my employer doesn't sponsor a group medical plan, then I'll purchase a low-cost individual medical insurance policy that protects me only against catastrophic medical bills. Such a policy will have a high deductible and won't pay much, if anything, for routine doctor's office visits. I'll also use the new HSA offering.

- If necessary and feasible, I'll take advantage of COBRA coverage. This allows me to continue group medical coverage from my most recent employer for up to 18 months after terminating employment.

Strategies after Age 65

- Once I make it to age 65, I can breathe a sigh of relief, since Medicare will take care of a large portion of my medical bills.

- At that time, I will purchase a low-cost Medicare supplement plan, or join a Medicare Advantage program.

- Of course, I will use group medical coverage through my work, if that is still available.

Strategies before and after Age 65

- I don't plan to buy long-term care insurance, for reasons I'll discuss in this chapter.

- I'll be an informed medical consumer, and will strive to buy only the medical services I really need, at the most effective price.

Now let's go into detail about each aspect.

I'll Use Medical Plans at Work

If I'm working anyway for all the reasons discussed earlier, then I'll seek employers that sponsor group medical plans.

Many such plans require a minimum number of working hours for eligibility, often 20 hours per week, but sometimes as high as 30 hours per week. Another possibility is that my employer might subsidize a smaller portion of the overall cost if I work only part-time. I'll take these things into account, both when selecting employers and when deciding how much to work. This is certainly a question I'll ask if I'm interviewing for work.

Some employers charge their employees a lot for medical coverage—sometimes the full cost. In this case, I might be better off with an individually purchased plan (which we'll discuss later). By knowing the cost and coverage of individually purchased plans, you can compare the cost and features to group plans.

How Can Recent Legislative Changes Help Me Now?

In December 2003, significant changes in Medicare coverage (i.e., after age 65) were made. However, there are also important changes that should have a positive effect on employer-sponsored plans for all employees, including those under age 65.

The Medicare Reform Act of 2003 created health spending accounts (HSAs). To be eligible for an HSA, we must participate in something called a high-deductible health plan (HDHP). This is a medical insurance plan with a deductible of at least $1,000 for an individual, or $2,000 for family coverage, that we must pay before benefits will be paid by the insurance policy. However, an HDHP can have a lower deductible for preventive services.

An HSA is similar to an individual retirement account (IRA). Each year, we can contribute amounts up to the plan's deductible, but no more than $2,600 per individual or $5,150 per family in 2004. These amounts are indexed in the future. Our contributions aren't included in taxable income, and the investment earnings aren't subject to income taxes.

We can use money in our HSAs to pay for the following expenses for ourself, our spouse, and our dependents:

- Medical expenses that aren't covered by our medical plan, including deductibles, co-payments, and co-insurance.

- Medical services that aren't covered by our plan, or for providers who aren't part of our plan's network.

- Certain premiums, such as COBRA premiums (we discuss CO-BRA in a few pages), long-term care insurance, medical policies while we're receiving unemployment compensation, and health insurance once we turn age 65 (except for Medicare supplement policies).

- Medicare deductibles, co-payments, and premiums.

Withdrawals from HSAs for eligible medical expenses aren't subject to income taxes at the time of withdrawal. If we withdraw from the HSA for other than medical expenses, then the amount of the withdrawal is subject to income taxes, plus a 10 percent excise penalty. However, this penalty doesn't apply once we reach age 65.

Here's the good part. If we don't use up our HSA funds in a year, we can carry the unused balances forward to future years until we can use them. For each year that we're covered by a high-deductible plan, we can contribute more money to the HSA, even if we have unused balances from prior years. Essentially we are able to use the HSA to build a financial cushion for our later years, when we are more likely to have higher medical bills.

The purpose of HSAs is to get us involved with paying for medical bills, and to encourage us to incorporate prevention into our lifestyles. As the theory goes, if we use our own money, we'll become better medical consumers. We'll do this by using medical services only when we need them, or by seeking the best deals when purchasing medical services.

I expect that more employers will begin to offer HDHPs to their employees, and will reduce required contributions compared to conventional plans with lower deductibles. If this happens, we can then contribute the resulting savings to our HSAs.

As of mid-2004, a few financial institutions offer HSAs, but not many employers have adjusted their medical plans accordingly. In addition, the federal government needs to provide guidance on these plans to fill in some details that weren't covered in the legislation. However, by early 2005, I fully expect investment and insurance institutions to offer a variety of HSAs, and employers to offer newly designed HDHPs. I plan to provide updates on my web site at www.restoflife.com.

If I Must, I'll Buy My Own Policy

In the future, there's a chance I might not have medical coverage from my employer, either because I'm not working enough hours, I'm self-employed, or I decide to retire full-time. In this case, I can still buy an individual medical policy. However, there are many products and choices to make, so I need to become an informed consumer.

One possibility to investigate is group insurance through a union, professional organization, club, or some other organization. Often I can get a better deal through the combined purchasing power of a group of people, compared to individual policies.

For individual policies, good sources of information and/or purchasing a policy are a trusted insurance agent, Blue Cross/ Blue Shield organizations, AARP (see www.aarp.org), and the Internet. You can use your favorite search engine and type in the

"Unfortunately, you have what we call 'no insurance.'"

words "individual health insurance," and you'll get plenty of references. Here are some sites that I found particularly useful:

- www.healthinsurance.org

- www.ahcpr.gov

- www.ehealthinsurance.com

- www.insure.com

These sites provide a lot of information, and with the last two we can get instant quotes that help us compare features and prices. If we must buy individual health insurance, we'll need to become informed and shop around. I'll share some important considerations and strategies, but we'll need to learn more and eventually make our own decisions.

There are two important decisions to make when selecting an individual insurance policy:

1. The type of plan—fee for service, health maintenance organization (HMO), or preferred provider organization (PPO). This influences the specific medical providers that are available to us.

2. The financial features, such as deductibles, co-insurance, and out-of-pocket limits.

Type of Plan

- A fee-for-service plan pays a specified portion of the fees we incur for medical services, including doctors, hospitals, and prescriptions. Usually deductibles and co-insurance payments apply. We can select any doctor or provider in any part of the country. For this reason, fee-for-service plans are usually the most expensive.

- With an HMO, normally we must use a doctor who belongs to the HMO. There may be alternative arrangements if we're traveling outside the HMO's geographic area. Usually there is a small fee each time we see the doctor, called a co-payment. Also, with an HMO, typically we must first see a primary care physician, who will then refer us to a specialist if necessary. HMOs are usually the least expensive type of insurance coverage, with one exception. It can be hard to find an HMO for only catastrophic coverage, while these are widely available with PPOs (see below). In this case, a PPO catastrophic policy can be the least expensive solution.

- PPOs are a hybrid between a fee-for-service plan and an HMO. We can use any doctor or medical provider as with a fee-for-service plan, but we have financial incentives to use a doctor or health care professional in the provider network. Usually these incentives include a lower deductible or co-payment. Also, typically we have a wider selection of doctors and medical providers in the PPO network, compared to an HMO. Finally, we have more control over the health care professionals we use, since we're not required to first see a primary care physician. PPOs are typically more expensive than HMOs, unless we buy a PPO policy that excludes routine doctor visits and has a high deductible. We're more likely to find a catastrophic plan with a PPO, compared to an HMO.

My preference is PPOs. The PPO represents a good compromise between an HMO and a fee-for-service plan, and is more likely to have a policy for just catastrophic coverage that I seek until Medicare kicks in at age 65.

The web site of the Agency for Healthcare and Quality—www.ahcpr.gov—has more information on the types of plans, along with a questionnaire that helps us decide which plan might fit best with our circumstances.

Financial Features

As mentioned, most likely I'd buy a PPO plan. In this case, or if I buy a fee-for-service plan, then I'll need to make decisions about deductibles, co-insurance amounts, payments for doctor visits, and annual out-of-pocket limits.

If and when I need to buy an individual policy (before age 65), my strategy is to buy insurance for only the truly catastrophic illnesses and accidents. These types of policies have the lowest costs. I only want to protect my retirement savings from getting wiped out. Catastrophic expenses typically result from hospital stays, surgery, and periods in convalescent facilities following a serious illness or accident. Costs for routine doctor's visits won't wipe me out, and the costs for most prescription drugs won't, either. This gives me some guidelines for analyzing individual medical policies.

Policies that reimburse for routine doctor's office visits and maintenance services, such as immunizations, charge the highest premiums. When insurance companies set the premiums for these types of policies, they typically assume the worst regarding the frequency of using medical services, and they build in their profit margins. So I'm actually paying for these routine services through high premiums, regardless of whether I actually use these services. If I take care of myself, as I advocate in the previous chapter, then I don't expect to go to the doctor, except for the periodic diagnostics and checkups that are recommended for our later years. I'm better off paying for these routine services directly than through a medical insurance plan. I can also use the money I save in premiums for my health investments—services that aren't covered by most medical plans, or providers that aren't covered by my insurance company's network. These will help me stay healthy, while paying for insurance premiums, by itself, won't do anything for my health. Finally, if I build up a cushion using an HSA, I can use it to pay for all of these expenses, instead of using an expensive insurance policy.

Here are some considerations for the financial features:

- I'll take a high-deductible plan—at least $1,000 so I can use an HSA, as described previously. This brings the cost down dramatically because it eliminates the routine doctors visits (see the examples in Table 8.1).

- I'll pick an out-of-pocket limit that I can afford—say $5,000. I'll save through an HSA so that I'll have this amount on hand if I need it.

- I'll pick a co-insurance amount of 20 percent or 30 percent.

- Some policies don't reimburse for expenses for office visits, as a way to reduce premium amounts. These are amounts paid for diagnosis and treatment of an illness or injury by physicians in their offices. Since office visits are at most a few hundred dollars, I can afford to pay them out of my pocket. If I don't go to the doctor very often, I can buy a policy that doesn't pay for office visits and save some money in my premiums.

■ The less expensive policies either don't pay for prescription drugs, require a high deductible or co-payment, or provide incentives to select generic drugs. Prescription drugs present a tricky problem. I won't need them if I'm healthy, or I can use alternative treatments. However, sometimes prescription drugs can be a lifesaver. Depending on my health, I'd either pick a plan that doesn't cover drugs or select a plan with a high deductible and/or incentives to use generic drugs.

Table 8.1 shows some sample quotes I obtained from the eHealth-Insurance.com web site (www.ehealthinsurance.com) to illustrate the costs of various features. These examples are for coverage just for myself, and not my family members. I picked from a variety of Blue Cross or Blue Shield plans that are available to me in California. My intent is to demonstrate the extent to which annual premiums can vary, depending on the financial features of the plan. The quotes also give you a ballpark idea of costs for a healthy, 50-year-old male. If you are in the market for individual coverage, your premiums would vary considerably by your age, sex, location, and how healthy you are. I encourage you to do your own shopping!
Here are a few observations on this table:

■ Note the huge variance in premiums. The lowest premium is $5,916 less per year than the highest. The difference between moderate and expensive policies is greater than $2,000 per year. If I'm healthy and don't need to go to the doctor, that's a lot of money that I can save in a HSA and invest in my health.

■ All of these policies will protect me from having to pay for catastrophic situations—extended hospital stays and surgeries.

■ The very cheapest policies pay little or nothing for doctor's visits and prescription drugs. Once again, these are usually not catastrophic amounts—in a really bad year, I might spend a few thousand dollars on these items, which I can afford if I've built up a cushion in an HSA.

TABLE 8.1. Sample Features and Costs of Individual Medical Policies

Deductible	Co-insurance	Out-of-Pocket Maximum	Doctor's Visits Covered? Co-payment	Prescription Drugs Covered? Co-payment	Annual Premium
$1,000	20%	$3,500	No	No	$1,572
$5,000	30%	$7,000	Yes—$35 co-payment	Yes—$10 for generics, otherwise higher	$1,620
$ 0	40%	$7,500	No	No	$1,788
$2,400	30%	$3,000	Yes—$45 co-payment	Yes—after medical deductible met, then 30% co-payment	$2,088
$5,000	20%	$7,500	Yes—$30 co-payment	Yes—$10 for generics, otherwise higher	$2,184
$5,000	30%	$7,500	Yes—30% co-payment	Yes—$10 for generics, otherwise higher	$2,280
$2,500	30%	$5,000	Yes—30% co-payment	Yes—$10 for generics, otherwise higher	$2,772
$2,000	30%	$5,000	Yes—$45 co-payment	Yes—$10 for generics, otherwise higher	$3,120
$1,500	30%	$4,000	Yes—30% co-payment	Yes—$10 for generics, otherwise higher	$3,600
$1,000	30%	$4,000	Yes—30% co-payment	Yes—$10 for generics, otherwise higher	$4,512
$1,000	30%	$4,500	Yes—$40 co-payment	Yes—$7 for generics, otherwise higher	$4,788
$ 750	30%	$4,000	Yes—$35 co-payment	Yes—$10 for generics, otherwise higher	$5,304
$ 500	30%	$4,000	Yes—30% co-payment	Yes—$10 for generics, otherwise higher	$5,496
$ 500	25%	$3,500	Yes—$30 co-payment	Yes—$7 for generics, otherwise higher	$7,488

Source: www.ehealthinsurance.com.

- Other considerations that are important for selecting medical insurance policies include the coverage of the provider network—do I have a reasonable selection of doctors? Also, what is the coverage for extended stays in a nursing facility after a serious illness?

- Another important feature is called "guaranteed renewable." This means that the insurance company can't cancel my policy as long as I pay my premiums. This is very important—if I don't have this feature, I might be healthy when I buy the policy, but then get sick, incur high expenses, and be in a bad position if the insurance company cancels my coverage.

One final consideration for buying individual policies relates to preexisting conditions. For many years, health insurance companies have reduced their costs by invoking a "preexisting condition" clause and refusing to cover a condition we had before we bought the medical insurance policy. Fortunately for us, a federal law gives us some protection. It's called the Health Insurance Portability and Accountability Act of 1996 (HIPAA). Its purpose is to protect employees who are moving from one job to another from losing coverage due to preexisting conditions.

HIPAA imposes limits on when group health plans can invoke preexisting condition clauses. As long as we have had qualifying medical coverage for at least 12 months, with no lapse in coverage for 63 days or more, then a new group health plan cannot invoke the preexisting condition clause.

Under HIPAA, we might also have the right to buy individual medical coverage after we lose group health coverage. For this protection, we must have had at least 18 months of qualifying coverage under a prior group health care plan, and have no other options available for group health care coverage. Unfortunately, there are no rules that limit the premiums that insurance companies can charge, so if we have preexisting conditions, we might be thrown into a higher-risk pool with high premiums.

These few paragraphs just raise awareness about the protection available to us with respect to preexisting conditions. If we lose group health coverage and think we might have preexisting conditions, there's a whole slew of rules about our rights and qualifying conditions that we should learn. Preferably, we do this *before* we change jobs or lose our coverage. I found a lot of information on-line about HIPAA and how it impacts individual and group health plans. I went to my favorite Internet search engine and typed in "HIPAA." I found these sites to be useful:

- *www.dol.gov.* This is the official site of the U.S. Department of Labor. Look for the section on health plans.

- *http://info.insure.com.* This is an online insurance broker that has a lot of useful background information.

These are some strategies for effectively managing our health and money that show how we can take into account medical expenses when developing our total expenses (see Section Three of this book for more on our expenses). This chapter gives me the knowledge and confidence to obtain the protection I need. If I can't afford the premiums for individual policies, then I'll need to work for an employer with affordable coverage. If I am able to afford the premiums, I'll buy the protection I need if I retire before age 65 or if I lose coverage from employment. Either way, I won't let the fear of losing medical coverage stop me from making important work/life changes.

What Is COBRA Coverage?

COBRA stands for the Consolidated Omnibus Budget Reconciliation Act of 1985. COBRA is a federal law that requires employers to offer medical coverage to employees and their dependents who have terminated employment for any reason. COBRA coverage is also available to spouses who lose coverage due to a divorce or death of the covered employee, or if the employee-spouse retires and is eligible for Medicare. In most cases, the coverage can be continued for up to 18 months following termination of employment, although the period is extended to 36 months in some cases (spouses who lose eligibility for the reasons just mentioned). Some states require longer periods of coverage than the federal law requires.

The employer usually charges the full cost of the medical coverage—it doesn't need to subsidize part of the cost like it typically does for employees. As a result, COBRA coverage can be very expensive—premiums exceeding $300 per month aren't unusual. It's quite likely that COBRA premiums are higher than premiums for an individually purchased policy. It pays to compare! COBRA coverage must be elected within 60 days of the event that triggers the coverage—typically the date of employment termination.

COBRA coverage can be useful in the following situations:

- If I and/or my spouse are close to age 65, I can use COBRA coverage as a bridge until Medicare kicks in. Note that COBRA coverage ends when I become eligible for Medicare.

- I can use COBRA coverage as a stopgap until I have the time to shop for an individual policy.

- COBRA might make sense if I expect high medical bills during the period immediately following my termination of employment, or if I have preexisting conditions that might put me in a higher-risk category for individually purchased policies.

If I lose group medical coverage due to termination of employment, the death or retirement of my spouse, or divorce, then I'll learn more about my COBRA rights. I found much good information online by going to my favorite Internet search engine and typing in the words "COBRA coverage." The same web sites mentioned previously were helpful:

- *http://info.insure.com*. This web site also identifies states that require more generous coverage than the federal law.

- *www.dol.gov.*

As with HIPAA, I'll learn about my COBRA rights before I terminate or retire.

What about Medicare?

Medicare is a federal health insurance program for people age 65 or older, who are eligible for Social Security retirement benefits or railroad retirement benefits. Medicare pays for a significant portion of our medical bills after age 65, so it's an important part of our financial security. However, Medicare doesn't pay all medical bills—in fact, by some estimates, it pays only a little more than half of seniors' medical costs. So, there's no excuse to stop taking care of ourselves, both for financial and for quality-of-life reasons.

It's pretty easy to find educational material on Medicare, so I won't duplicate it here. I have some background information on Medicare on my web site, www.restoflife.com. You can also go to the official Medicare web site, www.medicare.gov, or AARP's web site www.aarp.org.

To summarize Medicare, it's an important part of our financial security. I recommend that we sign up and pay for the optional coverages, Medicare Parts B and D, as soon as we are eligible. My reasons are on my web site. In addition, Medicare coverage is not complete, so I recommend supplementing the coverage with private insurance, unless we participate in one of the new Medicare Advantage (MA) plans (see my web site if you're not familiar with this term).

Medicare Supplement Policies

We can buy private health insurance policies that fill in the gaps in the Medicare coverage. Hence the common name Medigap plan. The gap in Medicare is indeed large. According to a study conducted by the Kaiser Family Foundation, Medicare covers only 56 percent of total health care expenditures for people age 65 and older, and as a result 87 percent buy some sort of supplemental policy.

If we participate in a Medicare Advantage plan, then we don't need a Medigap plan. In fact, it is illegal for anyone to sell us a Medigap plan if they know we are enrolled in a Medicare Advantage plan.

Several pages ago I identified resources for individually purchased health care plans—we can use the same resources for Medigap policies.

There are 10 standardized Medigap plans, A through J. Each plan has a different set of benefits. Plan A covers only basic benefits, which are included in all the plans. Plan J provides the most generous benefits, with the highest premiums. Not all insurance companies offer all the Medigap plans, and all types of plans may not be available in certain states or geographic areas.

One nice feature of Medigap policies is that they must be guaranteed renewable. This means that if we keep paying our premiums, the insurance company cannot cancel our policy, regardless of how sick we get.

The Medicare Reform Act prohibits Medigap policies from covering prescription drug expenses in 2006. As a result of this and other features of this new law, we can expect significant changes in Medigap policies in the future, which I'll discuss on my web site, www.restoflife.com.

Here are examples of budgets for annual premium amounts in 2004 for Medicare and private insurance, once we turn age 65. This is just an example for budgeting our total *rest-of-life* expenses, which we will do in later chapters. I had to mix apples and oranges, because Medicare coverage for prescription drugs won't be available until 2006. For Medigap insurance, I used a policy offered in 2004—a generous plan that doesn't cover prescription drugs, since Medicare will cover drugs beginning in 2006. During 2004, monthly premiums for these plans ranged from $100 to $200—I used the higher number for the budget in Table 8.2.

The out-of-pocket costs are for medical expenses that aren't covered by any of these plans. For example, if we are heavy users of prescription drugs, we might need to include estimates of amounts not covered by Medicare. I just used an estimate of $300 per month, which one study identifies as average out-of-pocket expenses. If we take care of ourselves, we might be able to reduce this significantly, perhaps close to zero.

These fees aren't cheap! It's one important reason to consider a Medicare Advantage plan. See my web site for details on these new programs as they emerge. It's also a good reason to take care of ourselves and to build a financial cushion in an HSA.

TABLE 8.2   Sample Annual Budget for Medical Costs

Premium for Medicare Part B (coverage for physicians)	$ 800
Premium for Medicare Part D (prescription drug coverage)	$ 400
Premium for Medigap policy	$2,400
Out-of-pocket costs	$3,600
Total	$7,200

Should I Buy a Long-Term Care Policy?

I've been interested in this subject for awhile, particularly as I got older. Once I looked into these policies, the short answer to the above question became "no." I'll tell you my reasons, so you can make up your mind for yourself.

Scary ads from insurance companies urge us to buy their long-term care policies. They go something like this:

> The odds are one out of three that you will need to go into a nursing home at some point over your lifetime. And nursing homes can cost over $50,000 per year. A prolonged stay can wipe out your retirement savings.

At best, this argument is misleading. At worst, it's a good example of that famous quote from Benjamin Disraeli about statistics: "There are three kinds of lies: lies, damned lies, and statistics."

Each statement has validity—it's the combining of the three statements together that creates the deception. Yes, the odds might be high that at some time in our lifetime we'll need some sort of assistance with living; however, that might not mean a nursing home. Yes, nursing homes can cost over $50,000 per year. And yes, an extended stay in a nursing home can severely damage a retirement nest egg. However, let's take a closer look.

First, let's look at some other statistics. According to a study in the *New England Journal of Medicine,* 86 percent of men and 69 percent of women will never need a nursing home. The 2000 census shows that only 4.5 percent of people over age 65 live in nursing homes, and only 18.2 percent of seniors over age 85 live in them. On the other hand, a study by the U.S. Department of Labor estimates that people who reach age 65 have a 40 percent chance of entering a nursing home at some point, and that 10 percent of those will stay for five years or more.

All of these statistics can get very confusing. One problem is that a nursing home can be defined differently by different researchers. Regardless of the study I choose to believe, the odds are easy to beat if we take care of ourselves. Most conditions that put people in nursing homes—heart disease, cancer, Alzheimer's, osteoporosis—are preventable or their symptoms can be delayed and mitigated through diet, exercise, and lifestyle.

And even the last statistic—that 10 percent of people entering nursing homes will stay for five years or more—shouldn't create fear. Multiply 40 percent by 10 percent and the result is 4 percent. This means that only one person out of 25 will be in a nursing home for five years or more.

Next, let's get some terms straight.

- Generally, a nursing home refers to a facility that provides a variety of personal care and health services. Such services include assistance with bathing, dressing, and using the bathroom.

- A skilled nursing facility goes way beyond a typical nursing home, and provides a level of care that must be given by or supervised by registered nurses. Such care can include getting intravenous injections, tube feeding, assistance with medications, and rehabilitation.

Now, let's look at a few considerations.

- It's very unlikely that we will spend a year in a skilled nursing facility or rehabilitation facility. Most of the time, a stay in a skilled nursing facility is brief—a month or less. Either we recover or we die.

- If we stay in a skilled nursing facility immediately following a hospital stay, Medicare will pay a significant portion of the costs for up to 100 days.

- There are many alternatives to a full-blown nursing home that are much less expensive. These include home health services, adult day-care centers, and that timeless solution—friends and family.

Let's go on to look at some features of typical long-term care policies that can cause problems.

- They are very expensive. If I start paying premiums in my fifties, the annual premium can easily exceed $2,000 per year. If I start in my sixties, I can be paying more than $3,000 per year. If I never need the policy, I've thrown a lot of money down the drain. A better idea is to simply invest the annual amount that I would have spent on premiums. For example, suppose I skip a long-term care policy. Instead, I invest $2,000 per year starting at age 55 and earn 5 percent per year. Most likely I won't need long-term care until my eighties or beyond. By the time I'm age 80, my long-term care investment account will have grown to over $95,000. While this might not cover all nursing home costs, it will go a long way, and it might be more than typical policies will pay in benefits.

- The policies have lots of catches and fine print. They can go to great lengths to make sure we use alternative sources, as mentioned previously, before they will pay the benefits promised by the policy. Insurance companies may require a physical with their own doctor before permitting benefits to be paid, and these doctors have the goal of keeping costs down.

- Most policies reserve the right to raise premiums. It's possible that I can initially afford the premiums, but if they are raised significantly, I can't afford them anymore, and I'll be forced to discontinue the policy.

I found a great deal of information about long-term care policies by simply going to my favorite Internet search engine and typing in the words "long-term care insurance." Many sites are sponsored by insurance companies and insurance agents, and will pitch their policies. However, I still learned a lot by perusing the web sites. One site that simply has a lot of good information and is not trying to sell anything is www.longtermcarelink.net.

A *Consumer Reports* article in November 2003 was critical of long-term care policies. I found it at www.consumerreports.org. It's worth a look—it does provide tips on buying these policies, if you still think you need such a policy.

After conducting my research, I concluded that I would simply set aside $25,000 to $50,000 of my retirement savings as my long-term care insurance, and let it grow with investment earnings. I won't touch it until I need it for this purpose. Hopefully, the investment earnings will keep pace with inflation in nursing home costs. As I've said repeatedly in this book, the best insurance is to take care of myself, and have a rich network of friends and family who might provide help if I need it.

I'll Be an Informed, Intelligent Medical Consumer

Even if I take care of myself, I still expect to need professional medical help occasionally. In this case, I'll strive for the most cost-effective treatments.

Here's another area where I'm glad to share some ideas developed by Watson Wyatt. Our clients are very interested in educating their employees to be informed medical consumers, as one way to save costs. Here are some tips we have developed as part of this work.

- Shop around! Ask medical providers how much they charge. If we need an expensive treatment such as a surgical procedure, compare prices. I've always been astonished at the variance in prices, and price is no indication of quality. Look for centers of excellence that specialize in certain procedures; often they have higher quality and lower prices, compared to facilities that perform only a few procedures per year. For really serious treatments, it may pay to look outside our geographical area.

- I'll only go to the doctor when I really need it. I won't rush to the doctor for colds, the flu, and other temporary afflictions. Many insurance companies and employers' medical plans now have hotlines that are staffed by nurses who can help us determine if we need to go to the doctor.

- If my physician suggests expensive surgery or prescription drugs, I'll ask about the scientific evidence that supports these treatments. It's possible that the evidence isn't convincing, or that the treatments don't significantly improve the medical outcomes. I'll also ask about the side effects, which can be as bad as the cure. These thoughts can be particularly true with regard to prescription drugs, which are often marketed aggressively to physicians by large drug companies.

- I'll be informed of alternative treatments, and discuss them with my doctor. Can I use natural treatments such as diet, exercise, and supplements? Do I need this treatment now? What will happen if I simply wait to let my body's natural healing power run its course?

■ A cutting-edge service offered by some employers and insurance companies is a resource on alternative treatments for various conditions. For example, one company, called Consumer's Medical Resource, puts together individually tailored reports on request for people who have serious conditions. These reports are prepared by doctors, and summarize the research that has been conducted on various treatment alternatives. The main goal is for the patient to have an informed discussion with the physician about the most effective means of treatment, using the latest research.

WRAP-UP

As with other subjects in this book, for the rest of my life, I'll keep up-to-date with the latest insurance products and Medicare. I'll always be protected, but at the best price.

When I have a medical condition, I'll become informed about alternative forms of treatment. Whenever possible, I'll let my body's natural defenses protect me—this is the cheapest, healthiest approach! This will be another area of lifelong learning for me.

The main point of this chapter is that I won't let the fear of high costs for medical insurance prevent me from living the life I want. I have the tools and knowledge to manage my fear of high medical bills.

SECTION THREE

MONEY MATTERS

How many things I can do without!
> —Socrates, on looking at a multitude
> of goods displayed for sale

N ow that we've discussed what will make us happy and fulfilled in our later years and how to stay healthy, let's finally turn to money. After all, this subject got me started on this book, and it may be the reason you originally bought it. For most people, this is a confusing, complicated, yet boring subject. I've done my best to simplify the strategies to be easily understandable, and keep you amused at the same time.

We face an intimidating challenge: how to make our financial resources last the rest of our lives. If we follow the advice in the first two sections, most likely we will prolong our lives into our late eighties, nineties, or even to 100 and beyond. This will put additional strain on our financial resources, particularly the balances in our 401(k) plans. Living to 100 will not be enjoyable if we run out of money at age 80. So, in this section I discuss how to support the lifestyle we want, taking into account the possibility that we might live a long time.

In the preceding two sections, I describe my intense interest in learning more about happiness and health in our later years, and my quest for more information. This section is a little different.

I've consulted to large corporations for nearly 30 years on these topics. Over the years, I've had many discussions and heated debates with my friends and colleagues Larry DiFiore, Cary Franklin, Dave Hoak, and many others about how to finance our retirement. The subjects of working lunches for normal people might be politics, our children, sporting events, or the latest fashions, but we debate asset allocation, the status of Social Security, and whether to take a lump sum or life annuity from a defined benefit plan. These are very exciting lunches—I wish you could join us sometime!

When we were in our thirties and forties, these discussions were mostly theoretical, since retirement age was far in the future. However, now that most of my colleagues have reached the third quarter in life, these discussions have become more focused and intense, as we're thinking about our own retirement. Actually, my colleagues are changing their thinking from retirement to *rest-of-life*, as I discuss my research for the first two sections in this book.

So here I share many professional lifetimes—mine and my colleagues—of thinking about financing our *rest-of-life*. I've taken advantage of data and tools that Watson Wyatt uses when consulting to America's largest corporations. I had my thoughts and chapters reviewed by many experts within Watson Wyatt, and I ended up learning a lot in the process.

We'll discuss how to invest our savings and withdraw them, to minimize the chances of outliving our financial resources. This subject requires paying attention to a number of issues: how much to withdraw, which investments to use, which financial products to use, which institutions to give our money to, and how to minimize taxes along the way. Please keep in mind that you may have to read these chapters once all the way through to get the whole picture, and then go back and reread some chapters to fully understand the strategies. It's a complicated subject, but one you can understand if you just take the necessary time.

I'll also cover how to maximize our income from Social Security, from defined benefit pension plans, and from other financial resources. Finally, I'll cover the other side of the picture—our living expenses in our *rest-of-life* years, and how to match them up with our financial resources.

How Much Is Enough?

Annual income twenty pounds, annual expenditure nineteen
six, result happiness. Annual income twenty pounds, annual
expenditure twenty pound ought and six, result misery.
— Charles Dickens, in *David Copperfield*

C an I retire full-time *now*? For most of us, this is the real reason for
asking the "how much is enough" question—at least it was for me.
And if I can't retire full-time, can I retire part-time? And if I must
keep working full-time, when *can* I retire?

Here we explore the methods and information to help us analyze the "when can I retire" question.

The traditional method—replacement ratio analysis—focuses
on building enough financial resources to replace our after-tax income that we received just before retirement. From this analysis,
we find statements like "You need 70 percent to 80 percent of your
preretirement income to have a comfortable retirement." I used
this analysis in *Don't Work Forever!*, but my thinking has evolved
since I wrote that book nearly ten years ago.

We frequently use replacement ratio analysis when working
with employers, to help them design their retirement plans. Our
clients want to make sure that their retirement programs deliver
adequate retirement incomes to their employees, and replacement
ratio analysis works just fine for this purpose. However, it is not the
best analysis for *individuals* to determine if and when they can retire. There are two shortcomings with using the replacement ratio

analysis for our own individual situation. It focuses on just half of our financial picture—income—and it ignores the other half—expenses. It doesn't take into account income from wages in our later years—it's based on the old twentieth-century all-or-nothing model of working and retiring.

Basically, the replacement ratio analysis tries to duplicate our life while we were working. However, we may want to reinvent ourselves in many ways in our later years, and our pattern of income and expenditures may change significantly. The traditional replacement ratio model works fine if we follow the old twentieth-century model of retirement. If this is the case for you, the ideas and methodologies in this book will still work for you. In addition, I point you toward resources that still rely on this old model, and may give you additional insights.

Can we find an effective, simple answer to the "how much is enough" question? After a great deal of investigation and thinking, my answer is . . . yes and no!

Yes, I found an effective, simple answer. No, because for most of us, the devil is in the details. We'll need a lot of effort to make it happen.

For most of us, this will be an iterative process for the rest of our lives. What do I mean by that? We will always be adjusting our lives and finances to accommodate new circumstances, new goals, and new points of view. Most of us won't put into place a strategy that will last untouched for 30 years.

Here's another possibility that happens for a lot of us. Initially, we do the analysis to determine if we can retire full-time or even part-time, and the answer is "no." We don't like the answer. So we go back and adjust our finances, points of view, and circumstances until we *do* like the answer.

Eventually in this chapter I'll get to the "when can I retire?" questions, but first let's look at . . .

The Magic Formula

Let's start with the simple answer, which gives us a framework for answering all of these questions. This answer is easy to say, harder to do. But it does give us the guiding principle for all of our thinking about our finances.

I need to arrange my life, and have enough financial resources, such that:

$$I > E$$

I is my annual income, and E represents my annual living expenses.

I need sufficient financial resources to sustain this relationship each year for the rest of my life.

If my I is greater than my E, then I'm okay. If not, then eventually I'll get into trouble unless I make some adjustments. The idea is as simple as that, although actually making it happen is more difficult.

The trick is to make my I as big as possible, and to *sustain it for the rest of my life*, however long that may be. This goal is intrinsic to all the strategies discussed here. Outliving my financial resources is an outcome I want to avoid at all costs. So I have spent a lot of time thinking about strategies to minimize this possibility.

Where does my I come from?

- Withdrawals from my investments, including income from dividends and interest, and, depending on my circumstances, withdrawals from my principal.

- Pension income, if I participate in a defined benefit plan.

- Social Security (after age 62).

- Wages.

- Other sources such as the equity in our homes, insurance, inheritances, and legal settlements from divorces.

On the other side of the magic formula, I need to minimize my E, and again try to contain increases over the rest of my life. Easier said than done! What are the most common and significant sources of E?

- Housing

- Food

- Transportation

- Utility bills

- Clothes

- Medical expenses

- Insurance

- Income taxes

- Property taxes

- Children and grandchildren

- Leisure

- Donations and charity

- Miscellaneous supplies and stuff

In this chapter, I present some general strategies and approaches to maximizing and sustaining our *I*. Then, Chapters 10 through 17 fill in the details, such as how to allocate our assets among different types of investments, how much to withdraw such that we don't run out of money before we die, strategies for maximizing our Social Security and pension benefits, and where to invest. Chapter 18 discusses managing our *E* during our later years. Chapters 19 and 20 put it all together, show several examples of how to make the *I* > *E* strategy work during our *rest-of-life*, and cover how much to save so that we can eventually retire full-time. These issues are all intertwined when answering the 'can I retire' question. To address these issues, I build on the *I* > *E* model for solutions. I suggest that you start with this chapter, read Chapters 10 through 20, and then come back to this chapter.

Managing Our *I*—the Big Picture

Near the end of Chapter 1, I set forth the idea that we might have two stages of retirement. In Stage 1, we continue to work, but we restructure our life to reconnect with the things that give us purpose and meaning, and take care of ourselves physically and emotionally. For many of us, this means cutting back our working hours—phased retirement—which frees up time to pursue other interests and activities. During this time, our wages are an important source of I. In Stage 2, we retire full-time, and live entirely from our financial resources.

How Long Should I Work?

I wouldn't feel comfortable planning to rely exclusively on my retirement resources—investments, retirement benefits, and Social Security—for more than 20 years of my life. I would feel comfortable only if my financial resources were large enough such that my I greatly exceeded my E, and I would expect this surplus to last for the rest of my life.

Why do I say this? Once I've cut the financial ties and income from work, I'm vulnerable to catastrophes such as stock market collapses, high inflation, personal illnesses, accidents or other disasters, wars—you name it. At least when I'm working, I can recover from any losses through future earnings. So, I want to limit the period when I'm vulnerable to my last 20 years, when I'll be least able to work. The worst possibility is to retire while I can still work, and then run out of money when I'm less able to work for income.

In Chapter 2, we saw that if we take care of ourselves, we could easily live until our late eighties or early nineties. Backing off 20 years puts me in my late sixties to early seventies for continuing some kind of work. And I might continue longer if my life feels like it is sustainable indefinitely—if the work still suits me.

When Should We Use Our Financial Resources?

During Stage 1, another big decision is the extent to which we use our existing financial resources, such as our 401(k) balances and other investments. And some of us may have earned a retirement income with a defined benefit plan.

Here are some possible strategies.

- *Let it grow.* We live entirely on our wages, and let our financial resources grow for the time when we need them.

- *Be cautious.* For our living expenses, we draw only the annual investment income—interest and dividends—from our 401(k) and other investments.

- *Draw it down.* For our living expenses, we draw more than our annual investment income, and start dipping into our principal.

Let's go into more detail on each of these strategies.

Let It Grow

We do this for a few different reasons. For example, we might really like our working situation and the wages are sufficient. Or our financial resources might be small enough so that we must let them grow for our eventual full-time retirement. If our wages are sufficient for us to continue to contribute to our 401(k) plan, so much the better!

For our other benefits—Social Security and defined benefit amounts—the reward for delaying is that we increase our monthly retirement income when we eventually start receiving payments. This is a very desirable goal—we want these to be as large as possible, since we can't outlive these benefits.

If we have earned a retirement income from a defined benefit plan, we should wait to start our benefits until there is no longer a reduction for early retirement. With most plans, this is no later than age 65, but it can be earlier. It would be foolish to delay receiving benefits if there is no financial reward for the delay. Chapter 15 covers this subject in more detail.

With Social Security benefits, the situation is a little more complex. As we will see in Chapter 14, it makes no sense to delay starting benefits beyond age 70. Before age 70, it depends on the amount of wages we earn (we cover this subject more in Chapter 14).

Be Cautious

For our 401(k) balances and other investments, living on just the investment income is a safe strategy that assures that we won't run out of money before we die. Chapter 10 covers this strategy in more detail, and we see how much income we can expect.

Draw It Down

We do this during Stage 1 only if we really need the money. While this is a viable strategy, it is also the trickiest, because we run the risk of running out of money. The more we withdraw, the greater this risk. Chapter 10 covers strategies for drawing down our principal and minimizing our chances of running out of money.

We might use a combination of these strategies. For example, we might delay drawing down our 401(k) accounts and other investments as long as possible, but begin receiving our Social Security benefits or pension benefits earlier. This is part of the iteration thing I mentioned earlier.

Which Strategy Is Best?

For the same reasons, I don't want to start drawing principal from my investments until my late sixties or early seventies. It comes down to this. When I start my full-time retirement, I want to have substantial balances in my 401(k) plan and other investments. If I start drawing down my principal too soon, I increase the chances of running out of money.

So my preference is that until my late sixties or early seventies, I'll arrange my living situation and expenses so that I can live comfortably on part-time work, interest and dividends from my investments, and Social Security. If I'm lucky enough to have a defined benefit pension, I'll start that when there is no longer a reduction for early retirement, which is usually no later than age 65, but can be earlier (see Chapter 14 for details).

The Worksheets

Here's a simple worksheet for calculating my I. Let's express it in annual income, before income taxes. We'll reflect taxes in our E.

Our total *I* is the sum of:

- Wages (see Chapter 17 for details): _____
- Draw from 401(k) balances (see Chapter 10 for details): _____
- Social Security (see Chapter 14 for details): _____
- Pension benefits, if any (see Chapter 15 for details): _____
- Other income, if any (see Chapter 16 for details): _____
- Total *I*: _____

Note that we may not be able to fill in these amounts until we read the chapters that follow. This is particularly true for drawing from 401(k) and other investments, since there are a few different methods. This is why I said earlier that you probably need to read Chapters 10 through 20, and then come back to this chapter.

Here's a simple worksheet for calculating my *E*. My total *E* is the sum of the following.

- Housing: _____
- Food: _____
- Transportation (not including car insurance): _____
- Utility bills: _____
- Clothes: _____
- Health insurance: _____
- Medical bills not covered by insurance: _____
- Car insurance: _____
- Other insurance: _____
- Income taxes: _____
- Property taxes: _____
- Entertainment, vacations: _____
- Children and grandchildren: _____
- Leisure: _____
- Donations and charity: _____
- Other expenses: _____
- Subtotal: _____
- Margin for error: _____
- Total *E*: _____

What's the margin for error? I find that I'm always too optimistic when calculating my expenses. I might forget to include something, or I'm not as disciplined as I'd like to be and spend more than I planned. To be safe, I'll estimate the margin to be 25 percent of the subtotal (multiply the subtotal by .25).

Note that calculating each of these might require some further breakdowns and details. For example, your utility bills might consist of several different services. Transportation could include repairs, gasoline, and public transportation. We go into more detail in Chapter 18.

As we have been discussing, the trick is to identify which sources of E we really need for a happy, meaningful life, and get rid of or minimize the rest. The happiest older people I know seem to be continually simplifying their lives. This usually means getting rid of things that are a drain on their time and money and don't add much to their happiness.

When considering a source of E, ask ourselves these simple questions:

- Do I need this E for my basic living needs?
- Is this E for my pursuit of happiness and meaning? Is it worthwhile?

If the answers are "no," then get rid of it! If one of the answers is "yes," then ask myself if I'm paying too much.

If my margin of I over E is tight, then I'll continually work at reducing my E to gain more financial comfort.

Finally, Can I Retire Now?

Yes, if my I is greater than my E, and this difference is sustainable for my lifetime. Calculate all of the amounts in the I worksheet as if they started now, using the strategies and methods described in the following chapters.

If my I is less than my E, then I'll need to earn enough wages such that my I is greater than my E, or look for ways of reducing my E. If I really want to change my life, I'll keep making adjustments to my I and E until my I is greater than my E. Chapter 19 provides some examples of figuring when I can retire.

Suppose I just can't get my I greater than my E. Now what?

When Can I Retire?

When my *I* grows to be bigger than my *E*!

Pick an age in the future when you think you might want to retire. Calculate all of the amounts in the *I* worksheet as if you started them at that age, projecting how much they will grow until then.

Note that I might need to save more in my 401(k) plan and other investments to get my *I* big enough. This leads to another important question: *How much should I save?*

For most of us, our 401(k) balances and other investments will be our primary source of financial security when we retire full-time. As we see in Chapter 14, Social Security benefits provide lifetime monthly benefits, but the benefits are modest and provide only a floor of retirement income. And most of us won't have generous lifetime incomes from defined benefit plans, either because our employers don't sponsor such a plan or because we didn't work long enough to earn much of a benefit.

This leaves the vast majority of Americans to rely on their 401(k) balances to supplement Social Security benefits. Social Security benefits keep us from sleeping on park benches, but not much more. For most of us, income from Social Security is not quite enough to meet basic living needs, but it is a very good start.

So, we'll need to build sufficient balances in our 401(k) plans and other investments to provide a comfortable living in retirement. How much should we save to build these balances? Chapters 19 and 20 cover this.

How Long Should I Work?

Even though I advocate earning some wages until our late sixties or early seventies, some of us might really want to stop sooner. Here are some thoughts.

I can go ahead and stop working now if I can live comfortably off my pension benefits, Social Security (after age 62), and interest and dividends without drawing principal. If my interest and dividends aren't enough, at least I can cut back on my work such that the wages, together with interest and dividends, are enough to live on.

If these situations don't apply, then unfortunately I need to keep working. I'll look for ways to improve my working circumstances.

WRAP-UP

There we have it! Answers to the "can I retire" and "when can I retire" questions.

This chapter presents a general framework for making our finances work for the rest of our lives. Now we have to do the hard part—figure out the details, which are in the chapters that follow. I expect that you'll revisit this chapter and continue to use the worksheets and make adjustments until you're satisfied with your situation.

Don't Die Broke!

For herein Fortune shows herself more kind
Than is her custom: it is still her use
To let the wretched man outlive his wealth,
To view with hollow eye and wrinkled brow
An age of poverty.
>   —William Shakespeare, in *The Merchant of Venice*

I f I could plan my future with perfect foresight, I'd spend my last dollar as I gasp my last breath. The worst possibility is to run out of money when I'm so old that it's hard to go back to work. The opposite side of this dilemma is to die with lots of money left. Whether this is an undesirable outcome depends on our outlook. Some of us may want to leave money to our loved ones or charity, so this outcome is fine. On the other hand, this could be money that we would rather have spent while we are alive, in which case this would be an undesirable result.

To manage our 401(k) balances and other investments, we'll need to make four important investment decisions:

1. The types of investments, such as stocks, bonds, real estate, and cash, that are most appropriate for our portfolio.

2. The investment products that deliver the best value.

3. The financial institutions that we can trust, such as mutual fund companies, banks, brokerage firms, insurance companies, and our employer's 401(k) plan.

4. The types of retirement investing programs that are most efficient for our *rest-of-life* portfolio, such as 401(k) plans, IRAs, tax-deferred annuities, and conventional investments.

Then, there's the decision that is intertwined with these four decisions—how much to withdraw for living expenses so that we don't outlive our money. This is the focus of this chapter. Chapters 11, 12, and 13 focus on the four investment decisions mentioned previously.

Also, this chapter focuses on the time when we *use* our retirement resources, not on our full-time working years when we are building our financial assets. We cover saving and investing during our preretirement years in Chapters 19 and 20.

There are three viable strategies for using our 401(k) balances:

1. Keep our money in a 401(k) plan or IRA, and use mutual funds or similar pooled funds that are invested in stocks, bonds, cash, or real estate investment trusts. Withdraw investment earnings and principal from these accounts in amounts that minimize the chances of running out of money.

2. Live off the investment income.

3. Buy an annuity from an insurance company.

Note that these strategies aren't mutually exclusive; there can be good reasons for doing two or all three. Also, one strategy might be appropriate at different stages of our lives. I'll elaborate on these thoughts later, but first let's go into the details of each strategy.

By the way, if we have worked at nonprofit organizations, we may have retirement accounts in 403(b) plans, otherwise known as tax-deferred annuities. Or if we have worked for state or local governments, the accounts might be known as 457 plans. The numbers—401(k), 403(b), and 457—all refer to the sections of the Internal Revenue Code that define the rules for these accounts. The considerations and rules for withdrawing from these accounts are almost all the same, with a few exceptions (covered in Chapter 13). So I use the term *401(k) plans* to encompass 403(b) and 457 plans as well.

The 401(k) Solution

The mechanics of the 401(k) Solution are easy—leave the money in our 401(k), 403(b), or 457 plan, invest using the options available to us, and make periodic withdrawals for living expenses. This strategy has some significant advantages.

- This is the only investment vehicle where the sponsor isn't trying to profit from our money. All other financial institutions are trying to make money from my investments, so their interests come first. Employers have our best interests at heart, and they run these plans solely for our benefit. Strict fiduciary standards apply, and employers get into legal trouble if they try to benefit financially from operating these plans. Most large employers (for example, those with 1,000 or more employees) are diligent about checking on the performance of the investment funds and effectiveness of the plan administrator. Often they hire companies like mine as watchdogs, to make sure that plan participants are getting the best deal. Smaller employers have this same fiduciary responsibility, but they may not have sufficient resources to hire outside consultants to help shop for the best deals.

- Most plans are set up to easily implement our strategy. We can access information about our accounts by telephone or the Internet. We can set up automatic investment and withdrawal instructions, so that our strategy is mostly on autopilot.

- Investment income is not taxed until we make withdrawals. This lets our money grow faster, so over the long run we will have more money if we leave it invested in a tax-sheltered program.

The two biggest challenges are deciding how much to withdraw, and allocating our assets among different types of investments, such as stocks, bonds, and cash. Here's where we can benefit from Watson Wyatt's asset/liability modeling (ALM) expertise. ALM is a powerful methodology that we use to help our clients decide how to invest their pension funds. We have used our ALM services for many Fortune 500 companies, including three of the four largest pension funds in the United States. Fortunately, we can bring the same methods to bear on our challenges, and I can share our experience and expertise to help you.

ALM deals with uncertainty. We don't know if the stock market will go up or down this coming year, and by how much. We don't know how high inflation will be. We don't know when we'll die. However, we can study the past to analyze historical experience, and construct some theories that adjust historical experience to devise assumptions for projecting into the future. These assumptions help us estimate the chances that these events will occur during our lifetimes. Based on this, we feed our assumptions into a large computer program, turn the crank, and forecast thousands of future scenarios for stock and bond market returns, inflation, and mortality experience.

For devising investment and withdrawal strategies for our 401(k) balances, the goal is to evaluate the odds whether a possible strategy will result in us running out of money before we die. We want these odds to be very small for an investment and withdrawal strategy that we might be considering.

In the next pages, I share results from my analyses of various investment and withdrawal strategies, and we can boil it all down to simple formulas. But if you're curious about how ALM works, here's a simple explanation of a very complex process. We tell the computer:

- How much money we have in our 401(k) accounts.

- How we allocate our assets among the different types of investments, such as stocks, bonds, and cash.

- How old we are, and whether we are male, female, or a married couple.

- How much we expect to withdraw each year for living expenses.

The computer then runs thousands of simulations of alternative future lives. For example, for the first simulation of our future life:

- The computer rolls the dice, where the dice is loaded for the chances of all the events we mention—investment returns on different types of assets, whether we die, and so on.

- The computer dice comes up with assumed investment returns for stocks and bonds for the first year, and rolls forward our account balances according to how we have invested our accounts.

- It withdraws the assumed amount for living expenses.

- The computer dice tells whether we died during the year or are still alive.

- It comes up with a projected account balance at the end of the year.

- The computer repeats this process for each future year, until the computer dice says that we died or that we have run out of money. It notes this age and which outcome—death or poverty!

The computer then repeats this entire process for thousands of future life simulations, each time noting when we die or run out of money. Some of these simulations have positive *financial* outcomes (the stock market does well and we don't live a long time), while some simulations have dire *financial* outcomes (stock market does poorly and we live a long time). And some simulations have the desired *life* outcomes—the stock market does well and we live a long time. Based on these thousands of simulations, the computer then calculates the odds of running out of money before we die. For example, if the computer runs 10,000 simulations, and 1,000 times we run out of money before we die, the odds are 1 out of 10 that this unfavorable outcome will result from the particular strategy we are considering.

See the box for an example of how this works.

Using Asset/Liability Modeling to Figure 401(k) Withdrawals

Suppose a single 65-year-old woman has $500,000 saved in her 401(k) account, and she's trying to figure how much to safely withdraw each year for living expenses. Let's further suppose that her accounts are invested 50 percent in stocks and 50 percent in bonds (this is called asset allocation, and we go into detail on this subject in Chapter 11). Finally, let's suppose that she wants to increase her withdrawal amount each year for inflation. With ALM, we can project two important items—the amount of money she will have when she dies, and the odds that she will run out of money before she dies.

She starts by assuming that she will withdraw 5 percent of her beginning balance during the first year (5 percent of

$500,000 is $25,000). We rolled the computer dice and turned the crank, and came up with these projections:

- There's a 50–50 chance she will have $112,000 left when she dies.

- There's also a 25 percent chance (one out of four) on the pessimistic side that she will have only $64,000 left, but another 25 percent chance on the optimistic side that she will have $177,000 left.

- There's an 11 percent chance (a little more than 1 out of 10) that she will run out of money before she dies.

For her, an 11 percent chance of running out of money seems too high, so for an alternative we looked at withdrawing 4 percent of her beginning balance—$20,000. Again, she'll increase this amount for inflation each future year. We turned the crank again, and here are the results:

- There's a 50–50 chance she will have $148,000 left when she dies.

- There's also a 25 percent chance (one out of four) on the pessimistic side that she will have $100,000 left, but another 25 percent chance on the optimistic side that she will have $239,000 left.

- There's a 4 percent chance (1 out of 25) that she will run out of money before she dies.

This example illustrates a basic dilemma. If we want to decrease the odds of running out of money, we withdraw less. Basically, we withdraw just enough so that we can withstand the outcome of living a long time while the stock market does poorly. However, if this dire outcome doesn't actually happen, then we die with money left in our accounts.

If we use the 401(k) Solution, we can't avoid this dilemma. We can't have our cake and eat it too. The only way to avoid this dilemma is to buy an annuity, which we discuss later in this chapter.

Table 10.1 takes a closer look at this example, for different rates of withdrawal.

TABLE 10.1   Odds of Running Out of Money for Different Rates of Withdrawal

Withdrawal Amount	Odds of Running Out of Money
3%	0.4%, or less than 1 out of 200
4%	4%, or 1 out of 25
5%	11%, or a little more than 1 out of 10
6%	23%, or a little less than 1 out of 4
7%	36%, or a little more than 1 out of 3
8%	49%, or almost 50/50
9%	59%, or well over 50–50
10%	67%, or about 2 out of 3

For 65 year-old woman, invested 50% in stocks and 50% in bonds. Withdrawal amount increases for inflation each year.

There aren't any hard-and-fast rules for using tables like this one. They should be just one input to our decision, which will eventually consider our personal circumstances, our comfort level, intuition, and ultimately gut feeling. I would be comfortable only with 4 percent or 5 percent withdrawal rates, which have odds of running out of money of 4 percent and 11 percent, respectively. I wouldn't feel comfortable with a 6 percent withdrawal rate, which has a 23 percent chance of running out of money—almost one out of four. If my I exceeds my E comfortably with a 4 percent withdrawal rate, I would use 4 percent. However, if I couldn't reduce my E and I needed a 5% withdrawal rate to make ends meet, I'd go with it.

The withdrawal amount need not be an irreversible decision. I can withdraw 5 percent initially, and if I find ways to reduce my E, I can cut back my withdrawals later. Or, I might not give myself a raise for inflation each year. I'll be more cautious if I'm making withdrawals at a "young" retirement age—age 65 or earlier—because there is so much time for things to go wrong.

We ran the ALM process for three different investment strategies:

1. Conservative: 33 percent stocks/67 percent bonds.
2. Middle-of-the-road: 50 percent stocks/50 percent bonds.
3. Aggressive: 67 stocks, 33 percent bonds.

We also looked at withdrawal percentages that ranged from 3 percent to 10 percent for a single male, a single female, and a married couple. The results are extensive and take up many pages, so I've put them in my web site (www.restoflife.com).

Table 10.2 presents the results as simple strategies, and rounds most of the withdrawal percentages to the nearest quarter of a percent. My web site has more details, showing results for different asset allocations and more precise odds of running out of money for various strategies.

Here are my underlying assumptions for Table 10.2:

- I don't want more than a 10 percent chance (1 out of 10) of running out of money.

- I will increase the withdrawal amount each year for inflation.

- As it turns out, it doesn't really matter which asset allocation I use—the safe withdrawal percentages don't change much.

These withdrawal percentages protect us from the worst future scenarios; if these dire scenarios don't happen, then we'll die with money in our 401(k) accounts to be left to our kids and charity. If my I is very close to my E, I really want to retire, and I don't mind taking a little risk, I might bump my withdrawals up by a quarter to half a percent. My web site shows the risks with this course of action.

TABLE 10.2 Withdrawal Percentages with Approximately 1 out of 10 Odds of Running Out of Money

Retirement Age	Single Male	Single Female	Married Couple Same Age
50	3½%	3¼%	3%
55	4%	3¾%	3¼%
60	4½%	4¼%	3¾%
65	5%	4¾%	4¼%
70	6%	5¼%	4¾%
75	7%	6¼%	5½%

Let's make a few comments and caveats on the 401(k) Solution:

- One drawback that isn't obvious at first is the continuing need to watch our investments and make sure we are withdrawing the correct amounts. This might seem easy when we're in our sixties and seventies, but this ability might start fading in our eighties or nineties. My sincere intent is that this won't happen to us if we take care of ourselves, but we may need to prepare for this possibility.

- It's appropriate only if we invest in mutual funds and other pooled funds that are typical of most 401(k) plans. This means that the funds are fairly liquid—they can easily be sold, and in small pieces. It might not work if we invest in assets that can't easily be sold, such as individual real estate properties or private businesses.

- This solution will also work if we invest in IRAs, the only disadvantage being that the IRA sponsor is trying to make money from our investments, so we need to watch out. See Chapter 12—"Where Should I Invest My Money?"

- I stated earlier that the safe withdrawal percentages don't change too much for different asset allocations. This doesn't mean that this decision is unimportant. If I minimize the odds that I outlive my money, this means that most likely I will die with money. The odds are that I will die with more money with higher allocations to stocks; the information on my web site illustrates this expected result.

- Finally, we can use Table 10.2 to adjust our future withdrawals to reflect our experience as it unfolds, with a "fresh start" approach. We determine the withdrawal amount by assuming that we will increase it for inflation each year. At some future year, we can take the withdrawal amount for that year, as adjusted for inflation to that time, and calculate it as a percentage of our 401(k) balance at the time. If the withdrawal percentage as calculated is less than the withdrawal percentage shown in Table 10.2 for our age at the time, this is most likely due to good investment returns. In this case, we might have room to increase our withdrawal amount to the withdrawal percentage for our age at the future year. This works in reverse as well—if the withdrawal percentage as calculated is greater than the withdrawal percentage in Table 10.2, this is most likely due to poor investment returns, and we may want to reduce our withdrawal amount accordingly.

- For 401(k), 403(b), and 457 plans, and for IRAs, we need to be wary of the IRS's minimum distribution rules. See Chapter 13 for more details.

One final note: The 401(k) Solution does involve selling principal—more than just the investment income—for living expenses. As such, there is some risk, however small, that we will run out of money. The more principal we sell, the higher the risk. Next we'll discuss a solution that carries no risk of running out of money.

The Income Solution

Here we live on just the interest, dividends, and other investment income that our assets generate. Since we don't sell principal, there is no risk of running out of money. However, the price we pay for eliminating this risk is that we'll have less money to live on, compared to the 401(k) Solution.

The Income Solution is fine if it generates enough money to live on, and if we want to leave money to our loved ones or charity. It also works well if the assets are fairly illiquid—they can't be sold easily—since we are living off only the income. This is characteristic of income property (real estate) or privately owned businesses.

So how much can we expect with the Income Solution? Let's look at yields of typical investments.

Here are some annual income and dividend yields that were available for various investments in mid-2004:

- Corporate bond mutual funds were earning from about 4.75 percent to 5.75 percent, depending on maturities.

- Government bond mutual funds were earning from about 3.75 percent to 4.75 percent, depending on maturities.

- Stock mutual funds that emphasized income were earning from 1.5 percent to 2 percent.

- Balanced mutual funds were earning from 2.5 percent to 3 percent, depending on the mix between stocks and bonds.

- Real estate investment trusts (REITs) were earning from 3 percent to 5 percent or more, depending on the mix of properties and the financial structure of the portfolio.

If I were relying on the Income Solution, I would use a mutual fund that invests in a mix of stocks and bonds, and possibly also invest in REITs. These provide a nice balance of growth and income. Looking at the percentages, I could pay myself about 3 percent of my balance each year and keep most, if not all, of my principal intact. Chapter 12 discusses balanced mutual funds and REITs in more detail. I could invest entirely in bonds, and the income would be higher than 3 percent. However, I'm leaving myself vulnerable to inflation. I might do this anyway if I feel confident about managing my E to contain future cost increases.

Let's compare this 3 percent payout rate to the withdrawal rates of 4 percent to 5 percent mentioned previously with the 401(k) Solution. Here's an example. Suppose I have $500,000 in my 401(k) plan, and I'm a single male.

- The Income Solution would result in an annual income of $15,000.

- If I use the 401(k) Solution and retire at age 55, Table 10.2 shows I can withdraw 4 percent, or $20,000.

- If I retire at age 65 using the 401(k) Solution, Table 10.2 shows I can withdraw 5 percent, or $25,000.

The reason for the higher withdrawals under the 401(k) Solution is that I am withdrawing principal in addition to investment income.

The Annuity Solution

Another possibility is to buy an immediate annuity from an insurance company. Here we give an insurance company a lump sum of money. The insurance company promises to pay us a fixed monthly retirement income for the rest of our life, no matter how long this is. This is the real reason for buying an annuity—it is insurance for living too long!

An insurance company can spread the risk of living too long among many policyholders. For example, for thousands of policyholders, mortality statistics say with accuracy how many people will die at each age. The insurer doesn't care *which* policyholders will live beyond their life expectancies. The insurer just knows that some will live beyond their life expectancies and some won't, and will price the annuities accordingly. We, however, don't have the luxury of not caring which people outlive their life expectancies. If we live a long time, we don't want to be broke, so it is smart to pass this risk to the insurance company through buying an annuity. This lines up our money with our life.

Another important advantage is that somebody else invests the money—we just get a check in the mail each month. Very user-friendly! We will really appreciate this advantage in our advanced years, when we might not be as sharp as we used to be. So this is another risk we pass to the insurance company—the risk that eventually we won't have what it takes to pay proper attention to our investments.

We can customize annuities to fit our life situation. For example, if we are married, we can continue payments to our spouse until both of us have died. If we're worried about inflation, we can elect to have the monthly income increase each year by a specified percentage. If we're worried about dying right after we give the lump sum to the insurance company, we can arrange for a death benefit to a designated beneficiary. All of these features increase the cost of the annuity, but they might be worth the price to fit our circumstances.

Let's discuss some factors that affect how much an annuity might cost. For a given monthly retirement income, the purchase price of the annuity—the lump sum of money we give to the insurance company—depends on a number of factors:

- *Whether we are male or female.* Females live longer on average and thus receive payments for a longer period, so the purchase price is higher than for males.

- *Our age.* The purchase price is higher for younger people compared to older people, because younger people live longer on average.

■ *Yields on bonds at the time of purchase.* Insurance companies typically invest the purchase price in bonds. The lower the yields on bonds, the higher the purchase price will be. The reason is that insurance companies use interest earned on the bonds in the future to help pay future annuity benefits. If interest rates are low, they need a higher purchase price for a given amount of monthly income.

■ *How we are buying the annuity.* We might pay high commissions to an insurance agent, or the insurance company might not be very competitive; we'll discuss the best ways to buy annuities in Chapter 12.

■ *The rated safety of the insurance company.* Generally, the stronger the company, the higher the purchase price.

Let's take a look at some examples based on annuity purchase prices mid-2004. These quotes come from www.immediateannuities .com, a good source of information about annuities. The examples show how much monthly retirement income we can buy with $500,000—the dollar amount of monthly income, also expressed as a percentage. This will help us determine if an annuity makes sense, for reasons that I'll explain. We start with buying an annuity for a male, with no special features like survivor benefits. (See Table 10.3.)

TABLE 10.3   Estimated Amount of Annual Annuity Income Purchased by $500,000 for a Single Male

Age Annuity Starts	Annual Income	Annual Income as Percent of Purchase Price
50	$31,344	6.3%
55	$33,540	6.7%
60	$35,880	7.2%
65	$39,024	7.8%
70	$44,076	8.8%
75	$52,176	10.4%

Source: www.immediateannuities.com.

Table 10.4 is the same except for a female, again with no special features like survivor benefits.

Here are two comments on these tables:

1. They use average purchase prices for illustration purposes—we can do a little better when we get actual quotes and pick the best price.

2. These quotes do not include premium taxes, which could apply in some states.

You might notice that the payout percentages shown for annuities are larger than the percentages shown for the safe withdrawal percentages with the 401(k) Solution. Why? There are two reasons:

1. The 401(k) Solution increases the withdrawal amount each year for inflation, while the monthly income with a basic annuity is fixed. Eliminating this difference brings the two solutions much closer together.

2. Insurance companies can afford to spread the risk among many policyholders. However, when each one of us uses the 401(k) Solution, we must take care not to outlive our money, so we must be overly cautious.

TABLE 10.4   Estimated Amount of Annual Annuity Income Purchased by $500,000 for a Single Female

Age Annuity Starts	Annual Income	Annual Income as Percent of Purchase Price
50	$30,288	6.1%
55	$32,256	6.5%
60	$34,224	6.8%
65	$36,744	7.3%
70	$40,776	8.2%
75	$47,364	9.5%

Source: www.immediateannuities.com.

What's the Best Solution?

Well, it depends on a number of things. We might use two or all three solutions, or use different solutions at different stages of our *rest-of-life*. Here we'll discuss strategies for combining these different solutions for various times and circumstances during the rest of our lives.

The underlying assumptions for this discussion are that I'll probably live at least until my late eighties or early nineties, and that I really, really want to avoid the situation where I run out of money.

As discussed in the previous chapter, I feel most comfortable living off just the income until my mid to late sixties or early seventies. The reason is to minimize the chance of running out of money and to keep substantial balances in my 401(k) plan and other investments.

This also applies if I'm buying an immediate annuity as part of my strategy, for a few different reasons.

- First, I'm relying on the financial strength of the insurance company, and a lot can happen in 20 years. We've seen companies go insolvent, when 20 years before they had good ratings from the rating agencies.

- Second, if I buy a fixed monthly income, after 20 years inflation can significantly cut the buying power of my annuity.

- Third, I lose flexibility by giving a lump sum to an insurance company. Once I do this, I can't ask for my money back. I am willing to give up this flexibility in return for passing to the insurance company the "living too long" risk and the "being too old to manage my money" risk. However, I don't want to do this too soon.

What's the Best Strategy When I Retire Full-Time?

If I have enough of a nest egg to live off just interest and dividends, I'll do so. I like the idea of leaving money to my children and charity. However, chances are good that I won't be so lucky. In this case, I plan on using a combination of the 401(k) Solution and the Annuity Solution. Note that with the 401(k) Solution, there is still a good chance that I will leave money to my children and charity, but there is no chance of this happening with an annuity (unless I name them as a beneficiary and reduce my annuity income).

The advantages and disadvantages of each solution complement each other nicely.

- With the Annuity Solution, I know I won't run out of money. And I don't need to worry about managing the money when I get really old. However, I can't access my principal for emergencies, and I run the risk that inflation might seriously erode the purchasing power of my monthly income.

- With the 401(k) Solution, I hedge my bets. I can access my money in case I have an unexpected emergency, and I protect myself against inflation. However, I need to manage this all my life, and this could get difficult when I'm really old. And if I withdraw too much or if the stock market collapses, I might run out of money.

For these reasons, I'll want to use both solutions. I'll take part of my investments and 401(k) balances to buy an annuity, and use the 401(k) Solution for the rest. How much annuity should I buy? Here are a couple of possibilities.

- Buy enough monthly income through an annuity so that, together with Social Security and any income from a defined benefit plan, I've covered most, if not all, of my basic living expenses. This way, I won't ever run out of money for the basics—I won't be sleeping on park benches! However, I don't want to use up all of my investments and 401(k) balances to buy an annuity, since I want to hedge my bets.

- So another possibility is to use no more than half of my investments and 401(k) balances to buy an annuity, and use the 401(k) Solution for the remainder. This gives me a hedge against inflation and the need for cash for unforeseen emergencies.

One way to think about an annuity is that it is like an investment in bonds. As discussed in Chapter 11, I always want some portion of my investments in stocks as a hedge against inflation and hopefully to realize higher returns; and some portion in bonds for safety of interest and principal. If I buy an annuity, I might adjust accordingly the split between stocks and bonds for the remaining amounts in my 401(k) plan and other investments. I might justify increasing my stock portion to two-thirds, since I have already invested in bonds through buying an annuity.

WRAP-UP

This chapter covers one of the most important decisions we can make—how to manage our 401(k) balances so that we don't run out of money before we die. This is a huge challenge, one that will take constant thinking and vigilance in the future. I present three possible solutions, and I will use all three in some combination throughout my future years. I will always be monitoring my progress and making adjustments to future events, such as changes in interest rates and volatility in the stock market. In other words, I will never be done with this challenge.

Now we'll examine asset allocation and determine which types of assets are appropriate for our later years.

Which Investments Should I Use?

Location! Location! Location! The three most important factors to consider when investing in real estate.

—Old real estate adage

Allocation! Allocation! Allocation! The three most important factors to consider when investing for retirement and the *rest-of-life*.

—Old actuarial adage

Our decisions on how much of our retirement investments to allocate among various types of investments (stocks, bonds, real estate, cash, etc.) have a far greater impact on our eventual wealth than our decisions on which stock to buy, which bond to buy, or which mutual fund to buy. Up to 90 percent of the total variability in my risk and return on my investments results from my decision on asset allocation. So, it's important that I spend some time figuring out how to divvy up my investments.

Why should we pay attention to our investments? Because doing so translates into extra money for the rest of our life! It's a good use of our time to get the most from our investments.

Let's look at an example. Suppose we have saved $100,000 for our retirement, and we decide to withdraw $1,000 per month. When do we run out of money? It depends on our investment return, as shown in Table 11.1.

If I earn 5 percent per year, I run out of money in 10 years and 10 months, but if I earn 10 percent per year, I run out of money in 18 years!

TABLE 11.1   Start with $100,000, and Withdraw $1,000 per Month

If I Earn . . .	I Run Out of Money in . . .
5% per year	10 years, 10 months
6%	11 years, 7 months
7%	12 years, 7 months
8%	13 years, 10 months
9%	15 years, 6 months
10%	18 years

Decisions, Decisions, Decisions, and Decisions

With our investments, we need to make four decisions, as shown in Table 11.2.

In this chapter, we'll discuss the first decision—which type of asset (stocks, bonds, etc.). Chapter 12 covers the next two decisions—the investment products we should use and the financial institutions we should trust. Chapter 13 covers the retirement investing programs we should use.

First, let's go back to school for some investment basics. (I call this Investing U—the Sequel.) Then we'll discuss investing strategies that are appropriate for our stage in life. Compared to the similar chapter from *Don't Work Forever!*, some material is the same, but some is different. In *Don't Work Forever!* I covered investment strategies for people in their thirties and forties—well before retirement. Now we're in our fifties and sixties and retirement is on the radar, so there are some important differences.

Here's our curriculum for Investing U—the Sequel:

- Investing 101: The Basics on Different Types of Assets.
- Investing 102: Risky Business.
- Investing 103: Strategies for Our Time.

TABLE 11.2   The Four Investment Decisions We Must Make

1. Which investments to use?
2. Which investment products?
3. Which financial institutions?
4. Which retirement investing program?

By the way, if you participate in a 401(k) plan at work, and have read the educational literature on different types of investments, Investing 101 and part of Investing 102 could be a review for you. Just skim material that looks familiar. However, don't skip this chapter entirely, particularly Investing 103, as I have some insights and considerations that you probably haven't seen in your 401(k) plan communications.

Investing 101: The Basics on Different Types of Assets

There are just five types of assets that I use in my retirement portfolio—excuse me, *rest-of-life* portfolio:

1. Stocks

2. Bonds

3. Deposits

4. Cash investments

5. Real estate

Note that these investments generate *I*. Another good use of investment money is to reduce or eliminate sources of *E*. Examples might include paying off my mortgage, investing in solar panels or insulation to reduce utility bills, and spending money on fruit and vegetable gardens and orchards to reduce food costs. We go into more detail on these types of investments in Chapter 19.

There are many variations within each category. Let's look at each category and its common variations.

Stocks, aka Equities

When we own stocks, we own a piece of a business called a corporation. This ownership piece entitles us to a prorated share of the business's financial success. There are two ways we can make money with stocks:

1. The price of the stock may go up after we buy it, so we can sell it at a profit. This is called capital appreciation.

2. The corporation may make enough money to pay a dividend, which gives income to its investors.

We can also lose money with stocks in two ways:

1. The price of the stock may go down below the price we paid for it (called capital depreciation).

2. The corporation may stop paying dividends, resulting in opportunity loss (which means we could have done better with bonds or bank deposits, which pay steady interest).

We need to distinguish between realized and unrealized appreciation or depreciation.

- Realized appreciation or depreciation is when we actually sell an investment, and get back more or less money than we paid for the investment. At that time, we owe federal and state taxes on any gain from the sale of the asset, unless it's held inside a retirement investing program such as a 401(k) plan or IRA.

- Unrealized appreciation or depreciation is when an asset has appreciated or depreciated in value, but we haven't sold the investment. In this case, the gain or loss is simply on paper and we don't yet owe any taxes.

Here are some common terms that we should know regarding stocks.

- *Blue chips* are stocks of large, well-established, and successful companies.

- *Income stocks* pay higher-than-average dividends.

- *Growth stocks* are stocks of rapidly growing businesses; they carry an expectation of capital appreciation. Growth companies typically plow back most of the money they earn into the business, so their stocks may pay low or no dividends.

- *Small-cap stocks* are issued by companies that are smaller than blue chips—the name refers to the relatively small capitalization or total market value of the company, compared to blue chips. We might also hear the term *micro-cap stocks*, which refers to stocks that are even smaller than small-cap stocks.

- *Cyclical stocks* are stocks of corporations that go through periodic ups and downs in their profits, often connected to the national economy. For example, most automobile manufacturers are considered to be cyclical, because their sales drop during business downturns, when people have less money to spend on new cars.

- *Defensive stocks* are the opposite of cyclical stocks; they often resist downturns because their products must be bought even when times are tough. Examples include food and drug companies.

- *Value stocks* are stocks of corporations with some inherent value that might be overlooked by investors. For example, the corporation might have valuable real estate or a successful division whose value is not fully reflected in the stock's price.

- *Preferred stock* is a special class of stock with a set dividend rate. Dividends must be paid on preferred stock before dividends can be paid on any other stock of the company. For this reason, preferred stock is considered to be safer than common stock.

- *Foreign or international stocks* are stocks of corporations in countries outside the United States.

Stocks can lose money, so they do carry risks. A particular stock can go down if the business doesn't do well, if the economy is doing poorly and drags the stock down with it, or due to financial events beyond the control of the corporation, such as rising interest rates. We'll discuss these risks in Investing 102.

Some common measures of stock market returns are announced daily in the financial news. These are average returns on groups of stocks that are representative of different types of stocks. Here are some common indexes:

- The *Dow Jones Industrial Average* represents 30 of the largest U.S. industrial companies.

- The *Standard & Poor's 500* (or *S&P 500*) are 500 large stocks representing a mixture of industrial, transportation, financial, and utility companies in the United States.

- The *Russell 1000* and *Russell 2000*, maintained by the Frank Russell Company, represent broad cross sections of 1,000 and 2,000 stocks, respectively.

- The *Wilshire 5000 Total Market Index* represents the broadest group of U.S. stocks, and is maintained by Wilshire Associates.

- The *NASDAQ Composite* represents a broad cross section of stocks sold on the stock exchange of the same name. These stocks are smaller than average, with a higher-than-average percentage of high-technology stocks.

- The *MSCI EAFE* represents stocks traded on the European, Australasian, and Far East stock exchanges, reflecting a mix of established companies outside the United States. It is maintained by Morgan Stanley Capital International.

If we hear that "the Dow was up 20 points today," this means that the overall value of the 30 stocks that make up the index increased during the day's trading. To figure this as a percentage increase, we would divide 20 points by the total points in the Dow Jones Industrial Average at the beginning of the day. If we hear that the total return on the S&P 500 was 10 percent during the year, this means that the total return considering both price appreciation and dividends was 10 percent.

One reason I mention these indexes is that they represent a benchmark for us to compare with our own results. If we own a portfolio of large stocks, hopefully we outperform the S&P 500 or Russell 1000 indexes. How to make these comparisons is discussed in more detail in the next chapter.

Stocks are important *rest-of-life* investments because they share in the financial success of companies and the economy, and because they have the potential to protect against inflation. Historically, stocks have outperformed all types of investments and have outpaced inflation, as we'll see in Investing 103. We should have a significant part of our assets in stocks, provided we are comfortable with the risks.

Bonds

Bonds are loans to either corporations or governments. Typically, we give the borrower a fixed amount of money (the principal) for a set period (the maturity period). The borrower promises to pay us a fixed amount of interest periodically, and to pay back the principal at maturity. We make the loan by buying the bond from the corporation or its financial intermediary—often a brokerage firm. We can buy the bond when issued by the corporation, at which point our money goes directly to the corporation. Or the bond can be sold later, in which case the buyer is entitled to the remaining interest payments and the principal repayment.

Here are some common terms that we should know regarding bonds.

- *Corporate bonds* are issued by businesses and corporations.
- *U.S. Treasury bonds* are issued by the federal government, and have maturities greater than 10 years.
- *U.S. Treasury notes*, also issued by the federal government, have maturities of 1 to 10 years.
- *U.S. Treasury bills* have maturities of one year or less.
- *Treasury Inflation Protected Securities, or TIPS*, are federal government bonds with a fixed interest rate, with the added feature that the principal is adjusted to reflect increases in the Consumer Price Index (CPI). As such, they give us some protection against inflation.
- *Government agency bonds* are issued by some agency of the federal government. It's important to distinguish whether the federal government will back the bond if the agency doesn't have the money to pay interest or principal. For example, the federal government guarantees the bonds issued by the Government National Mortgage Association (GNMA, or "Ginnie Mae"). Other institutions may sound like government agencies, but they're not, and their bonds aren't backed by the federal government. Examples include the Federal Home Loan Mortgage Corporation (FHLMC, or "Freddie Mac") and the Federal National Mortgage Association (FNMA, or "Fannie Mae").
- *Municipal bonds* are issued by states, counties, cities, or other local governments. Usually their interest is exempt from federal income taxes (and sometimes from state and local income taxes as well, if we live in the state where the bond is issued).

- *Zero coupon bonds* pay no interest. The maturity amount is larger than the price paid for the bond, so we earn all the interest in the difference between these two amounts.

- *Junk bonds* are from corporations that are small, relatively unknown, or weak financially. They pay higher interest than other bonds, to make up for the risk that we might not receive future interest payments and get back our principal.

- *Convertible bonds* let us convert our bond ownership to a stock purchase at a prearranged price.

- *Callable bonds* let the issuer buy back the bond from the owner prior to the maturity date, usually only if interest rates have fallen and the borrower can issue a new bond at a lower rate (an arrangement similar to refinancing a mortgage).

- *Foreign bonds* are issued by companies or governments in countries outside the United States.

Bonds are usually considered to be safer than stocks, because the borrower must pay back the interest and principal no matter how poorly it is doing. If a bond issuer doesn't pay back interest or principal, the bondholders can force the issuer into bankruptcy. With stocks, the corporation stays in business even if its stock price goes down or it skips dividend payments.

However, bonds do carry certain risks.

INFLATION RISK Our cost of living might increase at a rate higher than the interest rate on the bond. This means when we cash in the bond in the future, it buys less goods and services than today. This is the biggest risk with bonds, and it applies regardless of whether we hold the bond until maturity. Here's one important distinction for our later years: Many financial planners compare the interest rate on our bonds to the overall rate of inflation. A more useful comparison, although harder to quantify, is to our own personal rate of inflation. What are the cost increases for the stuff that we buy? We cover this more in Chapter 18.

INTEREST RATE RISK If interest rates go up, the value of a bond that we hold now will go down (capital depreciation), due to the law of supply and demand. Other bond buyers can get higher interest rates on new bonds, and are less interested in my bond unless the price goes down.

For example, suppose we buy a bond with a 10-year maturity that pays 6 percent interest. One month later, interest rates rise, and new bonds with similar maturity have interest rates of 7 percent. Bond buyers will be interested in buying my bond only if its price goes down such that the total yield becomes close to 7 percent (considering both the interest payments and repayment of principal when the bond matures). This will drive down the price of my bond by roughly 7 percent. If I paid $1,000 for the bond, now it will be worth $950 to $960. There would be higher depreciation if the maturity period was longer, and lower depreciation for shorter maturities.

This works in reverse as well: If interest rates go down, the value of my bond goes up. Fluctuations in interest rates are important if we sell the bond before maturity. If we hold the bond until maturity, we get exactly the yield we expected when we bought the bond.

FINANCIAL RISK If the borrower goes bankrupt, we will lose future interest and principal payments. Thus, the financial strength of the borrower affects the value of the bond. Rating services, such as Moody's Investors Service and Standard & Poor's, measure the financial strength of bonds. These services help me assess how safe my bond investments are. (See Table 11.3.)

The risk of losing money with bonds is considered low with investment grade bonds, and higher with speculative grade bonds. If a company becomes financially weak, the rating services will

TABLE 11.3   Bond Safety Ratings

Moody's	S&P	
Aaa	AAA	
Aa	AA	Investment Grade
A	A	
Baa	BBB	
Ba	BB	
B	B	
Caa	CCC	Speculative Grade
Ca	CC	
C	C	

downgrade the company, and most likely the value of its bonds will drop.

Bonds can be an important part of our assets, as long as we understand the risks. Over long periods of time, bonds have earned less than stocks, but more than deposits and cash investments.

Deposits

Deposits are loans that we make to banks or insurance companies, so they are like bonds. We give them money, and they pay us a fixed rate of interest. They pay back our principal after the maturity period. If we withdraw the money before the maturity period ends, usually we are penalized. Most deposits automatically roll over the account into a new deposit unless we specifically ask to be paid our money. Examples of deposits include certificates of deposit (CDs) and fixed interest rate investments in 401(k) plans, typically called stable value funds or capital preservation funds.

Deposits are somewhat safer than bonds, because the bank or insurance company guarantees that the principal will not go down. With banks, many types of deposits are insured by the Federal Deposit Insurance Corporation (FDIC). If the bank goes bankrupt, we still get our money back. This is not the case with all bank deposits, so we should ask before committing our money. Usually deposits with insurance companies are not guaranteed, so if the insurance company goes bankrupt, we're out of luck. In some instances, state guaranty funds may provide some protection. Deposits have the same inflation risk as bonds. But because of the certainty of interest payments and principal repayment, deposits have a place in our retirement portfolio.

Cash Investments

Cash investments pay a rate of interest that can change frequently, often daily. The rate is not guaranteed, but principal typically never changes. The most common examples of cash investments are savings accounts and money market funds. These are called cash investments because they're as good as cash—we can withdraw them at any time without penalty.

Over long periods of time, cash investments have had lower returns than stocks, bonds, or deposits. Money market funds have one advantage in that they usually track inflation fairly well, but they return not much more or less. We don't need most of our retirement investments on a daily basis, so we should have only a small portion of our portfolio in cash. There are two exceptions to this rule:

1. If we expect stocks and bonds to drop, we would park our investments in cash investments until the danger passes. This is called market timing, which is a bad idea for most amateurs.

2. If we expect to spend the money soon, say within the next six months, cash is a good place to park our money. For example, we might receive dividend payments from stocks or interest payments from bonds and not need the money for living expenses immediately. We should park the money in cash investments, to earn a little more income before we spend the money.

Real Estate

Real estate means property in buildings or land. We make money at owning real estate in two ways:

1. If the value of the property appreciates, we can sell it at a profit.

2. We might have rental income.

There are two types of real estate investments:

1. Our own home.

2. Any other property, called investment real estate.

Historically, real estate has realized favorable returns compared to inflation. However, I avoid individual pieces of investment real estate for my retirement assets. The reason is that we should know what we are doing when investing in real estate. It is like running our own business, so we need to have specialized expertise and spend a lot of time. Amateurs usually don't have the necessary time, patience, or expertise, so we lose money. Also, real estate is not very liquid, which means it can take a long time to sell and get our money out, if we need it for living expenses. Finally, we can have too many eggs in one basket with real estate investments. Most of us can afford to have only a few real estate investments, which leaves us vulnerable if we make a poor selection or if some disaster strikes our particular investment.

Some of you may have the time and expertise to invest in individual real estate. In this case, it is entirely possible you will make good money on these investments. If this is you, go for it!

However, the best way for most amateurs to invest in real estate is to leave it to the pros. With real estate investment trusts (REITs), I can pool my money with other investors and hire professionals to manage the investments. We discuss REITs more in Chapter 12.

The one exception to my advice about owning individual real estate is our own home. When we buy our own home, we protect a large part of our living expenses against inflation. And if we're lucky, we can make a profit when we sell.

Investments to Avoid

Half of the investment battle is *not* losing money. Here are investments that I avoid.

- Gold and other precious metals.

- Commodities.

- Options.

- Collectibles.

- Whole-life insurance or variable life insurance.

- Limited partnerships or tax shelters.

- Loans to relatives or investments in relatives' businesses. (This doesn't mean to refuse to help family—it just means I think of these transactions as gifts that I make for emotional reasons, and not as investments.)

- Hot tips from people I don't know.

I avoid these because they carry too many risks, and they take too much time and expertise for me to succeed. For every story about fortunes being made, there are many more stories about ordinary people like you and me who lose their money.

We might get pitched by an insurance agent to buy whole-life insurance or variable life insurance. These are usually poor investments, with high costs and commissions. It's much better to buy term insurance for the protection, where the premiums are much lower. I don't mix insurance and investments—I'd rather get the best deal for each.

Investing 102: Risky Business

All assets have some kind of risk—even those that are supposedly safe. Like the mythical free lunch, there is no risk-free investment. This section deals with the different types of risk, and how to protect against them.

Investing risks are like illnesses and accidents; they can happen in spite of the best precautions. Fortunately, we can take steps to minimize the damage. Some risks, like colds, flu, and stubbed toes, are nuisances, but we can recover if we just ride them out. Other risks eat away at our investments over long periods of time, and can be as devastating as a serious illness. Still others are like major accidents that most times can be avoided, but sometimes are serious or even fatal. In life, we can't guarantee that we won't have serious accidents, chronic illnesses, and temporary sicknesses, but we can certainly minimize the damage if we take precautions. It's the same with investment risk.

Let's take a look at different types of investment risk. Which are the serious accidents, chronic illnesses, and temporary sicknesses?

Here's a list of *serious accident* risks. Here we can suffer a financial fatality, where we quickly lose a large part, or all, of our investment.

- *Fraud risk*, where the institution, investment professional, or corporation intentionally steals our money.

- *Chump risk*, where the institution, investment professional, or corporation doesn't steal our money, but has little interest or competence in making money for us, and has clearly put their interests ahead of ours. Their expense and sales charges are usually far higher than average, and aren't justified by superior performance.

- *Amateur risk*, where the investments do poorly because amateurs are making the investment selections. Usually the amateurs are us!

- *Bankruptcy risk*, where the financial institution that has our money goes bankrupt, or the underlying asset is the stock or bond of a corporation that goes bankrupt.

- *Risk of really poor performance*, where the corporation that issues a stock or bond does so poorly that the value of the stock or bond depreciates significantly.

These risks are highest with stocks and real estate, although they exist for bonds as well. We protect against these risks with the following strategies:

- Be diligent in selecting investment institutions and professionals that have a track record of honesty, integrity, and good performance. I discuss this more in Chapter 12.

- Good investment professionals should minimize risk of bankruptcy or really poor performance through *diversification*. This is an effective strategy, and is the opposite of putting all our eggs in one basket. We spread the risk by using more than one investment institution or professional. With specific types of assets, such as stocks or bonds, we should have at least 10 stocks or bonds in our portfolio, and usually many more, to spread the risk of one stock or bond going sour.

Here's a list of *chronic illness* risks. Here we still lose value and money, but it takes a longer period for this to happen compared to serious accident risks. Also, we usually don't lose *all* of our money with these risks—the value simply erodes significantly over time.

- *Inflation risk*, where the value of our assets doesn't keep up with inflation. This means our investments buy less goods and services in the future, compared to today.

- *Liquidity risk*, where it is difficult to quickly sell our investments. If it takes a long time to cash out, the value of our investments might go down before we can sell them.

- *Tax risk*, where our federal and state governments take a large chunk of our investment return.

How do we protect ourselves against these risks?

- Inflation risk is highest with bonds, cash, and deposits. Historically, stocks and real estate have done the best job of outpacing inflation over long periods, so holding a significant portion of these assets is the best way to protect against inflation.

- Liquidity risk is highest with individual pieces of real estate, small stocks, and deposits (before maturity). Such assets have a place in our portfolio, but not a large place. The most liquid assets are cash, stocks and bonds of large organizations, and mutual funds in these investments. I like having enough cash investments to live for at least three or four months, and enough total liquid assets to live for at least 12 months, without needing to sell real estate and other investments that have liquidity risk.

- Tax risk is highest with investments outside tax-sheltered retirement programs, such as 401(k) plans and IRAs. So one important strategy is to put as much money as possible into these programs. If we still need additional retirement investments and we're in a high tax bracket, we need to minimize federal and state income taxes on investments that are held outside a tax-sheltered retirement program. Here are assets that meet this goal:
  - Stocks and real estate that are held at least one year, so we can take advantage of lower capital gains taxes.
  - Stocks that pay qualified dividends, that are taxed at a 15 percent rate for federal income taxes.
  - Municipal bonds, whose interest is tax-free.
  - Index funds, which don't generate much realized capital appreciation (these are covered in Chapter 12).

Corporate and government bonds are most vulnerable to tax risk, when held outside tax-sheltered retirement investing programs.

Here's a list of temporary sickness risks. Here our assets might go down temporarily for reasons beyond our control, or beyond the control of the corporations that issue our stocks and bonds. If we're patient, hopefully our assets will recover eventually, if history repeats itself.

- *Market risk,* where the economy does poorly for awhile, and our stocks and/or bonds depreciate.

- *Interest rate risk*, where interest rates rise, driving down the value of stocks and/or bonds.

Stocks and real estate are most vulnerable to market risk; bonds also are vulnerable, but much less than stocks. Bonds are most vulnerable to interest rate risk; stocks and real estate are also vulnerable, but less than bonds. Deposits and cash are not affected by market and interest rate risk.

Here's one more use of my accident/illness analogy on investment risk. Temporary illnesses like colds and the flu can cause problems for older people, particularly those in poor health. So it's not always easy to ride out these illnesses. It's the same with our investments! We'll elaborate in the next course, Investing 103.

Let's Sum Up about Investing Risk

As we can see, it's not possible to find an investment that isn't vulnerable to some risk. Here's a summary of strategies to reduce our investment risk.

- As much as possible, I'll use professionally managed funds in my 401(k) plan at work. These should protect against all the serious accident risks and all the chronic illness risks except inflation. We're left with inflation and the temporary illness risks.

- We can help protect against inflation risk by having a significant portion of our assets in stocks and real estate.

- Assets held outside tax-sheltered retirement programs are subject to tax risk. For these investments, I use stocks and real estate that are subject to capital gains taxes (which are lower than ordinary income taxes) and municipal bonds that are tax-free. When I'm living off the income from my investments, I'll use financially healthy stocks that pay generous dividends. The maximum federal tax rate on income from dividends recently dropped to 15 percent, and is lower than the tax rate on ordinary income.

- Most large employers (for example, those with more than 1,000 employees) monitor the investment institutions and investment professionals that manage our 401(k) plan investments, to make sure we are getting good performance. If we work for a smaller employer that doesn't do this monitoring, or if we invest in IRAs and other investments outside employer-sponsored plans, *we* need to do this monitoring. We must take the time to educate ourselves, and compare our investments' performance to alternatives. And we must be diligent against fraud and chump risk. We cover these topics in Chapter 12.

- *Diversify!* Note that we get this with carefully selected mutual funds and other pooled investments, which are discussed in the next chapter.

All of this takes some of our time, but it need not consume us. Initially we might spend a lot of time getting up to speed on investments, but once we're there, we should spend well under ten hours per month. I spend most of this time reading financial magazines or newspapers, to keep abreast of capital market developments and new investment products. I also read any article that discusses people who have lost money due to fraud or any other serious accident risk, just to be aware of the potential pitfalls. Here's another reason to work part-time in our later years, as I've advocated earlier in this book. We have the time to look after our financial health, as well as our physical and emotional health.

Now let's turn to some considerations for developing investment strategies during our *rest-of-life*.

Investing 103: Strategies for Our Time

Here I discuss three lessons, plus one concern. The goal of these lessons is to help us decide our target asset allocation—the portion of our portfolio that we dedicate to stocks, bonds, deposits, cash, and real estate.

After we review these lessons and my concern, I'll discuss possible appropriate asset allocations for our stage in life. I'll express these in ranges—no less than one-third of our portfolio in assets that protect us from inflation, such as stocks and real state, and no more than two-thirds of our portfolio in these same assets, which have temporary illness risks. I'll also summarize ideas and considerations to help us decide where we should fall in this range, and focus on our own asset allocation targets.

Lesson #1: Conventional Wisdom, Revisited

Here's a brief summary of the conventional wisdom that we see in most investment educational materials. I review this because much of the conventional wisdom is still appropriate for us. However, there are caveats and considerations that now apply for our stage in life, and we shouldn't blindly accept this conventional wisdom.

Over the long run, stocks outperform all other investments. Each year, our investment consultants produce the Watson Wyatt Asset Model. This represents our best professional estimates of average annual returns for the next 10 years for various types of assets. It takes into account historical returns, but it also reflects our view of how the future might be different from historical averages. Table 11.4 shows our forecasts for average annual future rates of return from the 2004 Asset Model.

TABLE 11.4   Average Expected Rates of Return on Various Types of Assets, from Watson Wyatt 2004 Asset Model

Type of Asset	Average Annual Return
Large and mid-cap stocks (similar to S&P 500)	9.6%
Small-cap stocks	10.2%
Real estate investment trusts (REITs)*	8.3%
Long-term government/corporate bonds	6.1%
Intermediate-term government/corporate bonds	4.7%
Treasury bills, representing cash	3.7%
Inflation	2.7%

*See Chapter 12 for explanation.

Table 11.1 showed us the importance of achieving higher rates of returns—that these higher returns translate into more money over our lifetime. So, why not put all our money in stocks? Well, we can also lose money with stocks, as we shall soon see.

Stock market returns come in bursts—up and down. Figure 11.1, a graph of annual returns in the stock market since 1925 for large company stocks, shows how much the returns can vary from year to year. Some years were great, like 1995 through 1999. Others were crummy with large losses, like 2000 through 2002. And some years were mediocre, like 1992 and 1994.

This graph illustrates what I call the "stock market double whammy." The first part: There are over twice as many up bars as down bars. The second part: On average, the up bars go up about twice as high as the down bars go down.

If only we could predict with certainty which will be the good years and which will be the bad years, we'd have it made! This goal is the holy grail of stock market analysts, but is rarely achieved. Unfortunately, it's inevitable that most of us are not

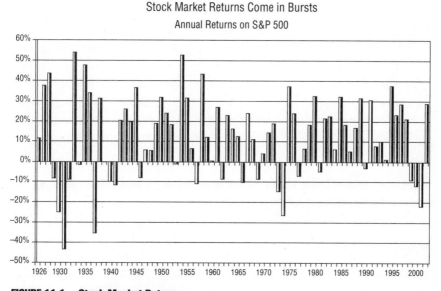

FIGURE 11.1   Stock Market Returns

sufficiently smart or prescient to sell our stocks just before they go down, and buy them back just before they go up. Realistically, all we can do is adopt strategies for surviving market downturns, which leads us to the next point.

Time is on our side. Stocks have their ups and downs, so to realize higher returns we need to ride out the down times. This is very good advice when we're in our thirties and forties, working and accumulating assets. During this period, retirement is far away, and we have the time to wait until stocks recover from temporary downturns. And we always can keep working to fill in any holes caused by investing accidents. However, once we're in our fifties and sixties, we have less time on our side. If we're not working, or are working only part-time, it's harder to make up for our investing misfortunes.

The Watson Wyatt 2004 Asset Model gives us insights into how much time is on our side for riding out temporary downturns. While Table 11.4 shows us the rate of return we *expect* to receive over a long period, we still need some insight into the odds that our expectations might be wrong—and in the wrong direction. The Asset Model can help us gain these insights.

For example, what are the odds that we will lose money with different investments? The answers depend on how long we are invested, as we see in Table 11.5. In this case, small answers are good!

Let's see what this means. The first numerical column shows that the odds of losing money over one year are highest with stocks—29.9 percent, or almost one out of three. These odds are somewhat smaller for bond investments. When we look at five years, the odds of losing money have decreased substantially, but

TABLE 11.5   Odds of Losing Money over Various Periods for Different Investments, As Predicted by Watson Wyatt 2004 Asset Model

Type of Investment	Odds of Losing Money over Period				
	1 Year	5 Years	10 Years	15 Years	20 Years
Large/mid-cap stocks	29.9%	11.9%	4.7%	2.1%	1.0%
Long-term government/corporate bonds	27.5%	1.8%	0%	0%	0%
Intermediate-term government/ corporate bonds	23.4%	0.1%	0%	0%	0%

the risks are still highest with stocks. For longer periods, the odds of losing money become small or nil for all types of investments.

If we consider only the odds of losing money, we'd pick bonds. However, let's look at the odds that stocks will beat the returns on bonds over various periods. In this case, we want the odds to be large (see Table 11.6).

The longer the period, the higher the odds that returns on stocks will beat bonds. By 20 years, the odds are roughly three out of four that stocks will beat bonds. This helps quantify the reason why we should consider taking some risk with stocks—to improve our chances of earning more money.

Your reaction might be that this is simple. Most of the time, stocks do better. Just like we discussed with our health, we can take action to beat the odds. If we're in a period when stocks will do poorly, pick bonds! Only buy stocks when they will go up! Alas, experience has shown that it is not possible to know in advance when we are in a time period when stocks will do poorly compared to inflation or other investments. The best way to protect ourselves is to take just enough risk so that we can recover from any misfortunes. Don't take risks that could ruin us!

THE RISK/RETURN TRADEOFF We all want an investment that has a high return with no risk. Yeah, and I wish the hair on my head would grow back! We can't have everything we want in life, and investments are no different. The only investments that provide the possibility of high returns also carry the risk that we might lose our money. The higher the expected return, the higher the risk of losing money. And vice versa—investments with guaranteed returns usually come with low returns. Figure 11.2 illustrates this by

TABLE 11.6   Odds of Stocks Beating Bonds over Various Periods, as Predicted by Watson Wyatt 2004 Asset Model

Type of Investment	Odds of Stocks Beating Bonds over Period				
	1 Year	5 Years	10 Years	15 Years	20 Years
Long-term government/corporate bonds	57%	66%	71%	75%	77%
Intermediate-term government/ corporate bonds	60%	71%	78%	82%	84%

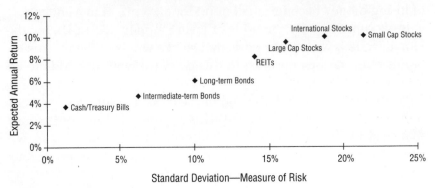

FIGURE 11.2   The Risk/Return Trade-off

Source: Watson Wyatt 2004 Asset Model.

plotting average expected returns for different types of assets with their expected standard deviation of the returns. For those of you who aren't actuaries or mathematicians, the standard deviation measures how far the year-to-year returns might vary, up or down, from the average expected return. The larger the potential variance, the larger is the standard deviation. If you didn't understand this, just take my word that the larger the standard deviation, the more risk we have.

The ideal place to be on this graph is the upper left-hand corner, with high return and low risk. This is the Shangri-la for investors, and is just about as difficult to locate. As you can see, there's a trade-off between risk and return—the higher the average returns, the higher the measure of risk, and vice versa.

So, we can pick assets with low risk and low expected return, or high risk with high expected return. We can get something in between by having a mixture of high-risk/high-return assets and low-risk/low-return assets. This is the purpose of paying attention to asset allocation—the mix of the different assets with respect to risk and return. Through asset allocation, we can control the amount of risk we take in our portfolio as a whole.

INFLATION IS OUR BIGGEST ENEMY   Once we see the risks with stock market investing, we might be tempted to put all our assets in safe investments, like bonds. The problem with this strategy is that inflation can erode the value of our investments. We've all seen the projections that show that, with moderate inflation, what costs a dollar today will cost a gazillion dollars 30 years from now. Over the long run, stocks and real estate have done the best job of outpacing inflation, provided we ride out the ups and downs. So, we should put a substantial portion of our *rest-of-life* portfolio in stocks and real estate. This is good advice for people in their thirties and forties; at this stage in life, we should be more worried about inflation than the temporary illness risk of losing our money from stock market declines.

In our fifties and beyond, we should still be worried about inflation. However, we should now have an equal balance of worry between inflation and the risk of losing money. The older we get, the more we should protect ourselves against temporary illness risks. We do this by increasing the portion of our assets that are invested in bonds and deposits.

When we're in our fifties, sixties, and beyond, it's time to take less risk, compared to our thirties and forties. When we're in our forties or younger, conventional wisdom says it's okay to allocate 75 percent or more of retirement portfolios to stocks. When we're in our fifties and sixties, I believe that no more than two-thirds—66^2/$_3$ percent—should be allocated to stocks, and often less is appropriate. Years ago, one popular rule of thumb said that our bond allocation should equal our age. For example, if we are 60, put 60 percent of our portfolio in bonds. This is a good rule of thumb, but it should be updated for improved longevity. Now I'd say that the bond allocation should equal our age minus 10 percent, if we want to use this rule of thumb. So if we're 60, put about 50 percent of our portfolio in bonds.

The stories of the centenarians from Chapter 3 make me reflect on the conventional wisdom about reducing our investments in stocks as we age. Moving most of our assets into bonds is an end-game decision—we acknowledge that we might die soon. Is it life-affirming to stay with stocks into our seventies, eighties, and nineties, because we believe we'll have the time to ride out the downturns? Does this state our intention and commitment to keep on living? I just might choose to believe this when I get there!

This finishes my review of conventional wisdom. Now let's turn to some practical considerations when deciding how to manage our *rest-of-life* portfolio.

Lesson #2: Don't Plan for the Averages

Many financial planners use spreadsheets based on averages when determining how much to save during our accumulation period, or how much to withdraw when we are living on our assets. They make assumptions like "Let's assume you earn 8 percent per year on your investments, which is what you can expect on average given your asset allocation." Or, "Let's assume you live for another 30 years, which is five years longer than your life expectancy."

It's dangerous to plan on the averages. With respect to life expectancies, we might live well beyond the averages. With respect to investment returns, we never earn the averages consistently each year. We'll have our ups and downs, and over a long period we might average 8 percent, but it's the volatility that can ruin us. Let's look at an example.

Let's suppose it is the beginning of 1973, and we are retiring at age 60. We have an imperfect crystal ball on the stock and bond market. We know what the returns will *average* for the next 30 years, but we don't know the actual year-by-year returns. We decide to put two-thirds of our money in stocks, and one-third in long-term corporate bonds. We do the math using average returns, and see that this portfolio will average a 10.5 percent annual return for the period 1973 through 2002. We also calculate that inflation will average 4.9 percent per year.

We've read Chapter 2, and see that on average a 60-year-old woman will live to 84.9 years and a 60-year-old man will live to 82.2 years. We are taking care of ourselves, so we decide to make sure we can live to 90 without outliving our money.

We have a buddy at work who is good with spreadsheets, and develops a spreadsheet that projects our account balances, plugging in average rates of return and inflation. He sets it up so we can plug in different withdrawal rates, to see when we run out of money. We assume that our account balance will earn the average rate of return, and that we will increase the amount we withdraw each year to reflect the average inflation rate. Our buddy plugs in these average rates and forecasts our account balances for various withdrawal rates. See Figure 11.3 for the results. (Actually, electronic spreadsheets weren't yet invented in 1973, but we'll just have to pretend we're at the movies and suspend disbelief for a while.)

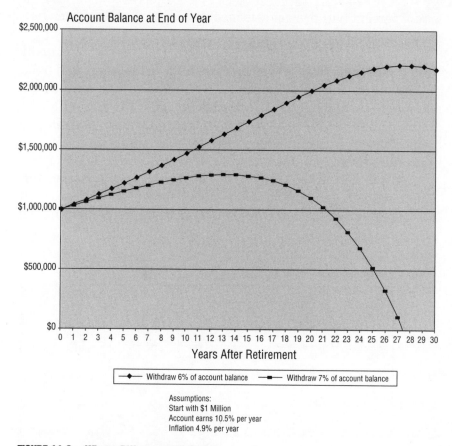

Account Balance at End of Year

Years After Retirement

— ◆ — Withdraw 6% of account balance   — ■ — Withdraw 7% of account balance

Assumptions:
Start with $1 Million
Account earns 10.5% per year
Inflation 4.9% per year

FIGURE 11.3   What a Difference 1% Makes

We see what our account will be at age 90, assuming that we start withdrawing 6 percent per year (which amounts to a withdrawal of $60,000 in the first year). Each year thereafter, we will increase the $60,000 amount by the average inflation rate of 4.9 percent. We see that with a 6 percent withdrawal rate, at age 90 we will have about $2.2 million. However, at a 7 percent withdrawal rate, we run out of money in 27 years, at age 87. So, we decide to use a 6 percent withdrawal rate, and we feel pretty safe because $2.2 million seems like a comfortable safety margin. By the way, this shows how sensitive the results are to small changes in our assumptions. The difference between a 6 percent and 7 percent withdrawal rate means the difference between out-living our money or not!

So, was our plan foolproof? Not quite. Let's see what actually would have happened if we had earned the actual stock and bond market returns since 1973, and if we increased our withdrawal amount for actual inflation during these years. The bottom line in Figure 11.4 shows the results. With a 6 percent withdrawal rate, we would have run out of money after 14 years, at age 74! Sadly, we must die at this point if we don't want to outlive our money.

Unfortunately, Chapter 10 wasn't available in 1973. It has a different method of determining how much to withdraw. If we could have used Table 10.2, we would have seen suggested withdrawal

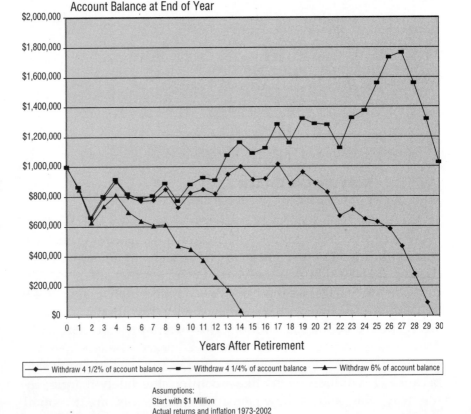

Years After Retirement

———◆— Withdraw 4 1/2% of account balance ———■— Withdraw 4 1/4% of account balance ———▲— Withdraw 6% of account balance

Assumptions:
Start with $1 Million
Actual returns and inflation 1973-2002

FIGURE 11.4   Using the Averages Can Be a Mistake

rates that have a low chance of running out of money. This table shows a suggested annual withdrawal rate of 4.5 percent for men and 4.25 percent for women. In this example, if we had withdrawn 4.5 percent per year, we would run out of money in 30 years, right at age 90. If we had withdrawn 4.25 percent each year, we would have more than $1 million at age 90—again, a demonstration of how sensitive the results are to small differences in withdrawal rates.

What's happening with this example? In the early years of our retirement, the stock market did poorly and inflation was high. Later on, the stock market recovered and inflation was much lower. However, we depleted our account balance so much in the early years that there wasn't enough account balance left to fully recover, and we ran out of money too soon.

This illustrates how the asset/liability modeling process described in Chapter 10 works. We do thousands of these scenarios, and see how many times we outlive our money. This process takes into account possible deviances from the averages for stock and bond market returns, inflation, and longevity.

You could argue that I picked a uniquely bad period for this example. The stock market did poorly in 1973 and 1974, and inflation was high for several years thereafter. My answer to this objection is: yeah, but it actually happened, and it could happen again. In fact, I'm more than a little worried that this scenario could be repeated in the future. Before the market declined in 1973, it had risen to a high level (similar to today, even with the recent market declines). And the high inflation of the 1970s was preceded by large budget deficits and shocks from the oil crisis. Given the budget deficits we are running now and instability in the Middle East, it could happen again.

In fact, people who retired in 2000 or 2001 are living this nightmare right now, as they have seen substantial declines in their retirement portfolios. One actuary friend who retired in this period is constantly forecasting his assets and living expenses. He tells me that he now needs to die about five years earlier than he had previously planned when he retired, due to the stock market declines in 2000, 2001, and 2002. While he has a good sense of humor, it's no laughing matter.

Let's go back to this example for one more lesson.

Now let's suppose that we withdraw $4^1/_2$ percent of our initial balance, and increase our withdrawal for actual inflation each year. The bottom line in Figure 11.5 shows the same result as from Figure 11.4—we run out of money in 30 years, at age 90. Let's compare this to a reverse universe, where everything is exactly the same, only time runs backward. The order of the investment returns and inflation is reversed, and we experience 2002 first and 1973 last. In the first year of retirement we earn the actual investment return from 2002, in the second year we earn the investment return from 2001, and so on. We earn the same returns for 30 years, just in reverse order of what actually happened. Obviously, this will have the same average rate of return for 30 years, compared to

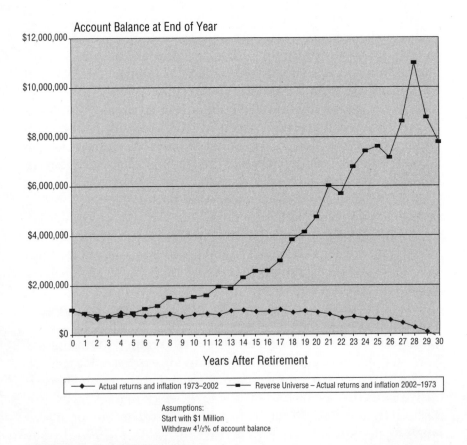

Account Balance at End of Year

Years After Retirement

◆ Actual returns and inflation 1973–2002 ■ Reverse Universe – Actual returns and inflation 2002–1973

Assumptions:
Start with $1 Million
Withdraw $4^1/_2$% of account balance

FIGURE 11.5   Stock Market Craziness

what actually happened for 1973 through 2002. The top line in Figure 11.5 shows the result. Instead of running out of money in 30 years, we have nearly $8 million!

How can this be? How can we have such dramatically different results at the end of 30 years, when we have the same average rate of return? It comes down to the timing of the bad years. The period 1973 through 2002 had the bad years at the beginning of the retirement period—poor returns and high inflation. The portfolio got so battered that there wasn't enough left to recover when the markets eventually turned around. The reverse universe had this bad period near the end, and the assets had grown enough to withstand the battering near the end.

The point of all of this craziness is just that—there is a lot of craziness in the stock market!

Here's a corollary to this lesson: *Don't sell when we're down.* If we put ourselves in a position where we must sell assets when they are temporarily depressed, then these assets won't be there when the market recovers. Selling stocks and real estate in a down market because we need them for living expenses is a recipe for disaster. That's why I prefer living on the income from these investments for as long as possible. This way, I don't care too much about temporary fluctuations in the value of these investments, as long as the income is reliable and my long-term outlook is that these investments will eventually recover.

The extreme sensitivity of these projections to small changes in withdrawal rates or to small changes in our assumptions points to the uncertainty involved with living on our lump sums for long periods of time. It also points to the consequences—if things go bad, we don't know it until late in life. By the way, this extreme sensitivity works both ways. If the stock market does well, then my account balances will grow nicely and I will have lots of money at the end. For me, this reinforces why I want to work part-time for awhile and enjoy my work in the process. This lets me see how the markets are doing, and if they are doing poorly, I can keep working a little longer. This also helps me delay withdrawing principal for as long as possible, which helps protect me from outliving my money.

Finally, don't get me wrong about the uncertainties and craziness of the stock market. We should still have a portion of our assets invested in stocks during our *rest-of-life*, because most of the time we achieve returns that are higher than for other investments, which translates into more money. The trouble is, it's most of the time, not *all of the time*. So, to protect ourselves from outliving our money, we should carefully plan our withdrawal strategies, using the techniques described in Chapters 9 and 10.

When I reflected on this stock market phenomenon, it occurred to me that life is similar. Like the stock market, life itself is a lot richer if we take chances—*most of the time*. However, when we take chances, either in life or in the stock market, occasionally we get burned. The point is not to avoid taking chances, but to be able to survive the times when we get burned by taking the chances. That's the point of the recommended 401(k) withdrawal strategies—to invest in the stock market and hopefully achieve higher returns and have more money, *and* to survive the possibility of being burned. Bonds provide predictable returns, but usually result in lower returns and less money. If we adopt an all-bonds philosophy to life, we guarantee not getting burned, but our lives might be a lot less rich.

Lesson #3: Consider Our Whole Situation

The portion of my portfolio that I dedicate to assets that can fluctuate in value, such as stocks and real estate, can be influenced by other aspects of my entire situation. The following situations might be a justification for being on the high end of my suggested allocation to stocks and real estate. In these situations, I might be able to afford to take a little more risk, because I can ride out any temporary declines in value.

- If I am living on just the income from my investments, and don't need to sell principal.

- If I'm in my fifties and sixties, particularly if I'm still working.

- If I have a significant lifetime income from a defined benefit plan, or have purchased a fixed immediate annuity (discussed in Chapter 10), so that my lifetime income, together with Social Security benefits, covers a large part of my living expenses.

- If I have a wide margin of *I* over *E*, and I expect to sustain this difference for my lifetime. This can result from having a large retirement nest egg, or from having reduced living expenses dramatically, for example, by paying off the mortgage.

Of course, if my circumstances are the opposite of these situations, that might call for being near the lower end of the suggested asset allocation range for stocks and real estate.

Stocks and Real Estate—A Concern

There is a possibility that when we baby boomers all try to sell our stocks to fund our retirement, the mass selling might drive down the value of these stocks. The same might happen with our houses, at least the large family homes in the suburbs.

Note that this refers to the value that the *market* places on stocks and real estate. Appropriately selected stocks and real estate will still produce earnings and income. It's entirely likely that corporations will still be healthy, will still meet our needs for goods and services, and will still crank out profits. However, because we might have a surplus of sellers over buyers, the market prices of the stocks of these same companies might be depressed.

I am worried enough about this possibility to take some precautions:

- This is one more reason to live off the income from investments and delay withdrawing principal as long as possible. With stocks and real estate, withdrawing principal means selling these assets.

- With respect to stocks, I'll place a higher emphasis on income stocks, compared to growth stocks. I'll look for companies that pay solid dividends, and can be expected to sustain and grow these dividends in the future. I'll still have growth stocks in my portfolio, but as I get older, I'll place a higher proportion of my stock portfolio in income stocks.

- For my home, I have already bought a "demographic investment" (e.g., a townhouse that appeals to empty nesters). I no longer live in a large house in the suburbs—the kids have moved out! Chapter 18 goes into more detail.

- I'll make investments to reduce my E, such as paying off my mortgage. Since inflation is a big concern for our later years, I'll adopt strategies to reduce my own rate of inflation to below the official inflation rate expressed by the consumer price index (CPI)—discussed further in Chapter 18.

This is an example of the value of risk budgeting, a strategy used in our pension consulting for managing assets and liabilities of large pension funds.

- If I'm wrong about my concern, the precautions I advocate won't ruin me. The worst that will happen is that I could have made a little more money with my investments, compared to not taking these precautions. But my portfolio and assets should still be intact, and I can still do what I want with my life.

- If I'm right about my concern and I don't take these precautions, my financial security could be jeopardized. My assets might decline so much that I can't do what I want with my life.

So I'd rather take these precautions and then turn out to be wrong about my concerns, than not take these precautions at the risk of jeopardizing my lifestyle.

So What Should We Do?

Once we're in our fifties and beyond, we should normally allocate our assets within the following ranges:

- No less than one-third in stocks and real estate, to protect ourselves from inflation.

- No more than two-thirds in these same investments, to protect ourselves from volatility and temporary downturns.

- The remainder primarily in deposits and bonds, with not much, if any, in cash (say 5 percent or less of our total portfolio). Cash is primarily for an emergency reserve or for parking our money temporarily before we spend it or redeploy it in another investment.

- With the portion in stocks and real estate, we'll put at least half into income-producing investments, with the balance in growth investments.

- With the portion in bonds, we'll put all of the assets that are in tax-sheltered retirement programs into intermediate, investment grade corporate bonds, and stable value funds if they are available. When investing outside tax-sheltered retirement programs, we'll use municipal bonds if we're in a high tax bracket; otherwise we can use the same taxable corporate bonds.

I asked a few of our investment consultants, "How do you allocate your 401(k) balances, and how will this change as you get older?" As expected, there was a variety of answers, and we had some healthy debates. We looked at our research and cranked up our computer models. The fanciest models generate "efficient frontiers," which is consultant-speak for specifying how much risk we can afford and then finding the asset allocation that maximizes the expected return for that level of risk—in other words, gives us the biggest bang for the buck.

Here's what we finally settled on. Investment consultants use colorful names for asset allocations, like "60/40" and "50/50," which refer to the equity/bond portions of the portfolio. The equity portion includes all types of equity investments—large companies, small companies, international stocks, and real estate. Similarly, the bond portion includes all types of bonds and deposits. In keeping with the clever naming convention, I designate our suggested asset allocations 65/35 (Table 11.7), 50/50 (Table 11.8), and 35/65 (Table 11.9).

65/35

This puts almost two-thirds of our portfolio in equities, and a little over one-third in bonds. This mix might be appropriate in our early *rest-of-life*, say our fifties and early sixties, or if we are comfortable with a little more risk. It might also be appropriate if we have other resources that allow us to take more risk, such as a lifetime income from a defined benefit plan or annuity, or a home with no mortgage. Finally, if we have a large margin of I over E, we might be able to take more risk.

If we want to add real estate to our portfolio through REITs (as discussed in the next chapter), we could add 10 percent for REITs and take 5 percent each from small U.S. stocks and international stocks.

TABLE 11.7 The 65/35 Asset Allocation

Asset Type	Asset Allocation
Large U.S. stocks	35%
Small U.S. stocks	10%
Large international stocks	20%
Intermediate bonds	35%

50/50

This puts half of our portfolio in equities and half in bonds. This mix might be appropriate in our middle *rest-of-life*, say our late sixties and seventies, or if we have a balanced view between risk and security.

If we want to add real estate to our portfolio through REITs (as discussed in the next chapter), we could add 10 percent for REITs and take 5 percent each from small U.S. stocks and international stocks.

TABLE 11.8 The 50/50 Asset Allocation

Asset Type	Asset Allocation
Large U.S. stocks	25%
Small U.S. stocks	10%
Large international stocks	15%
Intermediate bonds	50%

35/65

This puts a little over one-third of our portfolio in equities, and almost two-thirds in bonds. This mix might be appropriate in our late *rest-of-life*, say our eighties and beyond, or if we are really concerned about safety. It might also be appropriate if we don't have other financial resources or have a house with a large mortgage. If we have a tight margin between our *I* and *E*, we might want to play it safe with this allocation.

If we want to add real estate to our portfolio through REITs (as discussed in the next chapter), we could add 5 percent for REITs and take 5 percent from international stocks.

TABLE 11.9   The 35/65 Asset Allocation

Asset Type	Asset Allocation
Large U.S. stocks	20%
Small U.S. stocks	5%
Large international stocks	10%
Intermediate bonds	65%

WRAP-UP

By now, I hope you get the message that asset allocation is part science, part art. I have become knowledgeable about the characteristics of different types of assets and their expected returns and risks, and I urge you to do so as well. But in the end, nobody has a magic formula. We just need to make an informed decision and move ahead with it!

There are a couple of practical matters with asset allocation. First, it should apply to all invested assets, both inside and outside tax-advantaged retirement plans. One challenge is that we might have a few different resources, so we should apply the suggested allocation across all our *rest-of-life* investments. For this purpose, I don't count money that we might have in cash investments as an emergency reserve.

The second issue concerns rebalancing. This means that our allocation gets out of whack over time, as one type of asset does well while another might lag. We should adjust our investments roughly every six months, to keep in line with our target asset allocation.

The next chapter discusses investment institutions and products that offer convenient, effective ways to implement our own asset allocation strategies and protect us against some of the risks mentioned in this chapter.

Lesson #3 describes situations and circumstances that might influence our eventual decision on asset allocation, and how much we should invest in stocks. There is one more consideration:

"Do ya feel lucky?"

How optimistic do we feel about our future, the economy, and the political landscape? As a nation, we need to be strong economically and politically for our investments to keep their value.

Where Should I Invest My Money?

Knowledge is power.

—Sir Francis Bacon

When it comes to selecting investment products and financial institutions, we need to be vigilant with our investments, and make sure that the financial institutions with whom we invest our money deserve our trust.

Fortunately, most institutions and professionals have integrity and professionalism. They balance their needs with ours in an ethical way, and their people are informed, trained, and qualified to help us. Unfortunately, there are also sharks who will take large bites of our wealth.

All we need to do is "pretty good" and we'll be able to live the life we want. I'd rather have a boring investment that makes pretty good money, than an exciting investment pitched by a sharp-looking professional who might be either an investing genius who makes lots of money for me, or a slick shark who will rip me off, but I can't tell the difference. Of course, I'll try to do better than "pretty good" but in the process I won't jeopardize my financial security. This chapter offers some strategies for doing pretty good and better, and tips and warning signs for avoiding the money losers.

For the rest of our life, we should be informed and educated on investment products and financial institutions. This is a good use of our time, although it doesn't need to be huge amounts of time. We should invest our money with professionals who work full-time to manage our investments. We can't work on this full-time—we've got better things to do with our time. Also, they are trained specifically for their task, while we have different skills and experience.

However, we should take the time to evaluate and select the *right* professionals and monitor their performance periodically, to make sure they continue to be the right professionals or to see if there are better products and institutions. And, we should never go unconscious and blindly accept their guidance and advice. We should always test it against our experience, knowledge, and intuition, to see if it feels right and makes sense for our circumstances.

At the beginning of Chapter 11, I mentioned the results of studies that show that asset allocation accounts for up to 90 percent of the variance in the risk and return of our portfolios. However, we can't use this as justification for getting lazy with respect to selecting investment institutions and their products. These studies started with the assumptions that we weren't getting ripped off and had not hired incompetent managers.

The preceding chapter summarized four decisions that we need to make with our investments, as shown in Table 12.1. This chapter discusses the second and third decisions—the investment products and financial institutions that are best for us.

TABLE 12.1   Investment Decisions

---

1.   Which type of assets?

2.   Which investment product?

3.   Where to put our money—with which financial institution?

4.   Which retirement investing program?

The Very Best Place for Our *Rest-of-Life* Savings

My employer, Watson Wyatt, has a great 401(k) plan. I invest the most that I can in this plan, and I intend to keep it there even after I stop working. Chances are good that many of you also have a good 401(k) plan at work where you can invest most, if not all, of your *rest-of-life* savings.

Why is it the best place? I summarize some reasons at the beginning of Chapter 10. Here are two more:

1. Most 401(k) plans protect us against the serious accident risks discussed in the preceding chapter. Our employers have a fiduciary obligation to shop for the best financial institutions and products that perform well for our savings. Often they hire firms like mine to help them carry out these obligations.

2. Our 401(k) plans also protect against two chronic illness risks—tax risk and liquidity risk.

Here's one caveat: Employers with fewer than 1,000 employees may not have sufficient resources for selecting and monitoring their 401(k) investment choices. This doesn't imply we shouldn't use these plans—it just means we might need to investigate how our employer selected these funds.

One decision that we will need to make when we change jobs is to roll or not to roll. The issue is whether we should leave our money in our previous employer's 401(k) plan or roll it over into an IRA or our next employer's 401(k) plan. Here are the key considerations:

- I wouldn't roll over to an IRA, unless my previous employer has a bunch of money-losing funds or charges me for participating. The reason is that the institutions running IRAs are trying to make money from my money, while employers who sponsor 401(k) plans don't do this (in fact, they spend time and money to run these plans for our benefit). If your 401(k) plan charges former participants an administrative fee, I would compare it to charges from IRAs.

- If I have a new job, I can roll my balance from my previous 401(k) plan to my new plan. One advantage is that it is convenient to have all my investments in one place. One possible disadvantage happens if I want to access my 401(k) balances while I'm still working. The new plan might have restrictions on "in-service withdrawals," while these rules won't apply to my balances that I left in my prior employer's plan. See Chapter 13 for more considerations on the tax rules regarding 401(k) plan withdrawals and distributions.

Many of us don't have a 401(k) plan at work, or we need to save amounts above the maximum limits allowed in 401(k) plans. In this case, we need to learn about investment products and financial institutions.

Go with the Pros

The best investment products pool our money with that of other investors, and professionals are hired to manage the pooled investments. Examples of pooled investments include mutual funds, as well as investment funds and deposits offered by banks and insurance companies. All of these pooled arrangements can invest in one or more of the types of investments already discussed—stocks, bonds, deposits, cash, and real estate. The descriptions and marketing materials for a particular pooled fund should prominently describe the types of investments it holds.

By the way, many 401(k) plans offer funds that are individually managed by investment professionals. These operate like mutual funds, but they are available only through large employers, and are not available to retail customers. These funds typically have lower investment management expenses than retail mutual funds, so they are a good deal.

Properly selected mutual funds and other pooled funds will protect against all the serious accident risks and one chronic illness risk—liquidity risk—mentioned in the preceding chapter. However, I am open to amateur risk if I don't take the time and effort to select the right funds.

Other pooled arrangements, such as limited partnerships and tax shelters, are too risky, unless we have the time and skill to properly evaluate them.

All I Need to Know about Mutual Funds

Mutual funds put us in a pool with other investors. Any mutual fund has a stated investment objective, which indicates the types of assets the fund will invest in. We can use mutual funds to invest in stocks, bonds, cash, and real estate—all but one of the types of investments described in the preceding chapter. We won't use mutual funds for our deposits. There are thousands of mutual funds sold in the United States.

A mutual fund company hires investment professionals to manage our money. This gives us protection against amateur risk (although the mutual fund company might hire the wrong professionals). One of our jobs is to determine how good the investment manager is, and I'll discuss this evaluation later.

All mutual funds put their assets into trusts operated by independent trust companies. The trusts and operations of the mutual fund companies are audited by independent accountants. These safeguards make sure that our money will be used for its intended purpose—investing—and that the mutual fund operator won't take our money to Las Vegas. This protects against fraud risk.

A mutual fund company can go bankrupt, but the assets in the trust fund remain intact and belong to the investors—that's us! This protects us against the bankruptcy risk of the financial institution. However, we are not protected from the risk that a stock or bond held in the fund will become worthless because the underlying corporation has gone bankrupt.

Mutual funds offer many convenient services. We can access account summaries online, and perform most transactions such as buying, selling, and withdrawing our money. Usually we can talk with someone if we have any questions or special problems. Most mutual fund companies also offer a host of educational material on retirement planning and investing topics, both online and in brochures. For example, we can learn about investment strategies, withdrawal strategies, and the IRS rules that apply to retirement investing programs. Many have calculators that help us determine how much to save (covered more in Chapter 20).

The mutual fund company charges the fund for the expenses of operating the fund. The most significant expense is the money paid to the investment professionals. The level of these expenses is important and directly affects the value of my investments—I discuss this later.

I have my own savings with two large mutual fund companies, for a couple of reasons. First, I have access to more funds, and I can pick the best from both. No single mutual fund company has stars in every category; they each have their strengths and weaknesses. Second, each company's educational material is a little different, and I benefit by learning from both companies and their web sites.

There are a few ways to classify mutual funds. One important way is to identify the underlying assets in which the fund invests (usually this is obvious from the marketing materials). Other ways of classifying funds include the way the funds are sold and the way they are operated.

First, let's look at the two basic ways mutual funds are sold.

1. *No-load funds* are usually sold by mail, telephone, or through a sales representative employed by the mutual fund company. We can learn about them through advertisements, magazines, newspaper articles, and online. When we buy a no-load mutual fund for the first time, usually we send the mutual fund company a check in the mail. Once our account is established, we can direct the specific fund to invest the money. Subsequently, we can transfer our money to other funds, either by telephone or online.

    The mutual fund company will provide written information about the funds, and representatives will answer factual questions. However, nobody will give us advice on which fund is appropriate for us—we need to make this decision.

    Here's the most important characteristic of a no-load fund: All of the money gets invested in the mutual fund, which is not the case with load funds.

2. *Load funds* are usually sold in person by stockbrokers, insurance agents, or other financial advisers. Typically these advisers are not employed by the mutual fund company. To invest in the fund, usually we hand this person a check, which he or she then transmits to the mutual fund company. He or she should help us decide which funds are appropriate for us. This service comes at a price, since these advisers receive a commission, or load, from the fund. This commission can range from 1 percent to 8 percent or more of our investment. For example, suppose a fund has a 6 percent load. If I

give the adviser $100 to invest, $94 gets invested in the mutual fund, and the adviser pockets $6.

Which type of fund is best? For me, the answer is simple: no-load. I'm comfortable determining which types of assets are appropriate for me and selecting specific funds. My intent is for you to develop these skills and confidence as well.

Some of you may not feel comfortable making these decisions, and you may want the help of a financial adviser. In this case, you'll have to pay for his or her services, and one way is through investing in load funds. However, I'd rather work with an adviser who charges a flat fee or a percentage of assets under management (1 percent is common, while more than 1 percent starts to get excessive). This way, your adviser isn't tempted to move your money around frequently and get paid a commission for each transaction.

With load funds, there's an incentive for your adviser to churn your account by continuing to buy and sell funds in order to collect a commission each time. The adviser has no incentive to select a good fund and stick with it for years.

There is no convincing evidence that no-load funds outperform load funds, or vice versa. There are good and poor performers of both types.

Another classification of mutual funds is open-ended versus closed-ended. Another name for closed-ended funds is exchange-traded funds (ETFs). Here's an explanation:

- *Open-ended funds* expand and shrink the size of the fund, depending on how much money investors deposit and withdraw each day. The value of the fund equals the value of the underlying assets. As long as the fund is open to new investors, we can always send the fund more money to invest. Sometimes, these funds close to new investors when the fund operators think they can't effectively invest any more money.

- *Closed-ended funds* invest a fixed amount of money. Each investor is credited with a fixed number of shares in the fund. For new funds, we can invest directly with the institution that organizes the fund. The only way we can invest in an existing fund is to buy shares from a current shareholder. These funds are bought and sold on stock exchanges through stockbrokers and financial advisers. If there aren't any sellers, we can't invest in the fund. It is possible for the share price to be different from the underlying value of the assets; the share price is based on the supply and demand of buyers and sellers of the funds.

Which type of fund is best for us? There are advantages and disadvantages of each. I prefer open-ended funds, since they are by far the most common. It is easy to learn about them and to buy and sell them. While there is a lot of hype about closed-ended funds and ETFs, the advantages appear to be for traders and short-term investors. I haven't identified any advantages for long-term investors.

Most mutual funds protect against all the serious accident risks mentioned in the previous chapter—fraud, chump, amateur, bankruptcy, and really poor performance—and one of the chronic illness risks—liquidity. They do this by hiring professional investment managers and diversifying our investments. There are a few exceptions and things to look for:

- There's no guarantee that the professionals hired by the mutual fund company are good.

- Some funds have very high levels of expenses or very high loads so that the operators and sellers of these funds can make more money than we do. To protect against this risk, simply avoid these types of funds (soon I'll discuss how to do this).

- The underlying assets can become worthless if the corporation that issues the stock or bond becomes bankrupt. However, this risk is minimized if the fund is diversified.

- Most funds invest in many different securities, giving us diversity. Some funds purposely invest in few assets, exposing us to diversification risk. We can learn if this is the case by reading the fund's prospectus. Watch out if a single asset represents more than 5 percent of the total portfolio.

- Virtually all open-ended funds will cash out our investments on request within one day, so we are protected against liquidity risk. However, watch out for funds that charge a fee upon withdrawal—again this should be in the prospectus. With closed-ended funds, our ability to cash out our investment depends on whether there is a buyer. With larger funds, this usually isn't a problem, but it can be with smaller funds.

This is about all the general information we need to know about mutual funds. Next, let's talk about how to evaluate and pick mutual funds.

How Do We Choose Which Funds Are Best for Us?

With thousands of funds to choose from, it's easy to feel intimidated when we're selecting a mutual fund. But, as we'll see, we can quickly narrow down the candidates.

The mere fact that we're doing this on our own means we can forget about load funds; this eliminates hundreds of funds. We can then pick our funds with only two steps.

1. Determine our desired asset allocation and the types of investments we want—stocks, bonds, cash, real estate, or a combination of two or more of these types.

2. Pick one or more funds based on our evaluation of expected return, risk, and expenses.

Once again, I'll let the pros do the work for us. There are services that compile the performances of funds, as well as a wealth of useful information on these funds. They even rate the funds, based on past performance. Examples include Morningstar (www.morningstar.com), Value Line (www.valueline.com), and the Mutual Fund Investor's Center (www.mfea.com). All of these provide good information for free, and we can get additional information from Morningstar and Value Line for a subscription. Subscribers can conduct searches for funds that meet various criteria, and if we have a lot of money to invest, these subscriptions are worthwhile.

Now let's talk a little more about selecting funds for each type of asset: stocks, bonds, cash, and real estate.

Easy Answers: Hybrid Funds

Large, innovative mutual fund companies have given us a single easy answer: hybrid funds. They go by a number of names—

balanced funds, asset allocation funds, lifestyle funds, and target retirement age funds. With all of these, the mutual fund makes the asset allocation decision for us; they decide how much to allocate between different types of investments. All we need to do is review the marketing literature, and see if the fund's objectives and asset allocation are appropriate for our circumstances. They take it from there. Each of the types of funds is slightly different, so here's a brief synopsis:

- *Balanced funds* maintain a specific allocation among stocks, bonds, and cash. This allocation is usually stated in ranges. For example, a fund's stated allocation to stocks may never hold less than 33 percent or more than 67 percent.

- *Asset allocation funds* are like balanced funds, only the investment manager has the discretion to go all in stocks, all in bonds, or something between, based on his or her evaluation of capital markets. Sometimes these are funds of funds, where the manager selects among other mutual funds from the same company. For example, the fund manager might allocate among other stock, bond, and cash funds that the mutual fund company operates.

- *Lifestyle funds* are balanced funds with an identified lifestyle, which usually refers to the age of the investor. For example, such a fund might be targeted to people in their sixties and seventies, who need a balance between growth with its associated risk and security with its expected lower returns.

- *Target retirement age funds* are balanced funds that change the asset allocation as we approach the target year in which we expect to retire. For example, a fund might be identified as a 2020 fund, which means it targets the year 2020 as the retirement year. The fund operator moves more money from stocks to bonds as the target retirement year approaches.

I can use Morningstar's rating service to conduct a search of large, established hybrid funds: For example, I can tell the computer to use the following criteria:

- Current rank in highest two categories.

- Average five-year rank in highest two categories.

- Current manager with the fund at least five years.

- Expenses lower than average.

- No-load.

Keep in mind that there are different criteria that I could apply that could show different funds. For example, there are several highly rated funds whose manager tenure has been less than five years. Here I'm just showing how I might go about finding a list of funds to examine further.

Once I make a list of candidates, I'll look at each fund to determine its asset allocation limits and policies, expense ratios, and performance histories. After I've done this research, I need to make a decision, often based on my comfort level and feelings about each fund.

If you take the time to evaluate which fund best meets your circumstances and objectives, hybrid funds are worth considering. I prefer the balanced funds and asset allocation funds. The reason is that the lifestyle and target retirement age funds are based on the old model of retirement, where we retire full-time at a specific age and expect to live for only another 10 or 15 years. If we live to our nineties and continue to work for much of this time, it doesn't make a lot of sense to be changing our asset allocation in our fifties, sixties, and seventies. I believe we can select a balanced fund and stick with the specified asset allocation indefinitely. However, don't get me wrong—these are just slight preferences. Any of these types of funds can be appropriate.

We can combine hybrid funds with the Income Solution, described in Chapter 10. With a good hybrid fund, we should be able to withdraw 3 percent per year indefinitely for living expenses. If we don't want to think too hard about how much to withdraw and how to invest, this is a simple solution. It won't maximize our I, but it's a simple, relatively safe strategy. However, we shouldn't get too complacent—we should constantly monitor our hybrid fund, to make sure it continues to perform well.

Stock Funds

The first challenge is to understand all the classifications of stock funds. There are dozens of categories, and there can be hundreds of funds in each category. Here are common classifications that are appropriate for part or all of our stock investments:

- *Index funds* attempt to mimic the return on a specified index, such as the S&P 500, by investing in all the stocks that make up the index.

- *Growth funds* invest primarily in growth stocks.

- *Value funds* invest primarily in value stocks.

- *Equity income funds* invest primarily in income stocks.

- *Growth and income funds* invest in a mixture of growth and income stocks.

If we're picking our own funds, it's important to get diversification across different styles of funds. During any given period, one of the styles will outperform other styles. Studies show when growth funds outperform the market, value funds typically underperform the market, and vice versa. Like other forms of market timing, it's hard for amateurs to know in advance which styles will do well, so the best strategy is to be diversified across all styles.

Some types of funds have more risk than the common types listed earlier, but they expect increased returns to compensate for this risk. If we feel comfortable with these risks, we might put up to one-third of our stock investments in these funds:

- *Aggressive growth funds* attempt to enhance returns by investing in smaller stocks, stocks with growth potential, and/or stock options.

- *Small capitalization funds* invest in small companies with growth potential.

- *Global funds* invest in stocks all around the world, including the United States.

- *International funds* invest in stocks of other countries, excluding the United States.

I stick to broad-based funds that invest in a variety of stocks. I avoid specialty funds, such as gold funds or funds that invest primarily in one industry (called sector funds).

One decision to make is whether we choose passive funds or actively managed funds. This refers to a basic investment philosophy.

- *Passive funds* are index funds, which simply invest in all the stocks in the index. With index funds, we get almost exactly the return as the underlying index.

- *Actively managed funds* are the opposite. Investment managers try to beat the averages represented by the indexes.

Over periods of 10 years or more, index funds have outperformed most other funds, including actively managed funds. This seems counterintuitive, since index funds don't try to outperform any-body. Here are a couple of reasons why they are successful:

1. Index funds are fully invested in stocks at all times. All other funds have a portion of their assets in cash, for a number of reasons. The investment manager might think the time is not right for stocks, and parks money in cash until the manager finds some good stocks to buy. Another reason is to have cash on hand for redemptions. Regardless of the reason, cash dramatically underperforms stocks over the long run, so this part of the portfolio is a drag on returns.

2. Index funds have very low operating expenses because they don't do any analysis to pick stocks. Operating expenses come right out of our returns, so funds that spend lots of money actively managing stocks are at a disadvantage com-pared to index funds.

Most large mutual fund companies have one or more index funds, each of which might use a different index. I look for the funds with the lowest expenses, since that will determine most of the differ-ence in performance among these funds.

What's my take on the "passive vs. active" debate? There are convincing arguments for and against each approach. So, I split my money between both, to hedge my bets. Another approach uses enhanced index funds. These are funds that mostly track an index, but have a process for screening out stocks that are ex-pected to be the worst performers. For example, the Vanguard Growth and Income fund tracks the S&P 500, but has exceeded the return on the S&P 500 over the years through its quantitative process.

Also, I'm selective about the portion of my portfolio that goes into actively managed and passive funds. Many studies have shown that it's difficult to beat the average returns on large stocks, since so many professionals are in that game. The value with active management comes with smaller stocks or international stocks, where there isn't as much competition. This approach is called "core plus satellite." The money invested in large stocks goes into index funds, and the money invested in smaller stocks and international stocks uses actively managed funds.

Now that we understand the categories, how do we pick a specific fund? Here are some tips:

- Look at the rate of return over different time periods, covering both up markets and down markets. I look at returns over 1 year, 5 years, and 10 years and at specific years that the market dropped—2001 and 2002 are good tests. Has the fund consistently outperformed the appropriate index? I'll use the S&P 500 index for large company funds, and the Nasdaq Composite index for small company funds.

- I avoid funds with high expenses. Index funds should have annual expenses that are 0.2 percent per year or less. Expenses should be 1 percent per year or less for growth, growth and income, and equity income funds. Small cap funds or international funds should have expenses of 1.25 percent per year or less.

- I avoid all funds with 12b-1 fees (basically marketing fees that are excessive) or back-end loads. Back-end loads are applied when we withdraw our money. For example, suppose there is a back-end load of 1 percent. When I withdraw $100, I get $99, and the mutual fund company gets $1. The only possible exception to my avoidance rule is if the back-end load applies for only a brief period after I buy the fund, say 6 to 12 months. Some tax-managed funds have good reasons for back-end loads—they buy tax-advantaged securities that require investment over longer periods, and they want to discourage people from frequently moving in and out of the funds.

- I investigate the tenure of the fund managers. If the fund has performed well over long periods, have the current managers been with the fund all that time, or have the managers changed recently?

- I stick with established funds—those that have been around for at least five years, and have at least $100 million under management.

We can find all this information in a fund's prospectus, and with the rating services such as Morningstar and Value Line. In fact, Morningstar's rating service has a ready-made screen for large, no-load funds that invest in a blend of different types of stocks and have low expenses, experienced management, and performance in the top half of similar mutual funds. These funds can form the core of an equity portfolio.

Once I create such a list, then I'll look at each fund, including differences in active versus passive management and the degree of risk (which Morningstar also rates). Eventually I'll get comfortable with a certain fund and go with it.

Bond Funds

Like stock funds, bond funds have lots of classifications. These classifications depend on the type of issuer (e.g., corporate or government) and the maturity period. Here are common classifications that are appropriate for part or all of our bond investments:

- Bond funds can consist exclusively of government bonds or corporate bonds, or a mixture.

- *Short-term funds* consist of bonds with maturities up to five years.

- *Intermediate-term funds* consist of bonds with maturities up to 10 years.

- *Long-term funds* hold bonds with maturities over 10 years.

- *Municipal bond funds* or *tax-free bond funds* invest in bonds of state and local governments. The income is usually free of federal taxes, and sometimes state taxes as well.

Some funds give the manager the discretion to choose among different maturities and different issuers, depending on his or her outlook for the market.

I prefer intermediate-term corporate bonds that use investment grade bonds. These funds represent trade-offs in a few areas:

- The return is higher compared to government bond funds. Corporate bonds are riskier than government bonds, but if I stick to investment grade bonds I should be okay.

- The return is higher compared to short-term funds. Again, I take a little more risk, but it is limited. Long-term bond funds have higher risk due to the long maturities. If interest rates rise, long-term bonds will depreciate more than intermediate-term bonds.

One word of caution: As of the end of 2004, when this book went to publication, interest rates in the United States are near historic lows. If interest rates move in the future, they are more likely to go up than down, which would result in depreciation for long-term bonds.

Like stock funds, there are some specialized bond funds that have more risk than the funds already mentioned, but they expect that increased returns will make up for this risk. We may want to put part of our bond investments in these funds—say, up to one-third—if we feel comfortable with the extra risk. Here are classifications of these funds:

- *High-yield funds* invest in speculative grade or junk bonds. The yields will be higher, but there is additional risk that the principal and interest might not be paid.

- *International bond funds* invest primarily in foreign government or corporate bonds. They carry the risk that the currency of the bonds will drop relative to the U.S. dollar, leading to capital depreciation. This works the other way when the dollar depreciates relative to other currencies. Many foreign bonds pay higher rates of interest than U.S. bonds.

- *World income funds* invest in a mixture of U.S. bonds and international bonds, depending on the manager's outlook for the best investments. We still have the currency risk, but it's usually less than in funds that invest exclusively overseas.

Again, the rating services mentioned previously have a wealth of information that can help us choose a bond fund. Morningstar's rating service has a ready-made screen for taxable bond funds, meaning the investment income is taxed, so we would want to hold these in a 401(k) plan. The rating service selects funds with the highest Morningstar rating, low expenses, and managers who have been there at least five years.

Once I create a list of such funds, I'll look at each fund, including differences in maturities and safety ratings. Eventually I'll get comfortable with a certain fund and go with it.

Cash Funds

These funds, more commonly known as money market funds, invest in very short-term loans. The principal amount almost never changes, but the interest rate often changes daily. There are really only three types of money market funds:

1. Those that invest exclusively in Treasury bills and other loans to the U.S. government, and have the highest security.

2. All other *taxable* investments that make loans to corporations, with little or no investments in Treasury bills or other government-backed loans.

3. *Tax-free* funds, which invest exclusively in state and local governments, to avoid income taxes on the interest payments.

I prefer the second and third types, depending on how my investment income is taxed. I'll use a taxable fund if my investments are in a 401(k) plan or my income tax bracket is low. If my investments are outside a 401(k) plan and I'm in a high income tax bracket, I'll use the tax-free funds. I don't need the additional safety of government money market funds; few money market funds have ever lost money.

Occasionally a fund will lose money, though, either because it uses specialized investments called derivatives or because it concentrates too much in one type of asset. A fund should have no more than 5 percent of its money in one specific security, with the exception of U.S. Treasury bills. The fund's prospectus should have this information.

Most money market funds invest in the same types of assets, so the yield *before* expenses is usually similar for most funds. The largest difference in the net yield credited to us results from expenses. So it pays to shop around for the fund with the lowest expenses.

Real Estate Funds

As mentioned in the preceding chapter, I prefer not to invest in individual real estate properties. If I invest in real estate, I'll use pooled funds to gain the expertise of professionals to diversify my investments, and to increase my liquidity. It isn't always easy to pick a real estate fund, though. I will invest in these funds only if I'm willing to take the time to investigate them and monitor them periodically.

Many real estate funds are closed-ended funds, because it is hard to operate open-ended funds. Except for the very largest funds, managers find it difficult to buy or sell real estate according to how much money is deposited or withdrawn each day.

Some real estate funds are really limited partnerships; we pool our money with a small number of investors, and the fund buys a few properties. The performance of these funds is sporadic; there can be spectacular winners and losers, often from the same management company. If I would ever consider such an investment, I would investigate each property in the fund as if I were buying it alone. I'd also evaluate the real estate managers as if they were my own personal business managers. I'd find out if they are skilled and can be trusted. If it's too much work, I'll just pass on the investment.

For most of us, the most feasible real estate funds are real estate investment trusts (REITs). These are really stocks of companies that run real estate portfolios. To obtain special tax advantages, they must distribute 90 percent of their income each year to investors. REITs can produce income returns that compare favorably to bonds, yet have the potential to increase their payout with inflation.

Another advantage of REITs is that they provide diversification. Historically, for periods that stocks or bonds have done poorly, REITs have often done well. For example, during the three year period 2000 through 2002, the S&P 500 index dropped 31 percent, while the value of REITs jumped by up to 42 percent.

So, you might think, let's go load up on REITs. High yield, high potential for growth, great! Not so fast. Buying individual REITs is just as hard as buying individual stocks. We can't just buy the real estate market in America. The properties in REITs can include apartments, office buildings, hotels, factories, health care properties, warehouses, shopping malls, and even prisons! At any point in time, these properties are subject to market conditions and other significant events. Here's just one example: REITs specializing in hotels did poorly after 9/11 due to reduced travel demand.

To add to this complexity, we need to take geography into account. At any point in time, one area of the country might be doing better economically than another area, which can also have different impacts on the various types of properties. For example, office space may be in demand in one area, but factories might not be in demand if the area is not conducive to heavy industry.

The point I'm trying to make is that selecting individual REITs is not for amateurs. Once again, I want to leave it to the pros, which leads us to mutual funds that invest in REITs. These operate just like the mutual funds described previously for stocks and bonds. Professionals run a portfolio of REITs, considering their outlook for different types of properties and geographical areas. Such mutual funds are typically open-ended, which are liquid so we can get our money if we need it.

Here are some tips for selecting mutual fund REITs:

- Stick with large funds with a good track record. The fund should have at least a five-year history of providing above-average returns.

- Look for diversification. The largest single property should represent a small fraction—say under 5 percent—of the total fund. This way, one loser won't ruin the total return.

- Look for geographical diversification. If a recession hits one area, the total fund won't be devastated.

- Look for diversification across different types of properties—apartments, office buildings, shopping malls, retail stores, factories, and warehouses. Again, if one type of property doesn't do well, the total fund won't suffer very much.

You can find this information in the fund's prospectus. Also, the rating services like Morningstar and Value Line compile this information and rate the performance of many large REIT mutual funds.

Here's a refinement on the simple investment and withdrawal strategy described earlier with hybrid funds. I can boost my returns and diversify my risk by having part of my money with a hybrid fund, and part with a REIT mutual fund. In this case, I'd put no more than 25 percent of my total portfolio in a REIT mutual fund, and boost my withdrawal rate to no more than $3\frac{1}{2}$ percent per year.

Deposits

With these investments, we give our money to a bank, savings and loan, or insurance company. These institutions promise a fixed rate of return for a specified period. Our money is pooled with that of other investors and used for loans to other individuals and businesses.

Here are a few simple rules and tips regarding deposits:

- For my investments outside 401(k) plans, I'll make sure my deposit is insured by the Federal Deposit Insurance Corporation (FDIC). This means that if the institution goes bankrupt, the federal government will guarantee my original deposit and interest. FDIC insurance is good for only the first $100,000 of my total deposit at each institution. If I invest more than this amount, I'll spread it around to other institutions so that each account is insured. Only banks and savings and loans have FDIC insurance; insurance companies don't have it. Also, not all investments offered by banks and savings and loans have FDIC insurance, so I'll ask to see if I'm protected. It pays to shop around for the best rate. At any point in time, some institutions attract customers with high interest rates. A little extra interest can add up over a long time.

- For my investments in 401(k) plans, I don't require FDIC insurance for stable value funds or capital preservation funds. These usually spread the risk among a number of banks or insurance companies, offering us the protection of diversification. Once again, our employer usually spends time and money shopping for these investments, so most likely I won't need the protection of FDIC insurance.

- Usually, the longer the guarantee or maturity period, the higher our interest rate will be. I prefer guarantee periods of one to five years. Usually it doesn't pay to invest for longer guarantee periods; the extra interest won't compensate for the risk of tying up our money for so long.

401(k) Plans, Revisited

Does the process described earlier for selecting and monitoring mutual funds sound a little complicated? If it does, remember that our employer might do all this, and often a lot more, when it selects and monitors investment fund choices for our 401(k) plan. This is often the case with large employers, but less so with employers that have under 1,000 employees.

We should ask how our employer selected the 401(k) provider and investment choices. If the answer is something like "I have a brother in the business" or "my broker picked the provider," then we should do our own investigation on the investment choices, using the methods described in this chapter. It doesn't mean we don't use the 401(k) plan—it simply means we should take charge and do our own investigation. If our employer uses the methods described in this chapter, we might feel a little more comfortable.

Let me elaborate on one design feature of many modern 401(k) plans. Usually we're offered a core lineup of fund choices that have been subject to the due diligence just described. Many modern plans also offer a broker window, where we can choose from thousands of individual stocks, bonds, and other securities, as well as thousands of mutual funds. Unless I have the time and expertise to evaluate stocks, bonds, and mutual funds, I'll stick with the lineup offered by my employer.

Here's one more feature to watch in 401(k) plans. Often they let us buy our employer's stock as an investment. Sometimes our matching contributions are made in company stock. I try to limit the portion of company stock to no more than 10 percent of my total portfolio. It's simply a matter of diversification. If our company falls on hard times, not only does the value of our portfolio drop significantly, but we might lose our job as well.

So we've covered pooled investments in some detail. Now let's turn to annuities, both immediate and deferred. Both are specialized investment products that have specific uses in our *rest-of-life* portfolio.

How Should I Buy an Immediate Annuity?

In Chapter 10, I recommend immediate annuities as one investment product that protects against outliving our money. We might want to take the portion of our portfolio that we would normally invest in bonds and use it to buy an immediate annuity. Here we'll talk about how to pick the best annuities for us.

Only insurance companies can offer a lifetime annuity. We can buy them through a number of different intermediaries, but eventually we'll be dealing with an insurance company.

Let's make two more distinctions:

1. *Qualified versus nonqualified annuities.* If our money is coming from a 401(k) plan, IRA, or other tax-sheltered retirement plan, we buy what's called a "qualified annuity." If our money is not coming from one of these programs, we buy a "nonqualified annuity." Generally we can get better deals with qualified annuities compared to nonqualified annuities. Commissions must be disclosed with qualified annuities— not with nonqualified annuities. For this reason, I might restrict my annuity purchases to qualified annuities. However, I still might comparison shop for nonqualified annuities as well, and use them if I can get a good deal compared to a qualified annuity.

2. *Fixed versus variable annuities.* With a fixed annuity, the monthly payment is fixed for the rest of my life. With a variable annuity, the monthly payment is adjusted to reflect stock market performance. The problem with variable annuities is that they often have high expenses. Also, we're stuck with the same company for the rest of our life, which is a long time to stay with one investment manager and with one asset allocation. For the portion of my portfolio that is in the stock market, I'd rather go directly through mutual funds. I'd rather have the flexibility of a mutual fund, which I can change if I become dissatisfied with the performance or if I'd rather have a different asset allocation. I'd rather buy a fixed annuity for the safe portion of my portfolio.

There are only two considerations when buying an immediate annuity:

1. *Safety.* I don't want my insurance company to go bankrupt— if it does, I stop getting paid. Not good!

2. *Price.* Who will give me the highest monthly income for a given amount of money?

Unfortunately, we can't have our cake and eat it, too. We have to trade off between these two considerations. The most secure insurance companies bank on their reputation—literally—and don't have the best prices. Of the two, safety is more important. The only reason I'm buying an annuity is for lifetime security, so I don't want to take any chances. I might take some investment risk with my mutual fund investments, for the potential of higher returns, but not with my annuity.

Rating agencies such as Moody's and Standard & Poor's measure the security of insurance companies. You can get a lot of information online at www.moodys.com, and www.standardandpoors.com. For my own peace of mind, I'd use only insurance companies that have one of the highest four rankings by these agencies.

- For Moody's, this is Aaa, Aa1, Aa2, and Aa3.

- For Standard & Poor's, this is AAA, AA+, AA, and AA−.

If I'm really worried, I'd use only the top two rankings. Here's where a little judgment and shopping come in. Most of the time,

I'll get a better price by considering the top four rankings compared to the top two. However, once I get all my quotes, if there isn't much difference in price between an insurance company in the top two versus a company in the third or fourth rankings, I might take the company in the top two rankings.

With respect to price, we get the best deal by shopping around. Here's where the intermediaries come in. There are various ways we can buy annuities:

- We can go through an insurance agent who is a representative of one insurance company or just a few companies. Most likely, such an agent will take a large commission and steer us toward an annuity that makes more money for him or her. Not recommended!

- We can go through a stockbroker or bank, and get charged a commission of 4 percent or more.

- We can use low-cost annuities offered by insurance companies that are associated with large, no-load mutual fund companies, such as Vanguard or Fidelity. These can be good deals.

- We can use an Internet provider. I used my favorite Internet search engine, and typed in the words "immediate annuity." I found lots of sites that have good information on annuities. For example, www.immediateannuities.com provides an instant calculator that gives examples of how much we can buy with a given amount of money. Another useful site to consider is www.annuityadvantage.com. Many of these sites will help us shop among a number of insurance companies by providing quotes.

- Our 401(k) plan may have group contracts with one or more insurance companies, and we can directly transfer our money from the 401(k) plan to the insurance company to buy a qualified annuity. These won't charge commissions, but we might not get the best price because no shopping is involved.

- We could use a group insurance broker for qualified annuities. They will have group contracts with several large insurance companies, and will select the best price among their stable of insurance companies. They typically have lower commissions and expenses than the other intermediaries. One such broker is Brentwood Asset Advisors (1-800-642-2219).

The first four intermediaries are available for both qualified and nonqualified annuities. The last two are available only for qualified annuities and only if our money is coming from our 401(k) plan, so we need to do the shopping *before* we withdraw our money from the plan.

One last tip: Ask the intermediaries about the expenses and commissions that they collect. These come right out of my pocket, so I'll want these to be as low as possible. If they can't tell me, I'll go somewhere else.

Here's the process I plan to use when I buy an annuity:

1. I will split my annuity between two different insurance companies. This diversity gives me some protection against bankruptcy.

2. I'll do a test run. I'll get some quotes from a number of intermediaries—the mutual fund providers, Internet quotes, and, if available, my 401(k) plan and a group insurance broker. I'll only use the companies that have the four highest safety ratings. I'll try to get these quotes on the same day, since the prices can change daily.

3. Once I determine the best three or four prices, I'll go ahead with my purchase. I'll get real quotes on the same day, and then pick the two best prices (but using my judgment on price versus safety, as discussed previously).

This is a little trouble, but it's worth it. This represents part of my paycheck for the rest of my life!

Here's one last consideration. As I write this in 2004, interest rates remain near historically low levels. The price of annuities is inversely related to interest rates. This is actuarial jargon for the lower the interest rate, the higher the price, and vice versa. We may want to wait for interest rates to rise before locking in an immediate annuity.

Deferred Annuities

These are insurance company products that have both an accumulation period (preretirement) and a payout period (postretirement).

- During the accumulation period, we can allocate our investments among a number of pooled funds that have a variety of asset classes. The good thing is that the investment income isn't taxed while it is invested, so we have a tax advantage. This lets us build up more money for retirement. Unlike 401(k) plans, there's no limit to the amount of money that we can invest during the accumulation period.

- When we eventually withdraw our money, the investment income is subject to ordinary income taxes. Another rule: If we withdraw our money before age $59\frac{1}{2}$, the IRS imposes a 10 percent penalty on withdrawals of investment income.

- When we retire, we can convert the accumulated balances into immediate annuities.

Other retirement programs have better tax advantages—401(k) plans, 403(b) plans, 457 plans, and IRAs. The only situation in which to consider deferred annuities is when we have hit the maximums allowed by these other programs, and we still want to save more. In this case, I'm still very wary of deferred annuities, for two reasons:

1. Most of them have high commissions, expense loads, surrender charges, and death benefit charges. I'll never buy a deferred annuity from a stockbroker or an insurance agent. I don't need to pay commissions, and I can't trust them to shop for the absolutely best deal for me. The average annuity has annual charges well over 2 percent per year, while a typical mutual fund charges much less. The difference can be up to 1 percent per year, which adds up over time.

2. I'll avoid annuities that don't let me shop around to get the best immediate annuity when that time comes. I want the ability to withdraw all my money at once, so I can get the best price for an immediate annuity at that time.

The only advantage from deferred annuities is the tax sheltering of the investment income during the accumulation period. I can get similar advantages with no-load mutual funds—either index funds, tax-managed funds or municipal bond funds. Also, lower tax rates on capital gains and ordinary dividends can beat annuities, which are subject to ordinary income tax rates. Deferred annuities work best if I invest in them for at least 10 years, to overcome some of the expenses charged by the insurance companies.

So, I personally don't use deferred annuities. However, I am open to the products offered by the no-load mutual fund companies, which have deferred annuities with expenses that are far lower than average. Examples include Vanguard, Fidelity, and T. Rowe Price.

Which Financial Institutions Are Best for Us?

The best financial institutions offer the investment products recommended in this chapter—mutual funds, deposits, and immediate annuities. By far, the best institution is usually our employer's 401(k) plan, for the reasons mentioned previously.

We may need to choose financial institutions if we don't have a 401(k) plan at work, if we want to save more than allowed by 401(k) plans, or if we're self-employed. In these circumstances, we want the best investment performance available, at a reasonable price. If we are comfortable making investment decisions on our own after reading this book, then we won't need to pay for investing advice through loads or commissions. Instead, we'll want to use these institutions:

- No-load mutual fund companies for mutual funds.

- Banks and savings and loans for deposits.

- Insurance companies for immediate annuities (but consider annuities offered through insurance companies that are associated with no-load mutual fund companies).

Which of these is best? Among mutual fund companies, it's the company that offers the funds I want. I won't feel compelled to stay with one mutual fund company for all my investments; I can open accounts with different companies. My best bet is to take the time to analyze the funds with respect to their past performance and expense terms, using one of the services mentioned previously. To help narrow our search, I list some mutual fund companies with the following favorable criteria:

- They have many funds that are ranked above average by Morningstar or Value Line.

- They have no-load funds, or the loads are waived for retirement investing programs.

- Their expenses are at or below average.

- They offer a variety of funds that meet many different investment objectives.

- They have been around for many years, and many of their funds have lengthy, positive track records.

- They have robust web sites, with a lot of educational material and retirement planning calculators.

Based on these criteria as of the end of 2004, I like the following companies:

- Charles Schwab (a discount brokerage firm plus a lot more)

- Fidelity

- T. Rowe Price

- Vanguard

Once I pick a mutual fund company, I still have some work to do. Each of the listed institutions has above-average and below-average performers. Also, I won't be too intimidated by the number of available funds. I remember from the preceding chapter that most of my investment return is affected by the type of asset—my asset allocation—and not the specific asset that I select. I can't go too wrong if I pick a fund by a particular type of asset that is right for me and is ranked above average by the rating agencies. If I'm really stumped, I'll put a lot of money into index funds, which have beaten most other funds anyway over the long run. However, these simple solutions are intended just to keep us out of trouble, and I plan on doing better than just keeping out of trouble with my investments!

With deposits, I'll pick the banks or savings and loans that have the best rates, sticking to FDIC-insured products. Again, I won't be compelled to stick with one bank—I'll shop around for the best rates. Over the long run, I'll make more money through the time I spend shopping. One thing to watch for: When my CDs and deposits mature, I'll check around for the best rates. The banks would rather that we let our CDs and deposits automatically roll over into new CDs and deposits. I'll do this only if my bank still offers the best rates.

Picking an Adviser

My goal is to give you enough information and confidence to decide which types of assets are right for you, and to pick specific investment products. However, some of you might feel more comfortable with personal attention from a financial adviser. You want an experienced professional who understands your particular circumstances and doesn't try to sell you products you don't need. You'll need to pay them for their advice, but that should be a fixed fee or a percentage of your assets that they manage. I would prefer that they use primarily no-load mutual funds. If you have at least $1,000,000, you can consider professionals who will develop an individual portfolio for a fixed fee or percentage of assets, and who use a discount broker to execute their trades. However, even here I would be very wary.

For more strategies on finding an adviser and lists of situations to avoid, go to my web site, www.restoflife.com.

WRAP-UP

By now, I hope you understand that every investment has some risk. And the past is no guarantee of future results. The past is the only hard data we have, though, plus our interpretations of the past and how the future might be the same or different. Investing is part art and part science. The best we can do is learn from the past, forecast what might happen in the future, and move ahead.

Most of us spend lots of time understanding and buying consumer items such as clothes, cars, and gizmos. We take the necessary time to buy a house. We become informed consumers. It's the same with investments, and these will have a greater impact on our lifestyle and well-being during our later years than the clothes, cars, and gizmos.

Here's a suggestion. If you don't already know much about investment institutions and their products, spend a year learning about them. There are a lot of good sources. Read a few books and financial magazines. Look at the web sites of some large mutual fund companies. In addition, explore the web sites of rating services such as Morningstar and Value Line, or even subscribe to get additional information. Watch some financial shows. Pay attention to the investment education at work, through your 401(k) provider. Ask friends who are knowledgeable. Take an adult education class. You don't need to spend huge amounts of time—two hours per week will do. Make a resolution to do this for a year. Then, start on your own with selecting institutions and their products. Apply a simple test to a financial product. Ask about the risks, rewards, and expenses. Ask how the product operates. If you don't understand how it works, don't invest in it! Another suggestion: Do this with a buddy. Sometimes it helps to share insights, concerns, and questions.

The best financial products aren't that complicated, and can be explained easily, while the worst products are often hard to explain. If you don't understand a financial professional, go elsewhere. If someone speaks fast financial gibberish, just walk away.

We need patience, persistence, and the right professionals to help us, but anybody can do it. Including you!

Uncle Sam Wants to Help—Sorta

The hardest thing in the world to understand is the income tax.

—Albert Einstein

The federal government has the twentieth century model of retirement squarely in its collective consciousness. It firmly believes that full-time retirement is a good thing, and that all citizens deserve this as the way to finish life. It provides powerful incentives for saving for retirement, by allowing retirement investing programs that significantly reduce our taxes—for those of us who take advantage of these incentives.

However, the government also resembles an overly jealous spouse. It has lots of rules to prevent us from abusing the system for evil purposes, like using the savings for things other than retirement or for letting rich people hog all the tax benefits. These rules often are very confusing, get in the way, and discourage the very behaviors that the government wants to encourage. Also, the rules often conflict with emerging trends, such as people living longer and possibly working in their later years.

There's no doubt that the rules will change! Congress and the IRS constantly meddle with the rules, to respond to political and economic pressures and to fix what is perceived to be broken. For the past 30 years, Congress has made changes to the pension rules on average once per year. You need to continually keep abreast of these changes to see how they might affect your plan.

This chapter reviews how these retirement investing programs work and discusses the rules that will influence our saving behaviors, and the rules that we need to pay attention to when we withdraw money to pay for *rest-of-life* expenses.

I'll confine this chapter to defined contribution plans, which most of us will use to build a *rest-of-life* portfolio. Chapter 15 discusses defined benefit plans and their IRS rules. Here I'll cover 401(k) plans, 403(b) plans, 457 plans, and individual retirement accounts (IRAs)—both traditional and Roth. I'll also cover plans for self-employed individuals—SEP IRAs and SIMPLE IRAs.

This entire subject can be complicated, confusing, and deadly boring, even for accountants. Also, we can readily find a lot of information on these rules from our 401(k) communications and various web sites, such as www.aarp.org and www.smartmoney.com. I won't duplicate these resources here. Instead, I'll provide brief overviews of the rules, along with conclusions and strategies. If you're interested, you can find a much longer version of this chapter on my web site, www.restoflife.com.

Numbers Game—401(k), 403(b), and 457

These plans are for people who are employees, not self-employed individuals. As mentioned in other chapters, these plans offer substantial advantages, and are the best place for our *rest-of-life* portfolios. All of these names refer to the section of the Internal Revenue Code that describe the rules for each type of plan.

My advice is simple: Contribute as much as possible to these plans. If you are age 50 or older, the maximums can be up to $18,000 in 2005 and $20,000 in 2006 and thereafter. For most of us, this is all we can afford to save, so we don't need to go anywhere else with our *rest-of-life* savings.

Don't save for *rest-of-life* anywhere else until you have maxed out on these plans. There is possibly one exception for Roth IRAs, discussed later in this chapter.

The rules for these plans can be complicated, and if you run afoul of the rules, the penalties are high. For many of us, our 401(k) balances represent the biggest pot of money we'll ever see in our lifetimes. You should take the time to make sure you use the account appropriately to avoid the penalties. If you don't understand the rules, go to a professional, usually an accountant who specializes in personal finance.

The 401(k) plans can be offered by most for-profit and nonprofit employers, while 403(b) plans can be offered only by nonprofit organizations and educational institutions (including public school systems), and 457 plans can be offered only by government and nonprofit organizations. Federal government employees have their own savings plan, which is virtually the same as a 401(k) plan. This section uses the term "401(k) plan" as shorthand for all three plans, unless noted otherwise.

First, let's look at simple advice regarding putting money in the plan.

Don't put in more than the maximum allowed. The plan should automatically prevent you from doing this. However, if you have changed jobs during the year or you contribute to more than one plan, you need to provide your plan administrator with information on your contributions.

Now here are the details:

- Each year, we can contribute up to 100 percent of our pay or a dollar limit, whichever is lower. This dollar limit is $14,000 in 2005 and $15,000 in 2006. Thereafter, this limit is indexed for inflation. These are the IRS limits; many plans have lower limits, say 25 percent or 50 percent of pay, to ease administration of the plan.

- If we are age 50 or older by the end of a calendar year, we can make catch-up contributions. This means we can contribute up to the limits, *plus* the amount of the catch-up contribution. The amount of the catch-up contribution is $4,000 in 2005 and $5,000 for 2006 and thereafter. Adding up the regular dollar limit plus the catch-up contribution results in limits of $18,000 in 2005 and $20,000 in 2006 and thereafter. As long as our 50th birthday falls in the current calendar year, we can make these contributions during the year.

- The dollar limit applies to all of our contributions during the year, for all plans in which we participate. So, if we change jobs during the year or have two jobs, then the contributions for all plans combined count toward this dollar limit. In this case, each plan administrator doesn't know about our participation in other plans, so we have to provide them with this information to make sure we don't exceed the limit for our combined savings.

- If we're lucky, our employer will also contribute to the plan. However, that contribution counts toward the 100 percent of pay limit, but not the dollar limit. Also, matching contributions might be subject to vesting rules. This means that we must work for a minimum number of years before we own the matching contributions and their investment earnings. If we quit before meeting these vesting requirements, we might forfeit part or all of the matching contributions (but not our own contributions, which we always own). Common vesting requirements are 100 percent after three years of service, or 20 percent vested after two years, increasing 20 percent per year until 100 percent vested at six years of service. Fortunately, many companies don't have any vesting requirements, and we immediately own our matching contributions and their investment earnings.

- Only for 401(k) plans, complicated rules apply that make sure that highly paid employees aren't benefiting disproportionately from the plan. This means that additional limits might apply to the annual contributions, but just for highly paid employees. For the purpose of determining who is highly paid, in 2004 this means anybody who earns $90,000 or more during the year. Most likely this will increase in 2005, probably to $95,000.

- The penalties for contributing more than the maximum allowed are substantial. The amount of the contribution that exceeds the maximum allowed is taxed twice—once for the year the excess contribution is made, and again when it is withdrawn. If an excess contribution is made by mistake, it can be withdrawn within a specified time and avoid the double taxation. If this happens we should notify our plan administrator as soon as possible. Most of the time the plan administrator will make sure employees don't exceed the limit, but we must help if we participate in more than one plan each year.

- Our contributions are deducted from our paychecks, and aren't subject to income taxes when they are withheld. This reduces our federal and state income taxes that we pay during the year. For this reason, these contributions are also called pretax contributions. The contributions are subject to FICA taxes, which are used to pay for Social Security benefits (more on these taxes in Chapter 14).

- We cannot write a check to contribute to the plan—contributions must come from payroll deductions.

- A few plans also offer after-tax contributions. These work the same way, only the contributions are subject to federal and state income taxes when they are made. In this case, the contributions count toward the 100 percent of pay limit, but not the dollar limit. When we withdraw from these accounts, only the investment earnings are taxed. While these aren't as good as pretax contributions, they are still a good deal. Use these contributions if they're available, but only after you have maxed out on pretax contributions. However, as noted later, it might be better to contribute additional money to a Roth IRA, if you're eligible.

While the money remains invested in the plan, the rules are quite simple. The investment earnings aren't subject to federal and state income taxes. We won't pay taxes on investment income or capital gains.

These twin tax advantages—contributions aren't taxed when they go in, and investment income isn't taxed along the way—are substantial. We will have more money when we retire, compared to saving outside a tax-advantaged retirement plan.

Some plans offer loans, using our accounts as collateral. The most that can be borrowed is one-half of our vested account or $50,000, whichever is less.

> I recommend against loans from our 401(k) plan unless we have absolutely no other source of money and the need is very important, such as buying a house.

Loans make me nervous—if we terminate employment before paying back all the loan, usually we must pay the balance immediately. If we don't, the plan will forgive the loan by reducing our account balance, but this reduction will be treated like a distribution, and will be subject to penalties.

Most of the time, there are better places to borrow money than our 401(k) plan. For example, 401(k) loans must be repaid within five years; the only exception is for loans used to purchase a primary residence, in which case the term is specified in the plan's rules. Any other loan with a bank or other financial institution will let us take longer than five years to repay. If we own a home, we can take a home equity loan, and the interest will be deductible. If the bill is for college expenses, there are lots of low-interest student loans available. I would check all my sources for loans, and consider a 401(k) loan as a desperate last resort.

Now let's look at the rules regarding taking money out.

Withdrawal Rules

> Here are simple strategies for taking money out of these plans:
>
> - If we change jobs before needing the money from our 401(k) plan, either leave our account in that plan or transfer it directly to a rollover IRA or our next employer's 401(k) plan.
>
> - Don't withdraw the money before reaching age 55.
>
> - Start drawing the money out no later than age 70$\frac{1}{2}$. Using part of our money to buy an immediate annuity goes a long way to stay out of trouble with the applicable rules.

Please see my web site for background on the applicable rules, and for the reasons why I make these suggestions.

Next, a bunch of rules apply if we take out money too soon. In this case, the government assumes we are slothfully squandering our retirement resources for other purposes, so it discourages this behavior by applying penalties.

Early Payment Penalties

If we withdraw money before age 55, we are subject to an early payment penalty of 10 percent. This penalty is in addition to the federal and state income taxes. *My advice is simple—avoid the early payment penalty!* Many people terminate employment well before this age and take the money and run. Unfortunately, they don't get far, since Uncle Sam takes such a big chunk.

Special note for 457 plans only: There is no early payment penalty, like there is for 401(k) and 403(b) plans.

There are several important exceptions for the following situations:

- If we leave the money in the plan.

- If we roll it over to our next employer's 401(k) plan or an IRA.

- If we retire before age 55 and comply with certain rules.

- If payment is triggered by death or disability.

- If the withdrawal is to buy our first home, for certain medical expenses, or for college education costs.

Please see my web site for details on these exceptions.

Now let's look at the rules for taking money out too late. In this case, the IRS also assumes we are using these plans for purposes other than retirement, like leaving an estate to our children, so it wants to discourage this behavior.

Minimum Distribution Rules

- We must begin withdrawing money no later than April 1 of the year following the year in which we turn age $70\frac{1}{2}$. In each year thereafter, we need to withdraw the minimum amount during the year. One important exception to this rule: If we are still working for the employer who sponsors the plan, we don't need to start withdrawing money until we actually retire.

- The withdrawal amounts are taxed as ordinary income. Note that if we take advantage of the April 1 deferral for our first year, we will be taxed on two withdrawals in the next year—the minimum withdrawal for the previous year plus the minimum withdrawal for the current year. This could put us in a higher tax bracket. So, it may pay to make our first withdrawal during the year we reach age $70\frac{1}{2}$, so that we don't double up in the next year.

- We don't need to take out all the money, just a minimum amount—hence, the name "minimum distribution rules." We can also withdraw more than the minimum amount.

- Each year, the minimum amount we must withdraw equals our account balance at the end of the previous year, divided by the combined life expectancy for ourselves and a spouse 10 years younger. This is done even if we don't have a spouse! This usually gives us a break, and results in a smaller minimum withdrawal amount. In an effort to confuse us totally, the IRS allows three different methods for calculating this minimum distribution amount, and describes them in 42 pages of fine print. I'm not going to detail these rules here, but my web site provides an example to give us the feel for these rules. You should check with an accountant or other professional to verify that you're withdrawing enough.

- One note: If my spouse is more than 10 years younger than me, I'm allowed to use a higher joint life expectancy than the standard tables. In this case, it may pay to check out the special rules.

- If we withdraw an amount that is less than this minimum amount, the IRS takes 50 percent of the difference between the minimum amount and the amount we actually withdraw.

- These rules apply to our remaining account balance each year. So, in one year if we take out more than the minimum distribution, we don't get credit for this in future years. The minimum distribution amount is always based on the account at the end of the previous year.

■ If we buy an immediate annuity with our account, we automatically comply with the minimum distribution rules for the money we spend on the annuity. Any amounts remaining in our 401(k) plan must still comply with the minimum distribution rules. This is another good reason to buy an annuity. When we get much older, we might not pay attention to the minimum distribution rules, so it is helpful to buy a solution that automatically complies with them.

Obviously, I recommend complying with the minimum distribution rules, because the penalty is so high. By the way, the minimum distribution rules are an example of the government having the old model of retirement in its collective consciousness. It doesn't consider that people might live and work well beyond age $70\frac{1}{2}$.

Please see my web site for more details on the minimum distribution rules.

That's about all that most of us need to know about 401(k), 403(b), and 457 plans. There are plenty of additional details and exceptions to the rules that might apply in special cases. Check with your accountant when you're approaching the age when you will use these accounts, just to make sure you're doing the right thing. You can also consult online resources such as www.smartmoney.com.

If this weren't enough, there's more on the horizon. Starting in 2006, employers will be able to change their 401(k) plans to provide contributions that are like Roth IRAs. I will prefer these accounts over regular 401(k) accounts, so if my employer offers them, I'll use them. I discuss Roth IRAs in the pages that follow, including the reasons why I prefer them.

We're Owners!

Many 401(k) plans of large companies provide part or all of their matching contributions in company stock. Another variation, less common, is an employee stock ownership plan (ESOP). With an

ESOP, our employer contributes company stock to our account, regardless of whether we contribute to our 401(k) plan.

The government provides incentives to our employers for these plans and their special features. The government thinks it's a good thing that employees own company stock.

It is, with prudent limits with respect to diversification. We want no more than 10 percent of our *rest-of-life* portfolio in company stock. Otherwise we have too many eggs in one basket. If the company doesn't do well, not only does our 401(k) balance decline, but we stand a chance of getting laid off or receiving lower pay through reduced hours or smaller bonuses.

On my web site, I discuss a potential tax advantage that might influence me to leave more of my holdings in company stock. If I work for a very stable company, I might be willing to increase my holdings from 10 percent to 20 percent, but if I do I'll be nervous and watch the stock very carefully. We do have one advantage over other investors: Most of us are very familiar with our company and its prospects for the future. However, when balancing my priorities, I'll favor protection through diversification over tax advantages. I won't let tax goodies influence me to make a mistake.

Some plans let us diversify the company stock. They may make the match in stock, but we're immediately eligible to move it to other investments. In this case, I'll take advantage of this flexibility, and stay under my 10 percent rule.

Other plans force us to leave the matching contribution in company stock. After all, the company match is still free money, and we should be contributing to our 401(k) plan anyway. In this case, there's nothing much we can do, except wait until federal law requires my company to let us begin diversifying our account. This starts at age 55 with 10 years of service. Some companies allow diversification earlier—it pays to check the plans' rules.

Traditional and Roth IRAs

These are retirement investing accounts for anybody who works. They are particularly suited for people who work for an employer that does not sponsor a retirement investing program. However, all of us might be eligible, provided we meet the eligibility requirements. There are better programs for self-employed individuals, which I'll cover soon.

There are three types of IRAs:

1. Traditional deductible IRAs

2. Traditional nondeductible IRAs

3. Roth IRAs

Each works differently, with different rules regarding eligibility and withdrawals. We need to do a little work to decide which one best suits our circumstances. Here's what they all have in common:

- For 2005 through 2007, each of us can contribute up to $4,000 from our pay; a married couple can contribute $8,000. Beginning in 2008, the limits increase to $5,000 for individuals, and $10,000 for married couples. Thereafter, the limits will be adjusted for inflation.

- We can add $500 to these limits if we have attained age 50 by the end of the year (add $1,000 for a married couple where each has attained age 50). For 2006 and thereafter, the additional contribution increases to $1,000 for singles and $2,000 for married couples. The contribution must come from wages—we can't contribute more than we earn each year.

- These limits are the most we can contribute to all types of IRAs combined. So we can't contribute $4,000 to each of the three types of IRAs. We can split this amount—say $2,000 to a traditional deductible IRA and $2,000 to a Roth IRA, if we meet the eligibility criteria for each.

IRA Strategy Guidelines

- Contribute the maximum to a Roth IRA if eligible. But first, max out on 401(k) contributions that are matched by our employer, if available. Beyond this amount, if we have to choose between a Roth IRA and nonmatching contributions

(Continued)

to a 401(k) plan, we won't go wrong with either choice, although I prefer a Roth IRA. Of course, if we can afford to contribute to both, we should. This is the only exception to my rule to max out on 401(k) contributions. Note that our choice can affect the amount of our income taxes.

■ The only circumstance that makes sense for contributing to a traditional nondeductible IRA is if we're not eligible for a traditional deductible IRA or Roth IRA, and we're maxed out on any contributions to a 401(k) plan and still want to contribute more. Even in this case, it might make sense to invest outside a retirement investing program, due to the withdrawal restrictions on these accounts. If we're eligible for either a traditional deductible IRA or a Roth IRA, it makes no sense to use a nondeductible IRA.

■ We might contribute to a traditional deductible IRA instead of a Roth IRA, if we believe that our income tax rate will be much lower when we withdraw the money, compared to now when we contribute the money. This will happen only if we're not participating in a retirement plan at work, for the following reason. If we are participating in such a plan, we are only eligible for a traditional deductible IRA if we are currently in a low tax bracket, due to the income limits.

My web site goes into details about each type of IRA.

Here are a few good reasons why I like Roth IRAs better than traditional IRAs.

■ With Roth IRAs, there is no minimum distribution rule at age $70\frac{1}{2}$, like there is for traditional IRAs. Since I plan to live well beyond this age, I want the flexibility to leave this money invested for when I eventually need it.

■ With a traditional IRA, we only get income tax *deferral*. The Roth IRA gets us tax *avoidance* (of the investment earnings). Let me explain. When it comes to our contributions, we can deduct now our contribution to a deductible IRA, but we get taxed on it when we withdraw it. With the Roth IRA, it's the other way around. We get taxed on the contribution when we make it now, but not when we withdraw it later. Either way we still pay taxes on the contribution—either now or later. However, the goodies with Roth IRAs come with the investment earnings. With a Roth IRA, the investment earnings are *never* taxed, compared to an IRA, which only *defers* taxes until we withdraw them. This is tax avoidance. Normally, this advantage gives us more money when we need it, compared to a traditional IRA.

- I have more flexibility with a Roth IRA for early distributions, before age 59½. I can withdraw the original contribution amount without a 10 percent penalty, while this penalty applies for traditional IRAs.

The only exception to my preference for Roth IRAs might be if I expect to be in a much lower tax bracket when I withdraw the money, compared to when I contribute the money. Then a traditional deductible IRA might be better than a Roth IRA.

Let's revisit the first point in my IRA strategy guide from a few pages ago, where I stated that my preference would be for a Roth IRA over nonmatching 401(k) contributions. If I can afford to do both, that's great. However, if I'm limited in my funds and can do only one or the other, my choice will influence the income taxes I pay this year. Suppose I have $5,000 I can afford to save. If I put this in a 401(k) plan, then I pay no taxes on this contribution. If I put this in a Roth IRA, I will pay income taxes on the $5,000 amount; if my tax rate is 35 percent, this amounts to $1,750. If I don't have this amount lying around in other sources, I'll need to contribute $3,250 to the Roth IRA and keep $1,750 to pay the income taxes. However, when I later make a withdrawal, the original contribution to the Roth IRA is not subject to income taxes. On the other hand, if I used nonmatching 401(k) contributions, it is subject to income taxes at the time of withdrawal.

If all this weren't enough to think about, there's one more thing. We can convert a traditional IRA to a Roth IRA. Why are Roth conversions a good idea? For the same reasons I prefer Roth IRAs— investment income is never taxed, and we don't have the minimum distribution rules at age 70½. For details on Roth conversions, please see my web site.

Retirement Investing Programs for the Self-Employed

If we're self-employed, SEP IRAs or SIMPLE IRAs are better than traditional IRAs or Roth IRAs, because we can contribute a lot more. SEP stands for simplified employee pension plan, and SIMPLE stands for savings incentive match plan for employees.

Both SEP IRAs and SIMPLE IRAs have a good feature in common: They are simple to administer, without a lot of complicated IRS filings. If we want to stash away more money than the limits for SEP IRAs, we can use a defined benefit Keogh plan. However, these are complicated and more expensive to administer; we would use them only if we want to save a lot of money. In this case, we should see an accountant or retirement plan professional. My web site contains more details on SEP IRAs and SIMPLE IRAs.

If we're really hungry to save, we can set up a SEP IRA and one of the three types of IRAs mentioned in the previous section—Roth, traditional deductible, or traditional nondeductible. However, we need to meet the IRA eligibility requirements described previously.

One final word: You can get a SEP IRA or SIMPLE IRA at any of the institutions discussed in Chapter 12, including the no-load mutual fund companies. Just give them a call or visit their web sites. They are very helpful, and they make it easy for us to sign up and give them our money. They also help with the annual reporting requirements for the IRS.

WRAP-UP

These types of plans can help in building a *rest-of-life* portfolio. However, we shouldn't get too wrapped up in the rules and let them prevent us from saving or otherwise doing what we really want to do with our life. If we don't like the rules, we can always save the old-fashioned way, in a taxable account with a mutual fund company or any other institution. As mentioned in Chapters 11 and 12, we can get investment: with advantages that minimize our taxes, such as municipal bonds, tax-managed mutual funds, and tax-deferred annuities. There are alternatives to the tax-advantaged programs described here.

In addition, if we have maxed out on our retirement program contributions and want to save more, we shouldn't let the limits prevent us from making these additional savings. In my case, I have maxed out on my company's 401(k) plan. I save outside this plan, and I appreciate the flexibility of having some money without any strings attached like the early payment penalties and minimum distribution rules. With this money, I use investments with tax advantages mentioned in the previous paragraph.

Now that we have gotten these IRS rules out of the way, let's turn to the resources that Social Security can provide.

Social Security, or Insecurity?

Social Security is nothing more than a promise to a group
of people that their children will be taxed for that group's
benefit.

—Senator Russell Long

've had mixed feelings about Social Security for a long time. It
provides us with a monthly lifetime income that we can't outlive.
For most of us, this income isn't enough to live on, but it's a great
start. Also, the monthly benefit increases each year to keep up
with inflation. And finally, for most people, this income isn't subject to federal or state income taxes. For many of us, this might be
the only lifetime income we have, unless we are lucky enough to
have a defined benefit pension plan, or if we have an annuity (discussed in Chapters 10 and 12).

Medicare, which pays for a large portion of our medical bills
when we reach age 65, is also an important part of Social Security.
(See Chapter 8.)

However, I'm worried that the government has promised more
than it can deliver for the baby boom generation. Eventually it
may need to reduce the benefits, because of the way our government finances—or actually doesn't finance—future Social Security
benefits. The debate has raged for years inside and outside our
government about a looming crisis when the baby boomers retire.
Many experts have suggested remedies, but so far our government has made only minor adjustments, and hasn't been able to

reach a consensus for real change. My concern is that the longer we drag our feet in solving this problem, the worse it will eventually be for us and our children, who will be footing the bill.

Understanding Social Security is critical to planning for our *rest-of-life*. I believe it's a mistake to rely on the full value of benefits that the current Social Security program promises. However, it's also a mistake to be so pessimistic that we believe we will receive nothing from Social Security. The truth will lie somewhere in between.

In this chapter, I'll summarize the benefits under the current program. This gives us an idea of the most we can expect. It won't get any better than this, due to the financing problems. Along the way, I'll discuss important decisions we will need to make, such as the age at which we start receiving our Social Security income, and how Social Security benefits are affected if we work during our later years.

I'll also discuss the funding problems with Social Security, and what potential reductions might look like. We should be prepared to adjust our own plans if the government makes changes, which I think are inevitable.

First, let's take a look at the benefits.

When Can I Start Receiving Retirement Benefits?

The earliest age we can start benefits is age 62. However, if we start benefits at that age, Social Security reduces the monthly income, since we are starting them before our normal retirement age (NRA). Social Security increases our benefits if we start them after our NRA, up until age 70, after which there are no further increases. So there is no point in delaying our benefits beyond age 70. If we start our benefits on our NRA, then they are neither increased nor decreased.

Our NRA depends on our year of birth.

If We Were Born in . . .	Then Our NRA Is . . .
1937 or earlier	65 years
1938	65 years, 2 months
1939	65 years, 4 months

1940	65 years, 6 months
1941	65 years, 8 months
1942	65 years, 10 months
1943–1954	66 years
1955	66 years, 2 months
1956	66 years, 4 months
1957	66 years, 6 months
1958	66 years, 8 months
1959	66 years, 10 months
1960 or later	67 years

How Much Can I Expect?

Here I'll provide some estimates to give us a general idea about the monthly retirement income we might receive from Social Security under the current law. The actual calculations are quite complex, and take into account a number of factors, such as our pay over our career, our birth year, the age at which we start receiving benefits, and our marital status.

On the following pages, a series of tables show estimated monthly retirement incomes, depending on our year of birth and age at retirement. I've expressed these estimates in 2004 dollars; the actual benefits will be increased for growth in wages and cost of living between now and when we retire. In addition, once we retire, our monthly retirement income is increased each year to reflect increases in the cost of living.

These tables are just for illustration. If our year of birth is between the amounts shown, estimate an amount between the birth years that are shown. Do the same thing if our expected retirement age is between the ages shown, or if our salary in 2004 is between the salaries shown.

The first three tables show benefits for a single person. The next three tables show benefits for a married couple where only one person worked. This illustrates how Social Security pays more to a couple with one worker and one person who stayed at home, by paying an additional, special benefit to the spouse who didn't work. This feature has been described as unfair, because a single worker pays the same taxes as a married person, yet the married couple receives more benefits. If both the husband and wife work, then each is entitled to a benefit based on his or her own earnings (unless the special benefit for the spouse is larger, in which case the spouse gets that benefit).

So if we're married and both of us work a full career, most likely we can estimate our total Social Security income by calculating a single person's benefit for each, and adding the two together.

I had to make some assumptions when preparing these tables. Table 14.1 is for a single person who earned $25,000 per year in 2004, and has always earned similar amounts in the past (adjusted for average wage increases), and has always been covered by Social Security. The number in parentheses in the middle column is the NRA.

By the way, I put N/A for the person born in 1940 and retiring at age 62 because such a person is already past age 62 in 2004.

Table 14.2 is the same table, for a single person who earned $50,000 in 2004, while Table 14.3 is for someone who earned $87,900 in 2004. This is the maximum salary that is counted in 2004 for determining Social Security benefits; if we earn more than this amount, it won't increase our Social Security benefit.

Table 14.4 is for a married couple with just one wage earner who earned $25,000 per year in 2004, has always earned similar amounts in the past (adjusted for average wage increases), and has

TABLE 14.1   Estimated Monthly Social Security Income: Single Person, Earned $25,000 in 2004

Year of Birth	Retire at 62	Retire at NRA	Retire at 70
1940	N/A	$ 972 (65 years, 6 months)	$1,293
1945	$733	$ 978 (66 years)	$1,300
1950	$739	$ 986 (66 years)	$1,310
1955	$737	$ 994 (66 years, 2 months)	$1,307
1960	$701	$1,003 (67 years)	$1,250
1965	$706	$1,011 (67 years)	$1,259

TABLE 14.2 Estimated Monthly Social Security Income: Single Person, Earned $50,000 in 2004

Year of Birth	Retire at 62	Retire at NRA	Retire at 70
1940	N/A	$1,560 (65 years, 6 months)	$2,067
1945	$1,177	$1,566 (66 years)	$2,075
1950	$1,182	$1,574 (66 years)	$2,085
1955	$1,175	$1,581 (66 years, 2 months)	$2,074
1960	$1,114	$1,590 (67 years)	$1,977
1965	$1,119	$1,597 (67 years)	$1,986

TABLE 14.3. Estimated Monthly Social Security Income: Single Person, Maximum Earnings ($87,900 in 2004)

Year of Birth	Retire at 62	Retire at NRA	Retire at 70
1940	N/A	$1,882 (65 years, 6 months)	$2,577
1945	$1,438	$1,960 (66 years)	$2,643
1950	$1,487	$2,009 (66 years)	$2,676
1955	$1,503	$2,031 (66 years, 2 months)	$2,671
1960	$1,432	$2,050 (67 years)	$2,553
1965	$1,443	$2,064 (67 years)	$2,569

TABLE 14.4. Estimated Monthly Social Security Income: Married Couple, One Wage Earner Who Earned $25,000 in 2004

Year of Birth	Retire at 62	Retire at NRA	Retire at 70
1940	N/A	$1,458 (65 years, 6 months)	$1,940
1945	$1,075	$1,467 (66 years)	$1,950
1950	$1,084	$1,479 (66 years)	$1,965
1955	$1,081	$1,491 (66 years, 2 months)	$1,961
1960	$1,027	$1,505 (67 years)	$1,875
1965	$1,034	$1,517 (67 years)	$1,889

always been covered by Social Security. I assumed the husband and wife are the same age.

In Table 14.5 for the married couple, the wage earner earned $50,000 in 2004, while in Table 14.6 the wage earner earned $87,900.

Let's make a few observations on these estimates:

- The later we retire (up to age 70), the larger our benefits will be. This can make a big difference. For singles, the difference between starting at age 62 versus starting at age 70 can amount to $1,000 per month or more. For married couples, this difference can reach $1,800 per month or more. We will discuss this further in a little bit.

TABLE 14.5   Estimated Monthly Social Security Income: Married Couple, One Wage Earner Who Earned $50,000 in 2004

Year of Birth	Retire at 62	Retire at NRA	Retire at 70
1940	N/A	$2,340 (65 years, 6 months)	$3,101
1945	$1,726	$2,349 (66 years)	$3,113
1950	$1,734	$2,361 (66 years)	$3,128
1955	$1,723	$2,372 (66 years, 2 months)	$3,111
1960	$1,631	$2,385 (67 years)	$2,966
1965	$1,639	$2,396 (67 years)	$2,979

TABLE 14.6   Estimated Monthly Social Security Income: Married Couple, One Wage Earner Who Earned $87,900 in 2004

Year of Birth	Retire at 62	Retire at NRA	Retire at 70
1940	N/A	$2,823 (65 years, 6 months)	$3,866
1945	$2,109	$2,940 (66 years)	$3,965
1950	$2,181	$3,014 (66 years)	$4,014
1955	$2,204	$3,047 (66 years, 2 months)	$4,007
1960	$2,097	$3,075 (67 years)	$3,830
1965	$2,113	$3,096 (67 years)	$3,854

- Most likely these benefits are not enough to live on with no other income. At least, that's probably the case for single people or a married couple with just one wage earner.

- However, it might be possible for a married couple to live on these amounts, if both worked a full career so that they had two monthly Social Security checks, and if their E is small. This would probably require them to pay off the mortgage before retirement, or live in a tent.

- For a lot of people, it won't take a lot of additional income to get their I greater than their E, provided they make an effort to manage their E. So, Social Security is a great foundation to build on.

When completing the I worksheets in Chapter 9, I recommend that we use more accurate calculations than those shown in the tables in this chapter, reflecting our own special circumstances. There are a few ways we can do this:

- There's an official government web site on Social Security benefits (www.ssa.gov). It has online calculators that estimate our benefits, provided we input our salary history and date of birth. These online calculators show benefits only for three fixed retirement ages—age 62, our NRA, and age 70—not benefits for retirement ages between these ages, or the special spouse's benefit.

- The web site also has a more accurate calculator that we can download to our computer, and lets us pick our own retirement age and model the special spouse's benefit. This program and the online calculations mentioned above are the best sources for the most accurate estimates of our Social Security benefits.

- Each year we should receive a statement from the Social Security Administration that shows an estimate of our Social Security retirement income if we retire at age 62, our NRA, and age 70. This statement also shows a record of our earnings. It's a good idea to review it carefully, and report any mistakes to Social Security. We can do this by calling 1-800-772-1213, or by visiting a local Social Security office (we can find an office locator on the Social Security web site).

- You might want to purchase a retirement planning software package with Social Security benefits estimators.

- Some employers or 401(k) administrators provide retirement planning benefit statements or online calculators that will show estimates of Social Security benefits.

Let's turn to some key decisions we must make that will influence how much our Social Security retirement income will be. These decisions are:

- When should I start receiving Social Security benefits? As we'll see, the later our retirement age, the larger our benefits will be (up to a point).

- Should I work? If we are receiving Social Security benefits before our NRA and we work, it's possible that the earnings test will reduce our Social Security benefits.

As we will see, these two decisions can be intertwined.

When Should I Start Receiving Social Security Benefits?

The ideal, short answer is usually to wait as long as possible, to age 70 if we can make it. The reason is that benefits get larger the longer we wait. Let's take a closer look.

If I retire before my NRA, my benefit is reduced by $6^2/_3$ percent for each of the first three years that my retirement precedes my NRA, plus an additional 5 percent reduction for any additional years that my retirement precedes my NRA.

Here are some examples. Suppose I was born in 1950. Then my NRA is 66. If I retire at age 62, my benefit is reduced by 25 percent (three years times $6^2/_3$, plus one year at 5 percent). If I retire at age 63, then my benefit is reduced by 20 percent (three years times $6^2/_3$ percent).

Don't worry if these reductions seem complicated. I took them into account for the tables shown on the previous pages, and the Social Security calculators mentioned previously will also reflect these reductions.

If I retire after my NRA, my benefit is increased for each year that I delay, up until age 70. There is no increase after age 70. The amount of increase depends on my year of birth, as shown in Table 14.7.

Here's an example. Suppose my year of birth is 1950. My NRA is 66. If I postpone receiving benefits until age 70, they are increased by 32 percent (4 years times 8 percent).

Table 14.8 summarizes both the reduction for early retirement and the increase for postponed retirement.

For example, if I was born in 1950, my NRA is 66. If I start benefits at age 62, then my benefit is 75 percent of the benefit that would have started at age 66, or a 25 percent reduction. If I start at age 65, I'll get $93^1/_3$ percent of my NRA benefit—just a $6^2/_3$ percent reduction. If I start at age 67, I'll get 108 percent of my NRA benefit—an 8 percent increase. If I start at age 70, I'll get 132 percent of my NRA benefit—a 32 percent increase. Note that my benefit increases by more than 75 percent if I delay benefits from age 62 to age 70.

Again, don't worry if these increases are complicated. I reflected them in the benefit estimates shown on the prior pages, and all the retirement planning calculators will take them into account.

TABLE 14.7   Increase in Social Security Benefit That Starts after Normal Retirement Age

Year of Birth	NRA	Percent Increase for Each Year of Delay
1940	65 years, 6 months	7%
1941	65 years, 8 months	$7^1/_2$%
1942	65 years, 10 months	$7^1/_2$%
1943–1954	66 years	8%
1955	66 years, 2 months	8%
1956	66 years, 4 months	8%
1957	66 years, 6 months	8%
1958	66 years, 8 months	8%
1959	66 years, 10 months	8%
1960 and later	67 years	8%

TABLE 14.8 Percent of Benefit That Starts at Normal Retirement Age, For Retirement Age Shown

Year of Birth	NRA	Age 62	Age 65	Age 66	Age 67	Age 70
1940	65 years, 6 months	$77\frac{1}{2}$%	$96\frac{2}{3}$%	$103\frac{1}{2}$%	$110\frac{1}{2}$%	$131\frac{1}{2}$%
1941	65 years, 8 months	$76\frac{2}{3}$%	$95\frac{5}{9}$%	$102\frac{1}{2}$%	110%	$132\frac{1}{2}$%
1942	65 years, 10 months	$75\frac{5}{6}$%	$94\frac{4}{9}$%	$101\frac{1}{4}$%	$108\frac{3}{4}$%	$131\frac{1}{4}$%
1943–1954	66 years	75%	$93\frac{1}{3}$%	100%	108%	132%
1955	66 years, 2 months	$74\frac{1}{6}$%	$92\frac{2}{9}$%	$98\frac{8}{9}$%	$106\frac{2}{3}$%	$130\frac{2}{3}$%
1956	66 years, 4 months	$73\frac{1}{3}$%	$91\frac{1}{9}$%	$97\frac{7}{9}$%	$105\frac{1}{3}$%	$129\frac{1}{3}$%
1957	66 years, 6 months	$72\frac{1}{2}$%	90%	$96\frac{2}{3}$%	104%	128%
1958	66 years, 8 months	$71\frac{2}{3}$%	$88\frac{8}{9}$%	$95\frac{5}{9}$%	$102\frac{2}{3}$%	$126\frac{2}{3}$%
1959	66 years, 10 months	$70\frac{5}{6}$%	$87\frac{7}{9}$%	$94\frac{4}{9}$%	$101\frac{1}{3}$%	$125\frac{1}{3}$%
1960 and later	67 years	70%	$86\frac{2}{3}$%	$93\frac{1}{3}$%	100%	124%

One obvious strategy is to maximize my Social Security benefit, so that I have the largest possible lifetime income. For many of us, Social Security might be the only lifetime retirement income we receive. Remember—it's increased each year for inflation, and it is tax-free for many of us. So maximizing my Social Security income is a great idea, particularly if I have no other lifetime retirement income. This means arranging my finances, possibly including continuing to work, such that I can delay my Social Security benefits as long as possible, up to age 70.

This strategy works best if I'm in good health and expect to live to my life expectancy or beyond. The reason is that, over my lifetime, I'll receive more money from Social Security, because the increased benefits will make up for delay. If I'm not in good health, then the increase from postponing benefits might not make up for the delay.

The online calculators provided by the Social Security Administration show us the break-even age for postponing benefits. For example, suppose my NRA is 66, and I'm trying to decide whether to start benefits at age 66 or age 70. If I pick age 70, then the breakeven age is 82 and 2 months. This means that if I start my benefits at age 70, then I receive more lifetime income if I live to age 82 and 2 months or beyond. If I die before this age, I would have been better off starting my benefits at age 66.

Now let's see what happens if we work while we collect Social Security benefits.

What's the Earnings Test?

If we start our benefits before our NRA, our monthly Social Security retirement income might be reduced by the earnings test. Here's how this works.

- For calendar years *before* the year in which we reach our NRA, our Social Security benefit is reduced by $1 for each $2 that we earn over $11,640 per year. This is the limit in 2004—it is increased each year for inflation. Here's an example. Suppose we earn $21,640 for the year, which is $10,000 more than the annual limit of $11,640. Then our annual Social Security benefits are reduced by $5,000.

- For the calendar year *during* which we reach our NRA, our monthly benefit is reduced by $1 for each $3 that we earn per month over $2,590 before we reach our NRA. For the month during which we reach our NRA, and for each month thereafter, there is no earnings test. We can earn as much as we can and receive full Social Security benefits.

  Here's an example. Suppose we reach our NRA in April. Further, let's suppose we earn $4,090 for each month during January, February, and March, which is $1,500 more than the monthly limit of $2,590. Then our Social Security benefits are reduced by $500 during each month of January, February, and March. In April and thereafter, no earnings test applies and there is no benefit reduction.

- For calendar years *after* the year in which we reach our NRA, there is no reduction. We can earn as much as we can and still receive full Social Security benefits.

For the purpose of the earnings test, we count only wages from our job or net earnings from self-employment. Don't count pension benefits, withdrawals from 401(k) plans, or investment earnings.

For me, the implications of the earnings test are quite clear. Don't let it apply! If I start my benefits before my NRA, I'll make sure that I don't work enough to exceed the earnings limit. This strategy is consistent with the goal expressed earlier—to maximize my income by delaying the start of benefits. So now we have two powerful reasons to delay starting Social Security benefits at least until my NRA—to increase the income and to be able to work without worrying about the earnings test.

Other Features

Here are some other features of Social Security which can impact the amount of benefits we will receive.

How Long Must I Pay Social Security Taxes to Receive My Full Benefits?

The answer is 35 years. If we pay Social Security taxes for less than this period, our benefit will be reduced. When I prepared the tables of estimated Social Security benefits, I assumed we paid taxes for 35 years. The online calculators from Social Security make the same assumption, although the more sophisticated calculator that we can download lets us project benefits if we work less than the full 35 years.

What If I Work for a Government?

Some state governments don't participate in Social Security, and provide their own retirement programs. Public school teachers often are in this situation. In this case, we might not receive a benefit from Social Security, or our benefit may be reduced to reflect only the years we were covered by Social Security. It gets really tricky if we work for a nonparticipating government for awhile and also have a period of employment that is covered by Social Security. In this case, we should contact our local Social Security office to see how these features affect us. The Social Security web site has additional information on this situation.

Do I Pay Federal Income Taxes on Social Security Retirement Income?

Most people pay little or no federal income taxes on Social Security income. The rules are quite complicated, and consider income from pension benefits, 401(k) and IRA withdrawals, and investment income. My web site, www.restoflife.com, contains details on the rules.

One rule of thumb is that we won't pay much income tax on Social Security benefits until our retirement income from sources other than Social Security exceeds $50,000 per year. Here are some strategies for people in this situation:

- If, during our sixties, we have wage income that puts us well over the above threshold, this is another reason to delay receiving our Social Security benefits as long as possible, until age 70. By then, we might not be making as much other income, and we've maximized our Social Security income by delaying it until age 70.

- We should pay attention to the timing of large withdrawals from our 401(k) plan and IRAs. These can cause our total income to exceed the higher limit amounts.

- If we still have a mortgage on our house, we might be better off withdrawing from our 401(k) plan and/or IRA to pay off the mortgage before starting our Social Security benefits. This significantly reduces our E, while also reducing future I such that our Social Security benefits might not be taxed.

Let me repeat that we shouldn't let tax rules drive our lives. If our Social Security benefits are taxed, it's not the end of the world. We should first determine what we want to do with our lives, and then try to minimize our federal income taxes.

There's More!

Social Security provides still more benefits:

- If we were married for more than 10 years and are now divorced, we're eligible for an ex-spouse's benefit, similar to the special spouse's benefit.

- If our spouse is receiving the special spouse's benefit and we die, a widow's benefit goes into effect that is usually bigger than the special spouse's benefit.

- If we have dependent children or parents, they can receive additional Social Security income in certain situations.

- If we are severely disabled before age 62, we can receive special disability income benefits.

In each of these cases, the eligibility conditions and calculations get quite complex. The Social Security web site (www.ssa.gov) contains the details on these benefits.

What's Wrong with Social Security?

The short answer is that our government might not have enough money to pay the benefits. We will either need to raise taxes, cut benefits, or enact some combination of the two.

Each year, the Social Security Administration prepares a report from the trustees of the Social Security funds that includes a lot of projections on taxes collected and benefits paid. To prepare these projections, actuaries at the Social Security Administration make a number of assumptions on a variety of items, including the amount of benefits to be paid, longevity, productivity, immigration, birth rates, and so on. This report includes projections on three scenarios—pessimistic, optimistic, and intermediate. For the discussion in this chapter, I'll cite projections from the intermediate assumption scenario.

The first thing we conclude from the 2004 Trustees Report is that . . .

Social Security Is Really Big

Here's the opening paragraph from the Overview Highlights section of the 2004 Trustees Report. I added the words in brackets to make a point:

At the end of 2003, 47 million people [voters] were receiving benefits: 33 million retired workers [voters] and their dependents [voters], 7 million survivors [voters] of deceased workers, and 8 million disabled workers [voters] and their dependents [children whose plight profoundly influences voters]. During the year an estimated 154 million people [voters] had earnings covered by Social Security and paid payroll taxes. Total benefits paid in 2003 were $471 billion. Income was $632 billion, and assets held in special issue U.S. Treasury securities grew to $1.5 trillion.

When I hear the pessimists say that they will get nothing from Social Security, I think they're wrong. Too many *voters* have a big stake in Social Security. It might be cut back, but it won't go away entirely.

How Do We Pay for Social Security?

Social Security is financed with taxes paid by us and our employers. For the Social Security retirement income benefits, we each pay a total of 6.2 percent of our pay, up to something called the Social Security Wage Base (which is $87,900 in 2004). Any pay above this amount isn't taxed. When you add the tax paid by us and our employers, the total is 12.4 percent of our pay. To finance Medicare, we each pay an additional 1.45 percent of our pay, with no limit on the pay that is taxed. Adding up this tax for both us and our employer results in a total Medicare tax of 2.9 percent of pay. If you're self-employed, you pay the entire tax, although there is a slight break.

In 2004, if we make exactly the Social Security Wage Base, $87,900, we pay $6,724.35 in Social Security taxes. This is in addition to our federal and state income taxes. Many people pay more in Social Security taxes than they do for federal and state income taxes.

The government calls these FICA taxes; FICA stands for the Federal Insurance Contributions Act. To make us feel better, the government calls our taxes "contributions!"

What Does the Government Do with Our FICA Taxes?

The government uses our taxes to pay current benefits, and to build a reserve for future benefits when the baby boom generation retires. For much of the 1990s, the amount of FICA taxes exceeded benefits paid by many billions of dollars, and this surplus is expected to range from $50 to nearly $100 billion each year for the first decade of the twenty-first century. For example, in 2003, net taxes were $533.5 billion, while total benefits paid were $470.8 billion, for a surplus of $62.7 billion. While there are other measures of this surplus, I believe this measure makes the most sense.

As our population ages, the number of workers who are supporting older citizens through FICA taxes will shrink. Right now, there are about 3.3 workers paying FICA taxes for every person currently collecting benefits. At current tax rates, these workers are paying enough taxes to fund benefits for current retirees and to build the reserve. However, by 2030—prime-time retirement for baby boomers—there will be only about 2.2 workers for each retiree, and the FICA taxes paid by these workers won't be enough to pay for the benefits of all the baby boom retirees. This is why we need to build a large reserve to supplement the amount of FICA taxes paid by our children in future years.

While it sounds like the Social Security Administration has neatly planned for our retirement, there are still problems.

How the Government Invests the Reserve

The 2004 Trustees Report projects that the reserve will rise from $1.5 trillion by the end of 2003 to $6.4 trillion (in 2004 dollars) by 2030, and then start falling as the retirement of baby boomers gets into full swing. It predicts that the reserve will be exhausted by 2042. This seems very far in the future, which is part of the problem. No worries, mate—the problem is so far away! In fact, many politicians point to these projections as reasons for not taking unpleasant but necessary actions today.

Actually, a lot of us might be dead by 2042, so why should we worry? The problem is that the reserve isn't invested in the way that we normally think. It's not like our 401(k) plan or our employer's defined benefit plan, where there is a trust fund that can't be touched except to pay for our benefits.

In the case of Social Security, the taxes and benefits just become part of the overall federal budget. The official federal budget deficits that we see each year in the newspaper include

Social Security taxes and benefits. So, the official budget deficits published in recent years would be a lot larger if not for the surplus generated by Social Security taxes and benefits. For example, in 2003 the official federal budget deficit was $375 billion, but it would have been about $75 billion higher if not for the surplus generated by Social Security taxes.

Each year, the federal government issues bonds to the Social Security Trust Fund; the amount includes the Social Security surplus that we generate each year. These become the assets in the Social Security Trust Fund—the reserve mentioned previously. As we discussed in Chapter 11, bonds are basically loans from one party to another. When you and I buy bonds, we expect to be paid interest each year, and eventually be paid the principal as well. It's the same with these government bonds—eventually they must be repaid.

Here's another quote from the Overview Highlights section of the 2004 Trustees Report that illustrates the problem. The words in brackets are mine.

> Annual cost [benefit payments] will exceed tax income [FICA taxes] starting in 2018 at which time the annual gap will be covered with cash from redeeming special obligations of the Treasury, until these assets are exhausted in 2042.

What are "special obligations of the Treasury" and how will these be redeemed for cash to pay benefit payments? Let's take a look.

The problem is that the government is just loaning itself money. It is calling the loans "bonds," and counting them as "assets." Basically, these assets are just IOUs on paper. One part of the federal government (the part that spends money on government programs such as the military, foreign aid, government services, research, etc.) is borrowing money from another part of the government (Social Security). However, the government is ultimately on the hook for paying for everything, from Social Security to the military. No additional wealth is being created with these IOUs when we consider all the government's assets and liabilities. We have trillions in IOUs to ourselves, not real assets. In fact, we can argue that the existence of the Social Security surplus enables the government to currently spend more than it would have without the surplus, making the problem worse.

It's hard for us to wrap our minds around this problem, because the concepts are abstract and the numbers are mind-boggling. So, let's make a simple analogy. Suppose we have a family, and the parents loan $100 to a young child, who then spends the money. The parents count the $100 as an asset, calling it a "child bond." They add this to their child's college education fund, and feel good that they are preparing for their child's future. They expect their child to pay back principal and interest. As a result of this transaction, what is the effect on the wealth of the parents, the child, and the entire family? The parents have $100 in additional wealth, but the child is $100 poorer. Using Social Security accounting, the entire family would be the same, because the $100 expenditure by the child is balanced by the new $100 asset—the "child bond." However, the way you and I would normally think, the $100 is gone, and the family is $100 poorer. The $100 asset in the child's college education fund doesn't seem very real.

And where does the child get the money to pay back the bond? From future allowances. And where do future allowances come from? The parents!

Eventually the part of the government that owes this money will have to pay it to the other part of the government (Social Security) that will need it in the future. The mechanism for this is that interest and principal on the bonds will need to be paid. The bonds will come due. And how will the government find the money to pay off these bonds? It must come from general revenues—primarily income taxes. And this is the problem. Right now, the government is running huge deficits and spending the Social Security surplus. What will happen when this surplus no longer exists, and the government must add loan repayments on top of all its other expenditures?

When Will the Problems Start?

The 2004 Trustees Report projects that the annual surplus from Social Security will reduce to zero by 2018. If you're reading this book in 2005, that's only 13 years away! By 2020, the annual Social Security deficit (the excess of benefits paid over FICA taxes) is projected to be $85 billion in 2004 dollars. This will be the *addition* to the official federal budget deficit. The 2004 Trustees Report projects the annual Social Security deficit will grow:

2020	$ 85 billion
2025	$281 billion
2030	$512 billion
2035	$747 billion
2040	$960 billion (that's almost $1 trillion!)

And these amounts are in 2004 dollars. Remember that the 2003 official budget deficit was $375 billion, and politicians were wringing their hands over this huge amount. In 2025, the Social Security deficit will almost equal the entire 2003 federal budget deficit. By 2030 and beyond, the 2003 deficit will pale in comparison to the Social Security deficits, and we'll be reminiscing about the good old days in 2003. I'm planning to be alive then, so it affects me personally! And you, too!

Sometime around 2015 and thereafter, we'll be in big trouble. The government will need to either increase income taxes, increase FICA taxes, reduce other expenditures, run even larger budget deficits, or do some combination. And the problem will get much worse each year.

What Should We Do?

At the very least, I believe our government needs to better balance the budget in other areas, so it will have the financial resources to deal with looming Social Security deficits. However, we will need to do much more.

I think it comes down to the opening quote in this chapter. Social Security is a mechanism for working citizens to pay nonworking citizens. Nonworking citizens, by definition, don't produce goods and services. If the burden gets too big on the working citizens, something's gotta give.

Every recent President has assembled a commission to look into the problem, and we get a variety of possible solutions. These include raising the retirement age, increasing FICA taxes, increasing income taxes on Social Security benefits, and converting part of Social Security to IRA-like accounts.

Personally, I don't like the Social Security IRA solution. This just worsens the problem of outliving our 401(k) assets. I'd rather keep the current lifetime benefits, so that I have a core of financial resources that I can't outlive. I think we need a grand compromise between raising taxes and cutting benefits. Here are possible benefit cuts that would go a long way toward solving the problems:

- Raise the retirement age by three years.

- Reduce the average monthly benefit by between $200 and $400. This wouldn't devastate my $I > E$ situation.

Another possible solution would be to increase the number of workers relative to beneficiaries by allowing a lot of potential young workers to immigrate to the United States. This would work if we could gainfully employ all these new workers. However, as a nation, we haven't exactly been receptive to opening up the borders to large numbers of immigrants, so our mind-set would need to change for this solution to work.

WRAP-UP

I believe that Social Security's financial problems will be solved, one way or another. As a nation, we can't hide our heads in the sand forever. We all have a large stake in Social Security. It is in our own best self-interest to participate in the debate on the future of Social Security, and we need to support politicians who are brave enough to face the challenges.

Our security doesn't come from the IOUs that are accumulating on paper in the Social Security Trust Fund. It will come from future workers (our children and grandchildren) paying FICA and income taxes to fund our benefits and the interest on the IOUs. The real "trust fund" is the trust that our children will pay for our Social Security benefits. If we don't abuse this trust by placing too much of a burden on our children, we can count on this "trust fund."

Social Security benefits will still be an important part of our future financial resources. We can't count on Social Security as it exists today, but it won't be gone entirely, either. In fact, it won't even be cut in half from today's levels. If we follow the advice in this book, we can survive whatever changes will be necessary.

Too much reliance on the government is, indeed, social insecurity! Our real social security is our own talents and skills, our ability to earn wages, our financial assets, and our network of friends and family that we consciously build.

Getting the Most from My Pension Benefits

> If you don't know where you are going, you might wind up someplace else.
>
> —Yogi Berra

Most people's *rest-of-life* financial resources will consist mainly of Social Security, 401(k) balances, savings outside a 401(k) plan, and their house. If we're very fortunate, we'll also earn benefits in a defined benefit pension plan. These plans can be very confusing, and I often see people make mistakes when they decide how to use these benefits. To make optimal decisions, we need to know what we're doing. Knowledge is power!

No Respect

Defined benefit pension plans are the Rodney Dangerfield of retirement programs—they can't get any respect.

What a shame! Count yourself truly blessed if you participate in such a plan.

Most people don't appreciate the financial value in defined benefit plans. Here's a quick test. Suppose you're in your late fifties or early sixties. Which would you rather have—a balance of $200,000 in your 401(k) plan or an annual lifetime retirement income of $30,000? If you answered the retirement income, go to the head of the class! It's worth a lot more than $200,000.

The trouble that most people have is that $200,000 is a bigger number than $30,000, and it's hard to make a valid comparison. If you ask an actuary to make this comparison, he or she will want to calculate a present value of the retirement income, and will ask you which interest rate and mortality table to use for this calculation. At this point, most likely your eyes have glazed over and you're now thinking about lunch, last night's discussion with your spouse, yesterday's sports results—anything but mortality tables!

Here's a simple way to make this comparison. Multiply the lifetime retirement income by 20, which is a nice round estimate of your remaining lifetime. It is low—if we're in our fifties or sixties and take care of ourselves, we'll live much longer. But at least it gives us a very rough estimate of the total amount of money we might expect to receive over our lifetime. So for this example, multiply $30,000 by 20, and we get a low estimate of $600,000; we can expect to receive at least this amount over our lifetime.

The point of all this is to demonstrate that these plans pack a lot of financial value. Their big advantage is that they provide a lifetime retirement income, no matter how long we live. Another advantage is that they are very user friendly—the checks come in the mail each month or the money is deposited electronically in a bank account each month. I don't need to watch my investments and worry about what the stock market is doing. I might really appreciate this advantage when I get much older, and might not pay as much attention to my finances.

Let's keep these advantages in mind as we discuss two important choices that we must make regarding our benefits in these plans:

1. When should I start my pension?

2. What form of payment should I elect?

But before we answer these questions, let's review a few basics.

Defined Benefits 101

First, let's look at how these plans typically calculate the retirement income. All plans define a normal retirement age—the age when the retirement income starts. For most plans this is age 65, although some plans have earlier ages, say age 62.

All plans define the benefit as a lifetime monthly retirement income. There is a formula in the plan that calculates this amount. There are various breeds of plans that have different formulas for this purpose:

- A *final average plan* uses a formula that multiplies a percentage times our years of service, times our final average salary. This last amount is our pay, averaged over a relatively short time just before our termination of employment, say three or five years. For example, the monthly retirement income might equal 1 percent times our years of service times our final average salary for the last five years. There may be adjustments, or offsets, for Social Security benefits. If we work for a long time with one company and retire in our sixties or later, usually these types of plans provide the highest amount of retirement income, compared to the next three types of plans.

- A *career average plan* calculates the amount of retirement income that we earn for each year of service. Usually this is a percentage times our pay during the year. When we terminate employment, our total benefit is the sum of all the amounts we earned each year. For example, we might earn a retirement income of 1 percent of our pay during each year. When we retire, we add up the amounts we earned each year to determine our total retirement income.

- A *flat dollar plan* calculates the monthly retirement income by multiplying a dollar amount, say $40, times our years of service. These types of plans are common for union employees.

- A *cash balance plan* defines an account that is credited with contributions and interest each year. For example, the cash balance might be defined as the accumulation of a contribution credit of 5 percent of pay each year, credited with interest using rates on one-year Treasury bills. When we terminate or retire, we can elect to be paid this account in one lump sum, or we can have the account converted actuarially into a lifetime retirement income. Many employers switched to cash balance plans because the value of the benefit—a lump sum—is more readily apparent than a retirement income with a final average or career average plan. Also, these types of plans usually provide better benefits for people who work at various jobs throughout their lives instead of staying with one company for an entire career.

- A *pension equity plan* is a hybrid between a cash balance plan and a final average plan. It defines the benefit as a lump sum, by multiplying our final average pay by a percentage, times our years of service. For example, the plan might define the account as 5 percent of our final average salary for the past five years, multiplied by our years of service. We can then either take this amount as a lump sum or convert it to a lifetime annuity.

This process calculates our normal retirement income, the income we will receive if we start our benefits at our normal retirement age. However, many plans allow benefits to start earlier, which is called early retirement. Typical eligibility requirements might be age 55 with 10 years of service. Most of the time, the plan will reduce the amount of early retirement income, compared to the normal retirement income. The reason is that we can expect to receive payments for a longer period if we start benefits at an early retirement age.

In many cases, the plan calculates this reduction such that the expected value of the lifetime income is the same, whether we start benefits at early or normal retirement age. In this case, it is called an "actuarial reduction." In other cases, there is greater value if we start benefits early: Either the reduction is less than an actuarial reduction, or there is no reduction at all. This is called an "early retirement subsidy" because the employer is adding some value for people who retire before the normal retirement age.

Let's go on a quick detour about the reasons for early retirement subsidies. They were common when companies had the twentieth-century model of retirement in mind for the workers ahead of the baby boom generation. Companies commonly thought that employees were burned out in their late fifties and early sixties, and provided financial incentives to move them out of the workforce to make room for the up-and-coming baby boom generation. Recently, employers are removing these subsidies from their plans, as their mindset shifts to the twenty-first-century model of *rest-of-life*, along with the looming shortage of workers caused by the aging of the population. Lately, my clients are asking me how they can encourage older workers to *stay*, and they can't move fast enough to remove the early retirement incentives. Now back to the regularly scheduled program!

We should also talk about vesting. If we are 100 percent vested, we can quit and not forfeit our benefit. If we are 0 percent vested, if we quit we forfeit all of our benefit. Most plans have vesting requirements of five years, but shorter periods are possible. A few plans have partial vesting, which means that we might be 20 percent vested after three years of service, increasing 20 percent per year until we are 100 percent vested at seven years.

Just because we are vested doesn't mean we can start our benefit right away. We might get vested and quit at age 45, but we can't start our retirement income until age 55 at the earliest. Needless to say, we should be aware of our plans' vesting requirements, and make sure we don't quit just before we become vested.

All plans have alternative forms of payment. Most of the time, the formulas just described determine what is called a "single life annuity." This means we get paid for the rest of our lives, and when we die, payments stop. We can elect a joint and survivor annuity, which allows part or all of our income to continue after our death to a named beneficiary, usually our spouse or partner. We can specify whether the amount of income continued to our beneficiary equals 50 percent, 75 percent, or 100 percent of the income we received when we were alive. This income will continue for the rest of our beneficiary's life. Usually the plan reduces the retirement income for a joint and survivor form of payment compared to a single life annuity, since we expect benefits to be paid for a longer period of time.

Sometimes a plan will offer a "five-year certain and life" form of payment. This is a single life annuity, but if we die within five years of starting benefits, the income will continue to a named beneficiary for the remainder of the five years. We may also be able to elect a 10-year certain period instead of five years. Again, typically the income is reduced compared to a single life annuity, to pay for the potential death benefit. Usually, this form of payment makes sense only if we're in poor health and don't have a spouse or partner for a joint and survivor annuity.

Some plans offer a single lump sum payment in lieu of a lifetime retirement income. This will be the actuarial equivalent of the retirement income, determined in accordance with IRS rules, which specify the interest rate and mortality tables to use for this calculation. In theory, the lump sum is calculated the same way as the purchase price for an immediate annuity, as explained in Chapter 10. Let me warn you—I have a strong bias against lump sums. They are a trap for the unwary, and we'll talk more about this in a little bit.

All this can seem very confusing to people who aren't actuaries.

How Can I Learn More about My Pension?

Rather than trying to understand all the rules, *ask*! When you approach retirement, ask your plan administrator for an estimate of your retirement income under all the forms of payment. If you don't know who is the plan administrator, ask the human resources department.

Many companies have online benefit calculators that allow us to model our retirement income under different retirement ages. These are great, although it's easy to input the wrong information. I have to admit that I've done this with Watson Wyatt's own online calculator, and I'm an actuary!

Many companies have outsourced their benefits programs, which means a company like Watson Wyatt or one of our competitors administers the plan. Often there are people available on the telephone to explain the benefits. They won't give advice on which benefit form to take, but they should spend as much time with us as we need to understand the benefits.

When Should I Start My Pension?

Often this question gets muddled up with "When should I stop working?" These are two different questions. Usually it's possible to stop working on one date, and wait until a later date to start receiving our pension.

To answer the "When should I stop working?" question, here are some considerations:

- Since most plans use our years of service to calculate the amount of pension, the longer we work, the larger our pension will be.

- If the plan uses our final average earnings to calculate benefits, we should be aware of the years that will generate the highest average. This might be particularly important if we work part-time for an extended period of time. We might shoot ourselves in the foot if our final average earnings figure is based on part-time work instead of full-time work. Many plans have provisions to prevent this unpleasant result, but it pays to check this out if we are considering phased retirement.

- Many plans have so-called value cliffs. For example, there may be no reduction for early retirement if we reach a certain threshold, say age 62 with 30 years of service. Here's another common example. If we quit work before being eligible for early retirement, often we can still start receiving benefits once we are eligible for early retirement, but there's a steep actuarial reduction. However, if we work with the employer until we're eligible for early retirement, often there's a more favorable reduction for early retirement. In our business, we call the day we reach this value cliff "the biggest single payday in our lives." While it may be colorful, we're dead serious. So, if you're thinking about quitting, don't do it just before you reach the biggest single payday in your life.

- Speaking of value cliffs, some companies offer retiree medical plans, but only if we reach a threshold, again usually eligibility for early retirement. In this case, no benefits are paid if we quit before this threshold. This is also a valuable payday.

- Earlier I talked about vesting. Often we're vested well before we are eligible for early retirement. All this means is that we are entitled to an eventual benefit. Vesting is an important day, and we shouldn't quit just before we're vested. However, it's not the biggest single payday in our lives!

Having said all this, I let my life determine when I quit working. I'll work as long as I need the money and my job supports my life goals. I'll quit when both of these no longer apply. I will be aware of vesting days and big paydays—if I'm close I will hang on until I reach these days. But otherwise, if I really want to make important life changes, I'll go ahead after making sure I'm not hurting myself financially too much.

Note also that many pension plans will continue to count service even while we're working part-time, as advocated earlier in this book. However, there may be a threshold number of hours we need to work each week or each year, so we should check with our plan's rules for counting service if we are considering part-time work.

Now let's turn to "When should I start my pension?" With most plans, we can't start our pension until we completely quit working for the employer who sponsors the plan. The one exception is that a few plans let us start our pension at age 65, even if we work beyond this age, but these plans are unusual. Note that I can start the pension from a prior employer, even while I'm working for another employer.

Most plans will let us delay starting our pension after we quit working. Note that it is a dumb idea to delay once there is no reduction for early retirement. Normally this is age 65, but some plans allow for unreduced retirement incomes at earlier ages. The only reason we would delay our pension is to get a larger retirement income.

Since a lifetime income is so valuable, I want to make it as big as possible. So, I'll try to get wages and other income for as long as possible to make $I > E$, hopefully until there is no more reduction for early retirement. However, once again, I will let my life determine my decision, so if I really need the money from my pension plan to support my life goals, I'll start the pension.

Some financial planners and actuaries recommend starting the pension as early as possible, even with a reduction, to maximize its actuarial value. This might be at a date before we need the money, as I advocate. This strategy might make sense if the reduction for early retirement is very small—say 3 percent or less for each year the pension starts before normal retirement age. Otherwise, I'll wait until I need the money.

What Form of Payment Should I Take?

Here there are two traps for the unwary that should be avoided: One is the lump sum trap, and the other is the crafty insurance agent trap.

The Lump Sum Trap

About half of defined benefit plans offer a lump sum payment in lieu of a lifetime retirement income. A lot of people are tempted to take the money and run. Many stockbrokers, insurance agents, and financial planners will have very convincing arguments that we should take the lump sum and invest it with their products and services. I think this is a bad move, and I'll share my reasons.

Charlie Commander, a friend at Watson Wyatt, has a neat quiz called "You Bet Your Life." It goes something like this. Imagine you're in a room with 100 actuaries, each age 60. (Life doesn't get much better than this.) Each actuary is given a lump sum of $100,000 and is told that this is equivalent to a monthly retirement income of $825. Accordingly, each actuary deposits the $100,000 in an IRA and withdraws $825 per month. How many actuaries will *outlive* the lump sum?

A. 40

B. 45

C. 50

D. 60

E. 70

The answer is E, 70 out of 100 will outlive their lump sum! Not a happy result!

How many will outlive their lump sum by more than 10 years?

A. 15

B. 20

C. 25

D. 30

E. 35

Actually, the answer is halfway between C and D—27$\frac{1}{2}$! More than one-fourth will outlive their lump sum by more than 10 years!

If you got the first two questions right, let's go on to the bonus round. Suppose you're age 62, and given the choice of a lump sum of $250,000 or $2,000 per month as long as you live. You say, "Show me the money," and take the lump sum. You deposit it in an IRA and withdraw $2,000 per month. When do you need to die so that you don't outlive your money?

- If you earn 4 percent per year, you can live 13 more years, until age 75.

- At 6 percent per year, you can live 16 more years, until age 78.

- At 8 percent per year, you can live 20 more years, until age 82.

- At 10 percent per year, you can live 50 more years, until age 110. But note that this must be *exactly* 10 percent each year—if you have ups and downs and average 10 percent, you might run out of money a lot sooner, as we saw in Chapter 11.

Who wants to bet their life? I don't. I plan to take care of myself and live a long time, so I'll really appreciate a lifetime retirement income.

Here's another potential problem with lump sums. IRS rules dictate the interest rates and mortality tables that actuaries use to convert monthly retirement incomes into lump sums. These rates are fair to the recipients (that's us!). However, the IRS does not require that actuaries reflect the value of early retirement subsidies in this lump sum calculation. As a result, some plans reflect this value, and some don't. We should ask our plan administrator to see how the plan reflects early retirement subsidies when calculating the lump sum payment.

- If the answer is something like "The lump sum is actuarially equivalent to the age 65 benefit," and we are retiring well before age 65, then we're losing a lot of value by taking the lump sum.

- We're better off if the answer is something like "The lump sum is actuarially equivalent to the retirement income that starts immediately."

New regulations require plan sponsors to illustrate the relative value of lump sums and annuities, and these can help us realize how much value we might be losing by taking a lump sum. If I am considering taking a lump sum, I'll ask for a "relative value assessment." Such an assessment will attach a value to the annuity, and will compare it to a lump sum payment if it is offered. If the early retirement subsidy is not reflected in the lump sum payment, the lump sum will look less valuable than the annuity.

My opinion is that the whole purpose of defined benefit plans is to provide a lifetime retirement income. If we take a lump sum, we're defeating that purpose. I'd take a lump sum only if I was going to be shot at dawn tomorrow or given six months to live from my doctor. If I'm healthy and take care of myself, I'll be far better off with my lifetime retirement income. By the way, even if the relative value assessment shows the lump sum to be worth more than the annuity, I'd still take the annuity, for all of the reasons mentioned in this chapter.

"My pension has been renegotiated, and in lieu of a monthly check I'll receive a crateful of seasonal fruit."

There are four possible exceptions to my rule on lump sums:

1. This exception applies to highly paid people. The IRS places dollar limits on the benefits that can be paid from a tax-qualified retirement plan. This usually applies to people who make $200,000 or more per year. Many companies offer "makeup plans" that pay for benefits that are over the IRS limits. These makeup plans are not tax qualified. A tax-qualified plan has a trust fund with invested reserves, and there are complicated rules and requirements that help ensure that assets will be sufficient to pay benefits. A nonqualified plan usually has no trust fund; benefits are paid only from the employer's cash flow. This is fine while your employer is healthy, but a disaster if your employer files for bankruptcy—you usually lose your benefits. If you participate in a nonqualified plan and are worried about what can happen to the company over the next 30 or more years, you might take your benefits from the nonqualified plan in a lump sum. However, I'd still recommend you take a lifetime monthly payment from the qualified plan, since there's a trust fund that provides security for the benefits.

2. Some plans allow for partial lump sums and partial lifetime retirement incomes. If I have a very good need for a partial lump sum (to invest in a business, say, but not in a Winnebago), I might take just enough of a lump sum to meet this need. I'll make sure that the remainder of my lifetime annuity is enough to make $I > E$.

3. It is possible that I can take my lump sum and buy an immediate annuity that provides a greater monthly retirement income. If I shop around and am convinced that a safe insurance company can make this happen, then I'd go ahead. I need to make sure that the ultimate monthly benefit is higher, after all expenses and commissions have been paid. I'll do my own homework and won't let a sharp-talking insurance agent talk me into this course of action.

4. This exception applies in an unusual circumstance, although it is instructive. Suppose we are receiving a lifetime income

from a tax-qualified plan, the plan is underfunded (assets are less than liabilities for benefit payments), and the sponsoring employer files for bankruptcy. In this case, we might lose part of our monthly retirement income. If we think that these circumstances could apply, then we might want to take the money and run.

For us to fully understand this last point, we need a little knowledge about the Pension Benefit Guaranty Corporation (PBGC), which I cover later in this chapter.

The Crafty Insurance Agent Trap

If we are married or have a partner who depends on our retirement income, we should elect a joint and survivor benefit. This way, our spouse or partner also has a lifetime retirement income after we die. If we take the single life annuity and we die before our spouse or partner, they are out of luck. The only exception might be if our spouse or partner is in very poor health.

Here's where crafty insurance agents come in. They might say, "Yes, you need to protect your spouse, but you're better off taking the single life annuity and using the difference between a single life annuity and a joint and survivor annuity to pay premiums for a life insurance policy with my company." They might show complicated projections that supposedly prove that this is a good deal. Don't believe them.

Usually we're better off taking the joint and survivor benefit. These are calculated to be equivalent in value to the single life annuity. This means that the reduction in monthly benefit for a joint and survivor annuity equals the value of the death benefit to the spouse or partner. Life insurance companies use the same underlying actuarial principles to calculate life insurance premiums. They can't create additional value that isn't there to begin with. The last time I checked, insurance agents aren't magicians. Actually, if we read between the lines, what is really being said is: "Yes, you need to protect your spouse, and *I'm* much better off if you take the single life annuity and buy my life insurance policy, because I'll make a good commission."

What If I Start My Benefits and I'm Rehired?

Occasionally people have a "near-retirement experience"—they retire, start their pension, and then want to return to work. If we go back to work for a different employer, there is no problem. If we work for the same employer, then we might have a problem.

The IRS has some complicated rules called the "suspension of benefits" rules. These try to prevent the situation where somebody has a sham retirement—they quit for a day, start their pension benefits, and then start working again at the same job. However, there are legitimate situations where we might just change our minds and return to work. In this case, the retirement plan must suspend our benefit unless one of the following two circumstances apply:

1. We work sporadically, less than 40 hours per month.

2. We are age 65 or over.

If the plan suspends our benefits, then another complicated set of rules applies when we retire again and restart our pension. It's too complicated to explain here, other than to say that our pension usually is increased to adjust for the benefits that we didn't receive while we were working. Also, we might earn additional benefits during the period of reemployment. If this situation applies, the best course of action is to ask the plan administrator for an illustration of the adjustment of the benefit amount.

Pension Benefit Guaranty Corporation

The best way to describe the Pension Benefit Guaranty Corporation (PBGC) is that it is the FDIC of pension plans. The PBGC is a federal agency that guarantees the monthly retirement incomes of participants whose defined benefit plans are underfunded, and the employer no longer exists due to bankruptcy. The PBGC charges plan sponsors a premium, so that the PBGC has assets to pay for the insured benefits. However, ultimately the federal government stands behind the promises made by the PBGC.

In most cases, the PBGC insurance helps put our minds at ease about the security of our pension benefits. However, there are a few exceptions and limits, as follows:

- PBGC insurance applies only for tax qualified plans. It is not available for nonqualified plans that only cover highly paid employees.

- PBGC insurance does not cover the pension plans of any government—state, local, or federal.

- The PBGC has limits on the amount of monthly retirement income that it guarantees. These limits depend on a number of things, including our age at retirement, whether we elected a life annuity or a joint and survivor annuity, and the funded status of the plan when the sponsoring employer filed for bankruptcy. If our monthly income is higher than these maximums and the plan has insufficient assets upon the employer's bankruptcy, the most we will get from the PBGC is the maximum guaranteed benefit. In 2004, these maximums were as shown in Table 15.1 for a life annuity.

So, the nasty scenario is if we're being paid much more than these maximums, the sponsoring employer files for bankruptcy, and the plan has insufficient assets to pay benefits. In this case, the PBGC takes over the plan and makes the guaranteed benefit payments that are lower than what our pension plan has been paying. We don't have to worry if our employer never files for bankruptcy, or if the plan has assets that exceed the liabilities for benefit payments.

TABLE 15.1.   Maximum Benefits Guaranteed by the Pension Benefit Guaranty Corporation in 2004

Retirement Age	Maximum Monthly Guaranteed Benefit
55	$1,664.49
60	$2,404.26
62	$2,922.10
65	$3,698.86

How can we find out if our plan is underfunded? This isn't easy for a layperson to understand. We can see disclosures of assets and liabilities in our company's annual report, if it is publicly traded. Or we can ask the plan sponsor for a copy of the latest actuarial report, which has measures of assets and liabilities. Even if we get this information, it's hard to decipher and interpret. For example, many of these disclosures looked awful right after the market downturn in 2000, 2001, and 2002. However, after the partial recovery in 2003, these disclosures looked much better.

It's tricky to provide some rules of thumb here, but I'll try. Two measures of liabilities to consider would be the "accumulated benefit obligation" on financial statements, or the "present value of accrued benefits" on the actuarial report. If the market value of assets is less than these amounts by 20 percent or more, I'd worry. I wouldn't panic yet—I would inquire with my employer for an explanation. If the employer is the Rock of Gibraltar in financial strength, there's less to worry about. I should only worry with the combination of an underfunded plan, a financially weak employer, and benefit amounts that are well in excess of the PBGC guarantees. In this case, if I didn't feel good about the explanation I requested about the funded status, I'd consider electing a lump sum payment if it is available.

WRAP-UP

The messages in this chapter are simple. I'll make informed choices with regard to my defined benefit plan, while I thank my employer for sponsoring it. As we'll see in some examples in Chapter 19, having some lifetime income from a defined benefit plan can make the difference between working or not during part of our *rest-of-life*. We need to learn the rules, and stay focused on what's important to us. Take the time to fully understand the consequences of our decisions—it's time well spent!

Next, let's look at some potential miscellaneous sources of *I*.

Squeezing the Last Drop

From birth to age 18, a girl needs good parents, from 18 to 25 she needs good looks, from 25 to 55 she needs a good personality, and from 55 on she needs cash.

—Sophie Tucker

Many of us have other assets that we can use to generate *I* during our *rest-of-life*. Possibilities include tapping the equity in our home, inheritances, life insurance, and legal settlements, such as from a divorce. Here I'll talk about how to squeeze every last drop from these resources, to make them last the rest of our lives. To do this, we need to know what we're doing and focus on how we use these resources in the most efficient way to support the life we want.

Tapping the Equity in Our Homes

For most of us, our home equity represents one of the largest chunks of wealth we have. Many of us might need to tap into this resource, to generate *I* during our *rest-of-life*.

Of course, the simplest way to use the equity in our home is to pay off the mortgage, and just live there rent-free. Obviously this works best if we really like our current home. I'm a strong advocate of this approach, and I discuss this further in Chapter 18.

The next simplest way to use the equity in our home is to sell it, buy a less expensive house, and use the profit to generate income.

In this case, we can use the methods from Chapter 10 to estimate how much income we can expect from this profit.

For planning purposes, we should consider sales and closing costs, which can subtract up to 6 percent of the value of our house when we sell it. We'll also need to subtract the outstanding balance of any mortgage. A competent real estate agent can help us analyze the net profit we can make from selling our home. They will usually do this for free, since they want our listing. When I sell my house, I'll shop around among a few real estate agents, to get different perspectives, and to determine the difference in closing costs (often their commission is negotiable).

We might need to pay capital gains taxes on the profit from our homes. Federal law permits us to exclude from taxation the first $250,000 of capital gains if we are single, and $500,000 if we are married. Years ago, we needed to be age 55 or older for special capital gains treatment. Now, we can take advantage of this special treatment at any age and as many times as possible over our lifetime. The only requirement is that we need to live in the house for at least two of the last five years. There are many other rules and requirements, and clever accountants have strategies for squeezing the last drop out of the profit from the sale in our house. For example, all of the costs of remodeling and maintenance are deductible from the capital gain on our house. If we plan to sell our home and the profit is close to the limits, paying for an accountant is money well spent.

As mentioned earlier, the big homes in the suburbs may not hold their value when many are put up for sale as the baby boom generation ages and our kids move out. So we may want to seriously consider the "sell our house" solution before supply exceeds demand. I've already moved out of the big house in the suburbs, and live in a smaller townhouse, in a beautiful spot with nice recreational facilities. It's far enough away from downtown Los Angeles so that it's much less expensive, but it's close enough that I can get a taste of the big city when I need it. This is my demographic investment, as I think many baby boomers will do the same in the coming years.

Obviously this is not for everyone. Many of us will hold onto our homes for a variety of reasons—comfort, sentiment, or having room when the kids and their families come to visit. In this case, another way to generate income is to rent out a room or rooms. Not only do we generate income, but we get company at the same time. Of course, this creates obvious lifestyle issues—I'm just mentioning it here for our consideration. One fun way is to rent to students, particularly foreign exchange students. This way, we aren't committed for long periods of time, and if we get tired of the situation, we don't have to wait very long for them to move out.

What about Reverse Mortgages?

These are creative devices that can be useful for generating I, but only under the right circumstances. Here I'll summarize how they work and when they might work for us. My web site has more information if we want to explore this concept further.

Reverse mortgages work best when you don't want to move from your current house, and expect to stay there for many years.

Like a regular mortgage, you are taking a loan, using your house as collateral. The word *reverse* comes into play in two ways:

1. Instead of using the loan proceeds to buy a house, like a regular mortgage, we use the loan proceeds for living expenses or for any other purpose.

2. Instead of paying back the loan with monthly payments, we pay it back when we sell the house and move. We don't make any loan repayments as long as we are living in our house and meet certain other conditions described next.

There are a few ways to get a reverse mortgage:

- The most common is the Home Equity Conversion Mortgage (HECM), which is the only reverse mortgage that is insured by the federal government. HECM loans are insured by the Federal Housing Administration (FHA), which is part of the U.S. Department of Housing and Urban Development (HUD).

- Many state and local government agencies offer deferred payment loans (DPLs) for repairing or improving homes.

- Some state and local governments offer property tax deferral (PTD) loans. We can use the proceeds of these loans to pay property taxes.

- Banks, mortgage companies and other private lenders offer reverse mortgages with their own special features.

Here are some features that are common to all reverse mortages:

- We retain ownership of our home.

- Generally the loan must be primary. If there are outstanding loans when we take the reverse mortgage, they must be repaid. We can use the proceeds of a reverse mortgage to repay other outstanding loans.

- The loan balance grows over time with interest. When the loan is done, either we or our heirs must repay the original loan plus interest. If at that time the loan is worth less than the house, then we or our heirs can sell the house, pay off the loan, and keep whatever is left. Fortunately, the loan can never grow larger than the value of the house. The lenders have no other recourse for loan repayment—they can't attach our other assets or income. If the value of the house is equal to or less than the value of the loan, then we or our heirs receive nothing when the house is sold. Naturally the lenders take steps to prevent this from happening, since they lose money in this situation.

- The amount of the loan depends on our age and the value of our home. Generally, the older we are, the more cash we can get. Also, the more our home is worth, the more cash we can get.

- All reverse mortgages must be repaid when the last surviving borrower sells the home, dies, or moves out.

- Some lenders might require repayment if we fail to pay property taxes, fail to keep the home insured, or fail to keep it properly maintained and repaired.

At this point, let me point out the obvious. Reverse mortgages will reduce the amount of inheritance our children might receive when we die, since they eat into the net equity of our homes.

Another use for a reverse mortgage is to pay for nursing home expenses while keeping our current home. This might be useful if we expect to recover and move back home soon, or if we're married and one of us is ill while the other is healthy. If we don't need or want to keep our current home, though, we could sell it and use the profit to pay for nursing home expenses. This is one reason to delay using a reverse mortgage for as long as possible, so we keep our options open.

One good way to compare reverse mortgages is through total annual loan cost (TALC) disclosures. The federal truth-in-lending law requires lenders to provide the TALC for reverse mortgages. The TALC is useful when comparing and shopping for reverse mortgages. However, our actual costs may vary, due to the length of the loan and other factors. One thing is clear: Most of the time, reverse mortgages are a good idea only if we stay in the house for a long time, at least 10 years. The reason is that most reverse mortgages have high start-up costs, and it doesn't make sense to pay these if we live in the house for only a few more years.

Reverse mortgages can be a useful tool to draw down the "principal" of our home equity. As such, I would wait to use it until I retire completely, say in my late sixties or early seventies, for the same reasons in chapters 9 and 10 that I advocate waiting to tap into other forms of my principal.

An excellent resource on reverse mortgages is the AARP web site, www.aarp.org/revmort/. It provides loan calculators and an excellent downloadable summary called "Home Made Money."

Inheritances

The oldest generation is also the wealthiest. Some surveys report that two-thirds of Americans over age 65 own their homes free of a mortgage. This is the source of most wealth in the post–age 65 generation. It's easy to estimate how much income this might generate for us:

- Estimate the value of our parents' home and any other resources we might know about, and subtract any estate taxes that might apply. Estimating inheritance taxes is no easy feat, and these taxes are scheduled to change for the next several years. If our parents have a large estate, it might pay to learn more about estate taxes by visiting with an accountant.

- Divide the result by the number of brothers and sisters (include ourselves). This represents what each of us might inherit.

- We can now estimate how much I this lump sum amount can generate, using the methods from Chapter 11.

There are a couple of problems with the inheritance-for-retirement solution. First, the amount is usually not nearly enough to fund retirement. And second, the chances are good that one or both of our parents will be alive when we retire! This puts us in the awkward position of thinking, "Hurry up, Mom and Dad, I need the money. . . ."

Legal Settlements

Sometimes we get legal settlements that pay us a fixed amount of money for a specified period. Most likely these are from divorces, but there could also be a settlement as a result of an accident or a lawsuit.

Since these usually aren't lifetime payments, we need to consider how to use these for funding *rest-of-life* expenses. Here's one possibility:

- Estimate the total amount of cash we can expect to receive, by multiplying the annual payment by the number of years. Think of this as a lump sum.

- Estimate how much I this lump sum will generate, using the methods from Chapter 11. This is the amount we should use for living expenses. Save the rest of each payment for future living expenses.

Here's an example. Suppose I expect to receive $20,000 per year for 10 years, as a result of a legal settlement. Multiply these two numbers for a result of $200,000—the total amount I will receive. Using the methods from Chapter 10, I decide that at my age, I should withdraw 4 percent per year from a lump sum. Four percent of $200,000 is $8,000 per year. So I spend $8,000 per year and invest the rest of the $20,000 I receive each year. This way, I increase the chances that I can make this stream of payments last the rest of my life.

Whole-Life Insurance

Some of us have whole-life insurance or universal life insurance policies. Such policies build cash values while providing current life insurance protection. Generally I think these are bad investments, and I've never bought such a policy. I'd rather buy term insurance, which has far lower premiums than whole-life insurance policies, and invest the savings in premiums in mutual funds.

However, if you have such a policy, it's possible you might have some substantial cash values that have built up over the years. You might be able to stop paying premiums and withdraw the cash values, and use them to generate I. You can use these withdrawals like a lump sum, and use the methods described in Chapters 9 and 10 for generating I from lump sums. This strategy makes sense only if you don't have dependents who would need the death benefits. There's more about whole-life insurance in Chapter 18.

It's complicated to analyze whether it makes sense to stop paying premiums and withdraw cash values, and is beyond the scope of this book. I recommend that you ask your life insurance agent or insurance company for the amount of the cash value that is available for withdrawal. If this amount is more than $100,000, find an *independent* financial adviser to help you with the analysis. This can be tricky, because your insurance agent will want you to either keep the money with the insurance policy or convert it to an annuity with the current life insurance company. On the other hand, if your adviser makes commissions on the investment from the cash value withdrawal, you can guess what the answer might be. So you need to find an adviser who has no stake in the withdrawal—perhaps an accountant or other independent adviser.

Another possibility is a viatical settlement. With these, we sell the rights to the eventual death proceeds of our insurance policy to a third party, who in turn gives us money today. This can be done through insurance agents or other brokers. Naturally, the amount we get today is less than the death proceeds. What's really happening is that the third party is betting that we will die soon, and will pocket the difference between the death proceeds and what the third party pays us. I do not advise using viatical settlements for normal *rest-of-life* expenses. Often, these are bad deals, with deep discounts in the amounts that we would receive. Sometimes they are outright frauds. We should consider this option only if we have no other resources to pay for high medical or nursing home costs, when it seems obvious that the end is near. AARP's web site, www.aarp.org, has more information on the risks of viatical settlements.

Accumulated Vacation

Many employers allow us to accumulate vacation pay from vacation days that we don't use. This is paid in a lump sum when we terminate employment. If we know we're going to take a permanent vacation fairly soon (e.g., retire full-time), then we might want to accumulate our vacation pay to create some additional financial resources.

WRAP-UP

I'll be resourceful with my other assets, to squeeze out the most lifetime *I* that is possible. This can be a complicated subject, and it's easy to be talked into a bad course of action by somebody who will benefit from the transaction. We need to stay focused on what's important to us. I plan to take the time to fully understand the consequences of my decisions—it's time well spent!

Next, let's look at the practical aspects of working during our later years.

What, Me Work? —Revisited

I am a strong believer in luck, and I find the harder I work, the more I have of it.

—Benjamin Franklin

In Chapter 4, I make the case for working during our later years, for the additional income and to keep healthy and vital. I believe that keeping a sense of purpose in life is critical to one's well-being and longevity. However, I still have remnants of the twentieth-century retirement model in my mind, though, and it feels strange to think about working for such a long time.

So if I work during a good part of my *rest-of-life*, it will be on my terms.

My Way

What are these terms? This chapter covers some of the practical aspects of working during our later years.

For me, the most essential feature is reducing my work hours, so I have more time to do other things. I want the flexibility to work part-time in some manner. I prefer three full days per week, but others might prefer five half-days. Another possibility is to work full-time for several months of the year, interspersed with months of no work. Others might work at home, telecommute, or job share. I might be a contract employee with no benefits, or an outside consultant. The possibilities are endless—just work less than 40 hours per week, most of the time.

This usually requires that I step off the career ladder. What do I mean by that? I'll look for just enough income, the chance to do interesting work, and social contacts. I'm no longer working for prestige, that next promotion, a big raise. As a practical matter, part-timers aren't as important to the company as hard-charging full-timers, and there's a price I'll pay by going part-time. This is a small price that I'm willing to pay, but it can be a problem for some ambitious people, and the first step is to be fully conscious of it.

I'll also look for an effective, productive working environment. (Chapter 4 discusses some considerations and key questions.)

Another essential is easy access to work. I want to minimize my precious remaining lifetime hours in the commute to work.

Hopefully we've followed the advice of the health section of this book, so medical insurance is nice to have but perhaps not critical. For some people, though, it's essential. In any case, our medical insurance doesn't need to be the best, with low co-payments or the most comprehensive network. I just want the protection from really high medical bills, in case something drastic happens. If this is important to me, I'll need to check the plan's eligibility rules, to make sure that I work enough hours to be eligible for medical coverage.

I'll also look for *health benefits*, as opposed to medical insurance. Does my potential employer offer health risk assessments and other educational benefits to help maintain my health?

Another nice-to-have feature is a 401(k) plan, preferably with a matching contribution.

Defined benefit pension and retiree medical plans are in the "I must be dreaming" category, but if we run across them as part-timers, great!

Speaking of these plans, if we're leaving our current employer we need to watch for value cliffs, discussed in Chapter 15. I should be aware of the age and service eligibility requirements for retiree medical coverage and subsidized early retirement benefits. As we discussed, attaining these requirements can be the biggest payday in our lives. So, if this day will come soon, it doesn't make sense to leave now.

We should also be aware of a prospective employer's policies toward paid holidays, vacation, and sick leave. This might not be as important as when we were working full-time, but it is still nice to have. Paid time off will most likely be reduced for part-timers, but I wouldn't get too upset about this. After all, I'm getting time off just by being part-time!

The Age Advantage

How can we get all these wonderful things in our later years?

There's a lot of concern about age discrimination, and some stereotypes die hard. It's common to think that employers would rather have young, bright, cheap labor than us old farts who are set in our ways and won't learn new skills. While we need to be aware of these prejudices and challenges, they shouldn't stop us. Let's take a look.

First of all, age discrimination is illegal under the Age Discrimination in Employment Act (ADEA). The ADEA prohibits discrimination against any worker age 40 or older on the basis of age. Hiring, promoting, and firing decisions cannot use age as a criterion. Age discrimination does exist in some places, but not sufficiently blatant to get busted. This doesn't bother me; there are enough places that don't discriminate and do appreciate what I have to offer.

We have a lot of advantages over the young'uns. Here are just a few:

- We have life experience that gives us stability, confidence, and reliability.

- We might even be cheaper! Hopefully, our financial resources are sufficient such that we're willing to work for less, because we already have Social Security and other income. Our medical insurance might be cheaper, since the young employees often insure their entire family. If we want flexible hours, that might match well with employers who don't want to be locked into the financial commitment of full-time employment.

- A lot of businesses cater to the aging population, and it's important for them to have employees who look like their customers. While we're on this subject, we should make a point to support companies that hire older workers by giving them our business. In the process, we might make some valuable contacts.

- There's a lot of us, and not as many of them. In 10 to 15 years, there will be a lot of people in their fifties and sixties, and not nearly as many in their thirties and forties. They can't take all the jobs, and employers will need older workers.

- Finally, it's also interesting to note that the Supreme Court ruled in early 2004 that reverse age discrimination is okay. This means it's perfectly legal for an employer to discriminate *in favor of* older workers!

Another Barrier?

Our research on phased retirement often encounters a complaint that people can't work part-time and collect retirement benefits from the same employer. It is true that there are some antiquated government rules that were designed with the twentieth-century model of retirement in mind. Federal laws and regulations generally prohibit commencement of retirement benefits before age 65 for defined benefit plans, and before age $59\frac{1}{2}$ for 401(k) plans, while working for the employer who sponsors these plans. And employers often have more stringent rules that prohibit drawing any retirement benefits until termination of employment—no matter what age.

There are limited circumstances in which we can draw retirement benefits and work for the same employer. These fall under the IRS "suspension of benefits" rules mentioned in Chapter 15, where we work for less than 40 hours per month. This might be fine—maybe I don't want to work any more than that. However, the problem is that with 40 hours per month, I might not work enough hours to be eligible for medical coverage or to participate in the employer's 401(k) or pension plan. So there's a trade-off.

All of this doesn't bother me too much. There's no law that prohibits me from retiring from my current employer, drawing benefits, and working elsewhere. However, if we really like our current employer, this is a shame, and I'll set my intent to work around this problem. Actually, in my fifties and sixties, I'd prefer to let my retirement benefits accumulate and get bigger so I can draw them later in my seventies, eighties, and beyond when I might not work as much. So, if I really like my current employer, I'll manage my *I* and *E* such that I don't need my retirement benefits while I'm working. I'll find a way to live on the part-time wages.

More Phases

In Chapter 1, I suggest that we might have Stage 1 and Stage 2 of our *rest-of-life*, where we work part-time in Stage 1 (phased retirement), and retire completely in Stage 2. It's also possible that we might have two phases to Stage 1. In the first phase, I might work part-time in my current job or in a related field. Here the salary might be in the same neighborhood as my current pay, but reduced pro rata for part-time work. This can buy some breathing room for adjusting my *E* to accommodate my reduced *I*. It can also help me build up more financial resources to increase my *I* in later years, and maintain other goodies like medical insurance. I might do this until I reach eligibility for Social Security or Medicare. In the second phase of Stage 1, I might do something completely different, which gives me the freedom to accept much less money, and perhaps work on an hourly basis.

We have a lot of possibilities for transforming our work circumstances.

- We can stay with the same employer, but restructure our jobs to work part-time, and possibly pick and choose the activities and tasks that we want to do.

- If we like our work but our employer isn't flexible, we can go work for a competitor that is more flexible. And collect retirement benefits from our prior employer—poetic justice!

- We can work in a field related to our current work, where our current experience is valuable and we may have lots of contacts. In our current work, who are our customers, suppliers, or vendors? They might want to hire us for our experience and contacts.

- We can do temporary work, filling in when people go on vacation or when companies have temporary work surges. This can be in either our own field or a related field.

- We can have two part-time jobs, one in our current field and one in a new field.

- We can volunteer in our desired field to make contacts, or do an internship.

- We can go back to school and get retrained, or acquire new credentials.

- We can chuck it all and do something completely different.

And finally, there's one more important option.

Working on Our Own

We may need to start our own business, or work at home.

This might be our only option, either because we can't find a job or to pursue our bliss. No worries about age discrimination here! However, I've seen the sobering statistics on starting new businesses. Depending on which article I read, I see that well over half of new businesses fail, and the failure rate can get as high as 90 percent.

Should this stop us in our tracks? Nah! Many of these new businesses fail because they run afoul of the basic $I > E$ formula. The owners' E is big because they need to support a family or expensive lifestyle. They may need to pay for a large start-up loan. I have a few friends who have blown their *rest-of-life* portfolio on following their dream, to start a new business. When it failed, they went back to work at a regular job, disillusioned and depressed. This is something to avoid!

If I start my own business in the future, I won't spend much of my *rest-of-life* savings to do this. I'll be willing to risk some—just enough so that I won't ruin my life if I lose all of my investment. This is just my preference; you may wish to roll the dice. I'll look for businesses that require investment of my time, but not a lot of money. Working out of my home goes a long way to making this work. In addition, I don't need to make lots of money— just enough to supplement my Social Security and investment earnings.

There are plenty of service industries that provide these opportunities—training, education, health care, repair work, care for the elderly, just to name a few. A lot of these opportunities involve time—saving time for others or doing something that others don't have time for. One good way to find these opportunities is to look around our communities and see what needs servicing. Ask our friends and neighbors what services they would gladly pay for. Go to successful local businesses and ask if they are aware of their customers' needs that are not being met. If we have hobbies or interests with associated special interest groups, ask people in these groups for leads. Talk with other successful service business owners. See how they got started, and what are their challenges.

In my own circle of acquaintances, I know of several people who have been very creative with special service businesses, so I know it's possible. Here are some examples:

- A bicycle lover repairs bicycles in his garage. He also fixes seemingly hopeless bicycles that have been given to him, and he donates them to low-income families.

- An RV owner and former engineer visits with people who have recently purchased an RV, and helps them get set up with their new home.

- A former champion swimmer gives swimming lessons to children of affluent families in their own pools at home.

- An art lover has a studio at home, and gives art classes to young children.

- An avid fisherman takes people on fishing expeditions, using his knowledge of the local good spots.

- A childhood friend of mine who loves boats does "boat-sitting" for wealthy yacht owners who don't have time to look after their prize possessions.

- Avid windsurfers, baseball players, tennis players, golfers give lessons on . . . guess what?

- Hobbyists turn woodworking into businesses, making and selling furniture and crafts.

Some More Encouragement

If you're looking for work or self-employment income, *What Color Is Your Parachute?* (Ten Speed Press, 2003) by Richard Nelson Bolles is a great resource. It has tips and resources for the practical aspects of job-hunting or self-employment, and it lists helpful web sites. It has resume tips, practice for interviews, and advice on how to negotiate salaries. It also has great insights and exercises for finding our bliss (the book has a companion web site: www.JobHuntersBible.com).

Here's one enhancement of an idea featured in the Bolles book.

Persistence

The results of a successful job search could look like this:

> no no no maybe no no no we'll get back to you no no we'll see no no leave your resume no no no the job just got filled no no no you are very qualified but we have no openings now no no no yes but we only have openings 60 miles away no no no no no *this is getting discouraging* no no leave your resume no no no we'll call you if something comes up no no no *there must be something wrong with me* no no sixty people applied for one position no no no no *should I give up* no no no *this sucks* no no no no no no YES but the job is only for two days a week but it's a good start. Hooray!

Need I say more?

Reinventing Ourselves

Let's say we're 55, 60, or even 65, and we want to enter a new field. However, we don't have the necessary education, credentials, or certificates. Should our age hold us back from going back to school? We might think that this could take two to five years, and why should we do this at our age? Well, the time will pass regardless of whether we go back to school. In two, three, or five years, would we rather have our new credential or not? Do we have better things to do during this time? If we take care of ourselves and live vigorous, healthy lives until our eighties or nineties, we have time for a new 20-year career. There's plenty of time to get the necessary education and start over. Maybe we can do this while in our current position, if we cut back our hours so that we have time to go back to school.

Taking Inventory

An important part of working during *rest-of-life* is capitalizing on a lifetime of experience, skills, and contacts. It's very helpful to take inventory.

- What do we know? What technical knowledge and skills do we possess?
- Who are we? How do we get along with people?
- Who do we know? What contacts are valuable?
- What are our organizational and management skills? Can we get things done?

Which of these do we need to enhance to get the work we want? Again, the book *What Color is Your Parachute?* has great resources with more extensive worksheets on inventorying our skills and experience.

Define who we are and what we know, and then determine who we need to be and who we need to know. We've got plenty of time and patience.

Additional Resources

Just before my 50th birthday, I received an invitation in the mail to join AARP. My first reaction was, like hell, that's for old people. I wadded it up and threw it in the trash. A few months later I got another invitation. I cleverly told myself that I needed to join for researching my book, and sent in my $12.50.

Unfortunately the magazine doesn't come in a brown wrapper, so my mailman knows I belong. How embarrassing. And I sneak peeks at the organization's helpful web site, www.aarp.org, when nobody else is around.

But AARP is an invaluable resource. Its web site has lots of tips for finding work, and lists many links to job banks and other on-line job search resources. AARP is active in forming alliances with large employers to match members with jobs (Home Depot is a recent example). It sponsors the Senior Community Service Employment Program (SCSEP), and has chapters around the country. It gives annual awards to the Best Employers for Workers over 50. So swallow your pride and check it out.

The Great Oracle (Internet) is another valuable resource. One example of a good web site is the site of the Employment and Training Administration of the Department of Labor (www.doleta.gov). It has lots of information on the practical aspects of looking for work, and online links to job banks and other resources.

Remember, though, the Internet is great for obtaining *information*, but it is limited in its ability to actually land us work. To get to *yes*, you need to get face-to-face with contacts and prospective employers.

One More Suggestion

I haven't tried to duplicate the many valuable resources that help with making connections and developing our job-search skills. Instead, I've pointed you in the right direction. These three books are excellent resources:

- *What Color Is My Parachute?* (Ten Speed Press, 2003), by Richard Nelson Bolles.

- *LifeLaunch* (Hudson Institute Press, 1996), by Frederic M. Hudson and Pamela D. McLean.

- *Don't Stop the Career Clock* (Davies-Black Publishing, 1999), by Helen Harkness.

However, here's a practical suggestion. I won't underestimate the magnitude of the personal growth I am undertaking. At this age, I'm not too proud to seek help, and plenty of it. There are lots of other resources. If we work for a large employer, chances are good it sponsors an employee assistance program (EAP). These typically provide a handful of free visits with qualified counselors, to help with any personal problem. I've used these in the past with great success.

For much of our lives, we may have had very stable roles in our work or family situations. But when we're in transition, we'll feel uncomfortable and out of sorts. It helps to seek professionals and therapists who have seen these types of problems many times before.

The Power of Intent—Revisited

This refers to the end of Chapter 4.

Get up in the morning, look in the mirror, and tell myself:

■ I am successful at finding the work I seek.

■ I offer valuable skills.

■ Customers seek my useful services.

■ I recognize new opportunities when they arise.

■ I am open to different ways to find the work I seek.

Repeat as needed. Repeat as needed. Repeat as needed. Repeat as needed. Repeat as needed. Repeat as needed. Repeat as needed. Repeat as needed . . .

WRAP-UP

In the section on health, I made the point that investments of time and money in our health are as important as our investments in our 401(k) plans. Here I'll say the same thing. In our fifties and sixties, investing time, thought, and money in our avocation will be important for enjoying life in our sixties, seventies, eighties, and beyond. Such investments can include training and education, or just a lot of thinking and investigation. They can be just as important as our health investments and our investments in stocks and bonds.

Looking for work and reinventing ourselves takes time—lots of it! This is where our health weaves in: If we take care of ourselves, we'll live healthy, productive lives into our eighties, nineties, and beyond. We have plenty of time.

Here's one more personal story that gives a positive slant on this whole topic. As I'm writing this book, my son is graduating from college, and he's out on the job hunt. I'm giving him tips and insights, helping him think what to do, reviewing his resumes, talking about prospective employers, and rehearsing for interviews. Often I start a conversation with "If I were in your shoes, here's what I'd do." Then it occurs to me that I will be in his shoes someday, and what an advantage I have with my life's experience, contacts, and skills. Now I'm seeing my *rest-of-life* as similar to graduating from college—lots of potential—but with vastly more life experience.

This brings me to the main purpose of this chapter: motivation, disguised as practical guidance. I provide some suggestions for working during *rest-of-life*, plus real-life examples. This gives us confidence and understanding of what is possible. However, I don't intend for it to be a complete resource on finding work or creating self-employment. That's why I point you to additional resources.

It comes down to this. I'll decide what work I want and where I want it, and go after it. Then comes the hard part—following through and sticking with it!

Part of my quest involved listening to the life stories of people who have successfully worked during their later years. These stories, which you can find on my web site, www.restoflife.com, belie the popular image that productivity and fulfillment through work end with retirement. These people are into their second and third lives, and they are living examples of the Dalai Lama's advice about attitude being so important. Never once did I detect any bitterness at working during their *rest-of-life*, and in fact it was a basic part of their very being. And I'm amazed at their flexibility and resilience! They just keep on truckin', no matter what life dishes out. Their stories provide fascinating insights and motivation—don't miss them!

This ends our quest for *I* that we started back in Chapter 10. The next chapter turns to thoughts and strategies for the *E* part of the *I* > *E* formula.

Let's Spend Our Money!

I have enough money to last me the rest of my life, unless I buy something.

—Jackie Mason

n this section, I spend several chapters on generating *I*, and only this one on managing our *E*. However, this is not an indication of the relative importance of managing our *E* during our rest-of-life. It's just that for most of us, generating *I* that will last for our lifetime is a new skill, so we need to spend the necessary time to learn it. In contrast, most of us have plenty of experience at spending our money—in fact, too much experience!

In my own situation, I've always managed to spend most of what I earned. I suspect that I'm not different from most of you. I have used an effective strategy for saving for necessary things like my children's college education, large annual expenditures such as property taxes and car insurance, and my *rest-of-life* portfolio. I determined how much to save for these items, had them deducted automatically from my paycheck, and then felt okay about spending the rest. I figured that if I got into trouble financially, I could just cut back my spending for awhile and let future paychecks roll in and bail me out. As long as I have a steady income from wages, this strategy works okay.

No Steady Paycheck

The trouble comes when that steady paycheck is no longer steady.

When this happens, it's tempting to use what looks like large 401(k) balances to continue our spending habits. The money is there to spend, right? The trouble is, if we run into financial trouble, we won't have those future paychecks to bail us out. We'll need all of our 401(k) balances to generate I that lasts for the rest of our lives. Once I let this realization sink in, I knew I needed to change my spending habits.

By the time I was writing this chapter, I had already completed the research on happiness and fulfillment in life, as described in Chapters 3, 4, and 5. I realized that I have been spending too much money on the *pleasurable life*, and that puts me in a vicious circle. It forces me to keep working to support my spending habits. I work hard, so I convince myself that I deserve the *pleasurable life* as a just reward for my hard work, so I continue spending on the *pleasurable life*. However, when I thought about the activities that truly make me happy and fulfilled, I realized that they didn't involve a lot of money. I realized that I need *just enough* to meet my basic living needs and pursue the activities that provide meaning to me. True freedom comes when I have the time to pursue my interests and passions, and being more efficient with my spending habits is a small price to pay for this freedom.

So I set out on yet another quest to see how I could manage my E during my *rest-of-life*. My process for developing the ideas in this chapter was to do some research on the Internet, read some interesting books, and ask a number of older people how they make ends meet during their later years.

The successful agers confirmed what I just described—they found the sweet spot of spending *just enough* to lead a fulfilling life. Spend too little, particularly on our basic living needs, and we feel deprived. Spend too much, and at best we have this empty taste in our mouths that we wasted some of our money, and hence drained some of our life's energy. At worst, it creates fear that we might run out of money. *Just enough* has become my mantra, and it will be a recurring theme throughout this chapter.

There are plenty of resources and books on how to manage our spending, and I won't attempt to duplicate them here. Instead, I'll provide some different ways of looking at our expenses that are relevant for our *rest-of-life* and the themes in this book. Along the way, I'll also share some practical ideas. As has been my custom, I'll also identify resources that helped me.

The goal of this chapter is to help us balance our *E* with our *I*. We'll look at preparing budgets for our *rest-of-life*, so that we can address the *E* part of the *I > E* planning process. We'll explore ways to reduce our *E* without hurting our happiness and fulfillment. Actually, if we give some time and thought to our expenditures, we might increase our happiness and fulfillment while decreasing our *E*.

Before we turn to practical methods to manage our *E*, let's get some interesting insights on our *rest-of-life* expenditures.

Meditation on Money and Death

We can't get much more metaphysical than this!

Here's a thought exercise. Let's get comfortable, turn down the lights, make sure we have no distractions like the telephone. After we finish reading these instructions, put the book down and think about what we're about to read for at least five minutes. Jot down our thoughts, and share them later with our spouse or a close friend.

Imagine that we are 90 years old. We've taken care of ourselves, and we still feel pretty good. Sure, we're not as spry as when we were 70, but we still can move around, our mind is active, and we don't get sick that often. We have some aches and pains, but no chronic illnesses or debilitating conditions. We still have things we want to do. If we know anybody like this now, put ourselves in their position, based on what we've observed of them.

However, there's one problem. We depleted our 401(k) balance a few years back, and all we have now is our Social Security income. We're really struggling to make ends meet. We sold our house a few years ago, and are using the money to pay rent on a small apartment. We're imposing on our children or younger friends for help. We can't get around town without relying on somebody else for a ride, and we feel trapped. The world is getting narrower and narrower. It's affecting our health; we toss and turn at night, losing sleep. We can't afford as much fresh fruits and vegetables as before.

We cut back on our vitamins and supplements. We don't feel quite as energetic and vital as before. We wonder if it was worth it to take care of ourselves, and live this long.

We start thinking back on our expenditures in our sixties and seventies. Which expenditures still have meaning for us now, and which don't? The nice vacations. Some have fond memories, particularly the ones with our children and grandchildren. But the vacations where we sat in the sun in a tropical spot—that's another story. We wish we had the money now from those expensive vacations. What about our car? We wish we had cut back on this and bought the minimum necessary; it was just a means to get around. The club dues for our favorite hobby—that was money well spent. We had lots of fun, talking with friends who shared our interests. The dues weren't much money, either; we don't miss that money at all. The fancy clothes, watches, and jewelry. Bah, they don't mean anything now. We do just fine with a few basic outfits. What about the nice home decorations and remodeling? Our favorite 20-year-old chair and ottoman still work fine, but the other stuff doesn't mean much now.

The purpose of this exercise is *not* to get us fearful about spending money. No, it's just to encourage us to be thoughtful and deliberate about our expenditures. We no longer need to impress anybody but ourselves. What gives us meaning and purpose? What do we really need for our basic living necessities?

My goal is to spend *just enough* on my basic living needs, some on the *pleasurable life*, and then at that point shift my expenditures to the *good life* and *meaningful life*.

Just enough is a concept that we can apply to all of our expenditures. For each of us, *just enough* will be different. It's hard to tell anybody how much *just enough* is, and I certainly won't do it. This can seem very subjective, and it usually is. However, I do have one objective example.

There's a lot of consumer research on customer satisfaction with car purchases—*Consumer Reports* and surveys conducted by J. D. Power and Associates are two examples. We can compare customer satisfaction with certain base models to satisfaction with luxury cars that cost two to three times as much. The reported customer satisfaction with the luxury cars is only marginally greater than that of the less expensive cars, and it is never two or three times as much. There is diminishing return on the extra money spent on luxury features and gizmos such as automatic seats with memory, concert hall CD players, steering wheels that tilt seven ways, that extra 100 horsepower, and Global Positioning System (GPS) computers with a sexy woman's voice that tells us where to go.

Take Inventory

In Chapter 9, the following major categories of our spending were identified:

- Housing

- Food

- Transportation

- Utility bills

- Clothes

- Medical expenses

- Insurance

- Income taxes

- Children and grandchildren

- Leisure and recreation

- Donations and charity

- Miscellaneous supplies and stuff

I suggest that we take an inventory of what we spent on these items over the past year. I admit that some of us won't take the time to do this, but we might review the next few pages, take some ideas, and just wing it. Others of us will get quite focused about preparing this inventory.

Most of our expenditures will fall into one of six categories:

1. *Absolute bare living necessity* items.

2. *Living necessity items but I spent more than necessary*, for additional pleasure or comfort. Here I enter just the excess over

the absolute minimum, and enter my best guess on the minimum amount in the first category.

3. *Waste of money* items. These can be items that we think we need or want, but they are really a complete waste of money. Examples can include paying too much for a basic necessity, items that we could do or make ourselves, things we thought we needed but really didn't, and so on. As we go through this chapter, I'll identify a few common sources of wasted-money expenditures.

4. *Pleasurable life* item. Examples include any item or activity that goes beyond basic living necessities and is spent on the *pleasurable life*, as discussed in Chapter 3. This includes nice clothes that are more than *just enough*, car expenses more than *just enough*, vacations, entertainment, and so on.

5. *Good life* item. As discussed in Chapter 3, here we spend money on applying our strengths to work, love, and raising children. Examples of expenses can include work-related education and credentials for ourselves, money spent getting to and from work, money spent on our loved ones for support and gifts, college education for our children, and so on.

6. *Meaningful life* item. Here we spend money on causes and services greater than ourselves. Examples include donations to charity, money spent while giving our time and services to causes we believe in, and so on.

The goal of this exercise is to help differentiate our true needs versus our wants, and to distinguish expenses that provide meaning and fulfillment from expenses that don't. Most of us probably spend too much in the second, third, and fourth categories. Obviously, as much as possible we'll want to eliminate the "waste of money" category. Now don't get me wrong on the other items. I'm not advocating spending *nothing* on comfort and luxury items. If we have the resources to spend on these things, that's fine. The problem comes when we spend so much on these items that we don't spend enough on the *good life* and *meaningful life*, or if we are working so much to support our spending habits that we don't have time for the *good life* and the *meaningful life*.

For more insights and ideas on managing our expenditures, go to my web site, www.restoflife.com.

Now let's revisit each of these categories, with ideas for making our expenditures more effective and efficient during our *rest-of-life*. (Medical expenses are discussed in Chapters 7 and 8, not here.) These ideas may not be for everybody, but you'll start to get a feeling for what I mean by getting the most value from our expenditures.

Ideas for Managing Our Housing Costs and Living Situation

For many of us, our housing costs represent our largest single cost. The game is not an exclusive focus on reducing our costs, but getting the most value for our *rest-of-life*. Here is a good example of actions that we take in our fifties, sixties, and seventies that will affect our well-being and happiness in our seventies, eighties, and beyond. I advocate that we spend some time thinking about our housing situation, and act on our decision while we still can. Too often, I've seen people in their eighties or older who are stuck in an undesirable housing situation, because by then it's too difficult and stressful to move.

Do we move or not? That's the big question. There are pros and cons for both sides. Some people will want a smaller place, maybe even a different part of the country. Master-planned senior communities are springing up all over. And some people move abroad to take advantage of lower costs and fulfill their fantasies. All of these have their advantages, and if they appeal to you, I encourage you to do your research.

However, most older people tend to stay put. The census records show that about 60 percent of seniors who moved stayed in the same county, and 81 percent stayed in the same state. AARP conducted a survey in 2000 of people over age 55, and 81 percent stated a preference to stay in their current homes as long as possible.

There's a lot of value to staying where we've put down our roots. All of the advantages of moving might not compare to the value of the social network we have established. As we age, we'll be able to look out for each other if we stay in close proximity with our friends and family.

As we get older, proximity is very important—we might not want to or be able to drive long distances to see our friends and family. Some of us may want to keep the home in which we raised our families, for sentimental and emotional reasons, and to have room when they come to visit.

I intend to have a home where it's very easy to maintain current and new social relationships. In my case, I've bought a townhouse with plenty of recreational and social opportunities. It's close enough to my friends and family that I can see them often, and my day-to-day opportunities for social contact are abundant.

What are the downsides of staying put?

- A big house may become an albatross around our necks, with lots of time and money being spent on maintenance and utility bills for space that we don't need.

- We might need to tap the equity in our home to help generate I.

- We might be isolated. When we were younger, we got around by driving everywhere. When we don't want to drive as much, if we can't easily get to our friends and families, we become isolated. This is a big one for me. I've seen several older family members, huddled in the same big house and big yard. Opportunities for social contact are limited unless they make an effort to get out of the house, and the older they get, the harder this effort becomes.

After weighing some of the considerations, here's a list of ideas:

- Pay off the mortgage. Here's a great example of actions we take now that will pay off in our sixties, seventies, and beyond. One way to do this is to refinance with a 15-year fixed-rate mortgage. Another way is to simply pay more to principal each month; our mortgage companies can tell us how much to pay extra each month, such that the mortgage is paid in 15 years. Not only do we save a significant amount on interest costs over our *rest-of-life*, but once the mortgage is paid, our monthly E gets a lot lower.

- Move to a smaller house.

- Move to a less expensive area of the city, county, state, or country, or even abroad.

- Move into a large home with a group of friends. This is a great way to maintain social contacts and mutual support, and shave costs for housing and other living expenses. In our younger days, we called this a commune.

- Move into a condominium, townhouse, or other residential arrangement which shares insurance and maintenance costs, and provides opportunities for social contact and support.

- Rent out a room for extra *I* and companionship.

- Swap houses for vacations.

- House-sit for people on vacation.

- Be a live-in companion to an elderly person who needs basic living care.

- Move into a mobile home park, which is cheaper than regular housing and has plenty of opportunities for social contact.

By now you get the picture.

Here's an elaboration on the commune idea. Intentional communities are emerging as an alternative lifestyle. The basic idea is that a group of like-minded people band together to form a community, and share costs and donate time for running the community. In a prior era, we might have called it a tribe or a village. Many intentional communities share a common set of spiritual beliefs, or beliefs about lifestyles that are gentle on the planet. Many exist far from urban areas. One goal is to be as self-sufficient as possible. They might grow their own food, do their own repairs, and donate specialized skills and experience for commonly needed services, such as haircuts, financial matters, or education. The living costs can be quite low. I think that intentional communities might start expanding in number, location, and practices, as the baby boom generation ages and looks for creative living situations. We might see more in urban areas. It may be possible for a group of people who have nothing but Social Security income to band together for a less expensive but still fulfilling lifestyle, and I have an example of how this could work in Chapter 19. If you want to learn more, use your favorite Internet search engine and type in the words "intentional communities" or "cooperative living."

Ideas for Managing Food Costs

Here's another example of win-win. Fresh fruits and vegetables and whole grains are among the most healthy things we can eat and cost less than meat. Most meats are unhealthy when eaten in the quantities consumed by the average American. Per pound, fresh fruits and vegetables are also a winner in cost.

The same goes with processed foods. Compare the cost per pound of snacks, canned or frozen food, and other processed foods to fresh fruits and vegetables.

While we're talking about fresh fruits and vegetables, farmers' markets are springing up all around the country. I get most of my produce at these markets or at roadside stands. I pay less, get fresher fruit, make new friends with the proprietors, and have increased access to organic produce.

A growing trend is to subscribe to the produce from specific farms that will sell packages directly to consumers. This builds relationships between rural farmers and urban citizens. For more information, see the Community Alliance with Family Farmers (www.caff.org).

Another possibility is to form buying clubs. If we band together, we can buy large quantities at lower prices. This helps cut waste.

Finally, there's the old-fashioned garden and orchard. We get fresh produce, exercise, and assurance that it's organically grown. If we don't have a plot of land, we can explore a community garden, and make lots of friends in the process.

Ideas for Managing Transportation Costs

Here's where housing and transportation have some synergy. It's best to live close to most of our needs—shopping, friends and family, recreation, and medical care. The best situation is that these are a walk or bike ride away. Not only does this save a lot of money on car costs, but it helps keep us vital and healthy as well. Second best is a short walk to public transportation.

Here's another example of the value of *just enough*. Do we still need a fancy car that is never more than a few years old? My strategy is to buy a car model that has a great repair record, as measured by *Consumers Reports* and the J. D. Power survey, and then hold onto it for 10 years. I did a quick spreadsheet analysis and determined that, compared to trading in my car every five years, this strategy will save me from $25,000 to $50,000 over my *rest-of-life*. This alone buys me well over one year's worth of E, which translates to one year's worth of freedom.

To further reduce car expense, how about sharing one with friends and family? This works particularly well if we live in an intentional community as described earlier with housing. I've always wondered if this would work, as I observe with my older friends and family that their cars sit in the garage for long periods of time.

Ideas for Managing Utility Bills

Here's another reason to own a smaller house—it's cheaper to heat, cool, and water the lawn.

I'm also looking into ways to reduce my utility bills, through insulation, solar heating and electricity, and water-saving devices. Solar energy is finally becoming cost-effective, and innovative designs build it into roofing materials instead of ugly panels. If I can recoup my savings in 5 to 10 years with such an investment and I stay in the house for my *rest-of-life*, then I'm way ahead. These types of investments can be better than stocks and bonds and are yet another example of actions I take now that can pay off later.

Clothes

I've probably already ranted enough about clothes. Let me just say that I don't need as much clothing as I did when I was working and I had the money to spend. My goal is to wear out most of the clothes I have before buying new clothes. If I dig in the back of my closet, I often find stuff I haven't worn in years, and it still looks pretty good.

Now, if I go to a sale and I find something I really like at a really good price, I'll buy a few of them. I consider it a *rest-of-life* supply.

Spending *Just Enough* on Insurance

I believe many insurance policies sold are unnecessary or overkill. Many fall in the "waste of money" category, as identified in our inventory. One powerful reason for the overkill is that the people selling these policies, the insurance agents, usually have significant financial incentives to sell these policies. Their commissions can range from a few percentages of premiums to more than 10 percent. With these rewards, they devise very persuasive reasons to buy their products, and usually appear to be very trustworthy.

Before I go too far, let me say that I've also run into many agents who help me determine how much I really need, and direct me to the appropriate policies. After all, we do need some forms of insurance, and there are many honest and competent people in the business who aren't after *all* of our money. It's up to us to distinguish between the two.

First, let's take life insurance. Life insurance agents will gravely tell us that it's our duty to protect the ones we love. Well, yeah, that's right, but insurance isn't usually what's needed during our later years. We only need insurance when somebody depends on our income and financial support. This is necessary when we're raising a family and working for a living, and our death would cut off the future income stream. However, when the kids are on their own, the only one who needs our income is usually our spouse. In this case, we should ask if our death cuts off the future income stream. It doesn't with respect to 401(k) plan withdrawals. Our Social Security gets cut somewhat, but not by more than 33 percent. If we have income from a defined benefit plan, we can protect our spouse with a 100 percent joint and survivor form of payment.

Even if we need insurance, then we need to buy the right type. Term insurance has premiums that are usually far cheaper than whole-life or universal life insurance. This type of insurance is rarely a good deal.

Speaking of whole-life insurance, it's possible that you may have an old policy on which you've been paying premiums for a long time. In this case, you might have built up a large cash value. In many cases, it's a good deal to stop paying premiums and convert the policy to paid-up status. This means that the cash value pays for a reduced death benefit, but for the rest of your life. At this stage in life, the reduced benefit may be all that you need to protect your loved ones. So, this represents a chance to reduce your E without ruining your lifestyle.

Another possible use for the cash value is to convert it to an immediate annuity, to generate more *I*. In this case, if the cash value is large, I might also look at withdrawing the cash value altogether, and shop for an immediate annuity to get the best rate. Or I might just add the cash value to my investments and treat it like any other investment.

Chapter 8 discusses methods for buying medical insurance, and questions whether long-term care insurance is necessary. Careful selection of these policies will help keep our *E* to a reasonable level.

Another problem that Americans have is buying too much insurance. The original idea of insurance was to provide protection against truly catastrophic events, and not to pay for everyday expenses. I buy policies with the largest possible deductible for my car insurance and homeowners policies. Here's one way to analyze the savings: Look at the difference in premium between a policy with a $500 deductible and a $1,000 deductible. Often, this difference in premiums is a couple of hundred dollars. If I don't have a claim in two or three years, my savings in premiums exceeds $500, which is the difference in the deductible. I save the difference in premiums until it hits $500. This is a reserve for future claims. Then I've freed the future savings in premiums to spend on something else.

Speaking of car insurance, here's another reason to own a car for 10 years. Near the end, the insurance gets really cheap as the car's value declines. In fact, in the last year or two, I've found it's not worth it to insure for theft and collision. The premium savings are close to the worth of the car.

Finally, most of us need only basic medical, car, and homeowners insurance. We don't need flight insurance, cancer insurance, appliance insurance, pet insurance, insurance that pays our deductibles, and so on. If we are considering a purchase of insurance, we should ask ourselves two questions:

1. Am I covered for this event with my basic insurance? The answer is usually yes when it comes to flight insurance, cancer insurance, and so on, so these policies are unnecessary.

2. Would my life be ruined if the event occurs? While the answer might be yes if we are in a car accident or if our house

burns down, the answer is usually no if our appliances break down or if we need to pay the deductibles for our basic insurance.

Saving Money on Taxes

Paying too much taxes also falls in the "waste of money" category. Once we turn age 65, we get extra exemptions for our federal income taxes. Other than this break, there aren't many good strategies for reducing income taxes unless we have self-employment income.

The frustrating thing is that we still pay FICA taxes on our wages, even if we're collecting Social Security income and are eligible for Medicare benefits. If we work for a company or other employer, this amounts to 6.2 percent on our wages up to the Social Security Wage Base, which is $87,900 in 2004. We also pay 1.45 percent on all of our wages for Medicare. (Our employer pays this same amount.)

If we consider self-employment income to supplement our Social Security, 401(k) withdrawals, and pension, this gives us an opportunity for a number of creative income tax deductions that will reduce our taxes. Examples include transportation costs, supplies, and services. The distinction starts blurring between living expenses (usually not deductible) and working expenses (deductible). We can also set up our own retirement plan and make contributions to it, as described in Chapter 13. If we have substantial self-employment income, it pays to see an accountant who can help us determine what is appropriate.

However, if we're self-employed, the FICA tax can get worse. We pay both the employer and employee tax, for a total of 14.13 percent. We do get a deduction from our federal income taxes for part of our Social Security taxes, but we're still paying more than if we're working for somebody else. FICA taxes apply to our net income, which can be reduced for business expenses, so here's one way to reduce FICA taxes. If we have substantial self-employment income, it pays to see an accountant, who can help us find other ways to reduce our FICA taxes. These include converting some income to dividends, and using contributions to retirement and medical plans to convert taxable income to nontaxable benefits.

Here's one last idea. As we saw in Chapter 16, some states allow property tax deferral loans, which are one way to tap into the equity in our home to pay these taxes and reduce our E.

Children and Grandchildren

Here's another category where *just enough* is applicable. It's only natural to want to shower that cute baby with all kinds of stuff. However, I believe that sharing our time, life experiences, and wisdom are infinitely more valuable for both them and us. If and when I have grandchildren, I'll try to resist the urge to show my love by buying Gucci diapers, a Hummer stroller, Waterford crayons, a complete laptop computer system, and a Rolex baby watch. I hope that my children and grandchildren will have fond memories of the time we spend together, and the life experiences that I share with them.

Oh sure, I'll probably buy them some books, clothes, and stuff they need, but I'll be mindful about what is *just enough*.

College represents another huge cost for our children. I got quite intense about this and started saving when my kids were born. I didn't save enough to pay for all the expenses, but I'm very grateful for what I managed to save, because it was a lot less painful when the time came. We may also want to explore possibilities for financial aid and public colleges, which are a less costly than private colleges.

Leisure and Entertainment

Here's where we apply the lessons learned from Chapter 3, and distinguish among the *pleasurable life*, the *good life*, and the *meaningful life*. Time spent with friends and family need not be expensive, and the focus can be on being together, instead of on spending money.

Examples can include progressive dinners with friends, a dining club where a person or couple hosts a periodic dinner at their house, game night, video night, museum visits, and trips to places of natural beauty.

If I shift my focus from the *pleasurable life* to the *good life* and the *meaningful life*, I'll be spending less money on leisure and entertainment, with the goal of increasing my happiness at the same time.

Other Ideas for Managing Our *E*

Here I'll throw out a number of miscellaneous ideas for managing and reducing our *E*:

- Using the methods in this book, determine our *I* and think of it as our paycheck. In other words, there's nothing more than this to pay for our living expenses. Our 401(k) balance is not a source of paying for our *E*. It is a source of generating our *I*, and this is the source of paying for our *E*. The *I* becomes our paycheck, and we can't spend any more than our paycheck.

- I plan to set aside a permanent reserve for paying for unforeseen emergencies and other big-ticket items. Examples might include costs for nursing homes and future car purchases. I'll try to set aside $20,000 to $30,000 if I'm single, and $40,000 to $60,000 if I'm married, depending on my circumstances. This amount will grow with investment earnings, and I won't use it to generate *I* for my living expenses. Obviously, this is a subjective amount, and many of us won't be able to set aside this kind of money.

- As much as possible, I use cash or checking accounts for most of my purchases. I don't use credit cards very much, because it's easy to lose track and spend more than my *I*. This is an easy habit to fall into when we're working. If we spend too much money in a month, we can always cut back and let future paychecks bail us out. This won't work when the paychecks are no longer steady. When I use a credit card, I pay the balance each month, and don't let it accumulate.

- I don't go shopping for recreation. In fact, I don't shop much at all. I think many people go to malls and spend money just because they are there and have money in their pocket or room in their credit cards. If I need something, I pretend I'm on a mission to get the specific items and do so as quickly as possible. I admit that this strategy might not work for everybody. Here's yet another area where it's apparent that I'm just a guy!

- When I need something, I try hard to get it for less. I am always amazed at my savings when I shop around, search the Internet, and read consumer magazines. This is easier now that I have extra time.

- I take care of what I have. The most obvious examples are cars, appliances and home maintenance. Usually it costs far less to properly maintain these items than fix them when they are broken.

- I use things until they break or wear out. This applies to not only clothes, but to small appliances, tools, sporting equipment, and a whole host of stuff that we buy.

- Whenever possible, I buy on sale or get it used. Hooray for eBay and the local *Pennysaver*!

- An idea that I want to explore in the future is to put together buying and sharing clubs. A buy club will buy stuff in large quantities, to get lower prices. A share club buys and shares large-ticket items that might not be used frequently, such as lawn mowers, tools, sports equipment, and even cars. And in the process, I'll hang out a little more with my friends.

- I look forward to bartering and swapping services as another way to cut expenses and meet new people.

- I'll take advantage of my free time, and do stuff myself as much as possible.

- I'll take my leisure vacations at home. If I just want to spend time relaxing, reading books, and otherwise just hanging around, why go to the expense and stress of traveling somewhere else to do this? I'll arrange my immediate surroundings such that it is pleasant to do this.

What Does the Average American Spend?

The U.S. Department of Labor conducts periodic surveys of annual expenditures by Americans and provides various breakdowns of these expenditures by categories and by various demographic groups. This survey gives us some insights into what's possible with budgeting for E during our *rest-of-life*. If we can't do our own inventory, then we might use these numbers as guidelines.

For example, we see that in 2002, the average "consumer unit" (household) spent $40,677, broken down as shown:

Item	Average Expenditure in 2002
Food	$ 5,375
Housing	13,283
Clothes and services	1,749
Transportation	7,759
Health care	2,350
Entertainment	2,079
Personal care	526
Education	752
Contributions	1,277
Insurance and pensions	3,899
Alcohol and tobacco	696
Miscellaneous	932
Total	**$40,677**

Let's look at a breakdown from the lowest to the highest spenders. We'll just look at the totals; the breakdown by category is proportional, for the most part.

Group	Average Expenditures in 2002
Lowest 20% of spenders	$19,061
Second lowest 20%	$27,140
Middle 20%	$36,881
Second highest 20%	$50,432
Highest 20% of spenders	$79,199

Thus, a whole lot of people manage to make ends meet on $36,881 or less per year.

Now, let's look at the breakdown by age group:

Group	Average Expenditures in 2002
Age 55–64	$44,330
Age 65–74	$32,243
Age 75+	$23,759
All retired people	$27,535

Note that the people age 55 to 64 include many working people, while the category for people age 75 and over probably doesn't include very many workers.

Now, let's look at the breakdown by type of household:

Type of Household	Average Expenditure in 2002	Average Expenditure per Person
Single	$24,190	$24,190
Husband and wife	$45,557	$22,779
Five or more people	$55,501	$11,100

I included the last category to lend support to my commune idea.

Finally, let's look at the breakdown by geographic area:

Area	Average Expenditures in 2002
All urban	$41,600
All rural	$34,067
Northeast	$42,390
Midwest	$40,601
South	$37,281
West	$44,728

How do we compare to these averages now? How about when we're working much less?

WRAP-UP

I didn't intend for this to be a complete treatise on saving money with our expenditures for our *rest-of-life*. My goal is to provide ideas, tools, and information for balancing our E with our I in our later years. I focus on the larger costs, but there's a lot more that can be said on the subject. Here are a few resources that I have found helpful for managing my E:

- *Your Money or Your Life* (Penguin Books, 1999), by Joe Dominguez and Vicki Robin.

- *Consumer Reports* (see www.consumerreports.org).

- *The Complete Tightwad Gazette* (Villard Books, 1999), by Amy Dacyczyn, and the associated web site www.tightwad.com.

One idea I hope comes through loud and clear is that we don't necessarily need to support our current lifestyle during our *rest-of-life*. In fact, it might not be the most healthy lifestyle for us, both physically and emotionally.

I have been deeply influenced by Lynne Twist's book *The Soul of Money* (W.W. Norton & Company, 2003). She advocates that we use the flow of money through our lives to express our values, passions, and interests—who we are and what we stand for. We make powerful statements about these things through the choices we make when spending our money. My goal is to give us tools, information, and strategies that give us the freedom to make these statements.

Now, let's turn to putting together all of the ideas and information in this section on finances. The next two chapters show how we can make the $I > E$ methodology work to support our *rest-of-life*.

Answering the Three Big Questions—Examples, Tools, and Templates

Can I retire now?
When can I retire?
How much should I save?

—Average American

T his chapter brings it all together with respect to our finances, and making $I > E$ work for our *rest-of-life*. Chapters 10 through 17 cover strategies for generating I, and Chapter 18 discusses ideas for managing our E. Now, we'll look at examples, templates, and tools that put this all together to help answer the *three big questions*.

We'll go through several examples that show how to answer the three big questions. This is the best way to learn the methodology. I've purposely selected a variety of common circumstances, to illustrate what might happen with regard to when we can retire, or whether we should work part-time for awhile during our later years. I use statistics from Chapter 18 on average annual expenditures from the U.S. Department of Labor, and I also use representative 401(k) balances for people in their fifties and sixties. Some of the examples depart from these averages, but still are representative of circumstances that are common to many people. Maybe we'll see ourselves in some of these examples. They will reinforce some of the themes of the whole book, and I'll come back to this idea in the next chapter.

With this entire section on finance, my goal is to provide simple techniques that will help us put together a financial plan to get us in the ballpark. I truly believe in the KISS principle (keep it simple, stupid). I could have added refinements to the savings, withdrawal, and investment methodologies, but I believe that the extra complexities would not outweigh the benefits. Humans can be very flexible, so once we're in the ballpark, we can make minor adjustments to our *I* and *E* to support the life we want.

The *I* > *E* Methodology

This methodology is a process rather than a formula where we turn the crank and get simple answers. It will always have the following steps:

1. Select a target retirement age, either part-time or full-time (or one age for each).

2. Estimate our *I* at the target retirement age from existing resources. Include Social Security, income from existing retirement investments, wages, income from a defined benefit plan, if any, and any other assets.

3. Estimate our *E* at the target retirement age. The best way is to estimate our *E* now, and then adjust for inflation between now and the target retirement age.

4. If *I* > *E*, then we could be done, and we might not need to save any more.

5. If *E* > *I*, subtract *I* from *E* to determine our shortfall. Then, figure out how much total assets we will need at our target retirement age that will generate enough additional *I* to close this gap. Finally, estimate our annual savings amount that will accumulate this amount of assets.

In step 4, if *I* > *E*, we still might want to continue saving for the future. We should consider a number of factors, such as:

- The margin of *I* over *E*.

- Whether we are using the 401(k) Solution, which draws down principle, or the Income Solution, which is a little safer.

- How much control we have over our *E*—whether we expect high medical expenses, have paid off the mortgage in our house, and so on.

Now, I'll provide several examples to illustrate how this can work in different situations. I'll start with the simplest situations, and then provide examples that have more complicated life situations. Along the way, I'll introduce some tools and methods to help us.

To make these easy to read, for each example I highlight the assumptions and then the results of the analyses.

The first five examples illustrate the simplest situations, for single individuals and married couples with average account balances, at various ages, asking the question whether they can retire now.

TABLE 19.1 Can I Retire Now? Example #1: Assumptions

Situation	Single male, age 62
Current salary	$50,000, before taxes
Annual *E*	$30,000, not including income taxes—about average for a single or retired person
401(k) balance	$100,000—about average for someone my age
Defined benefit pension	None

After reading Chapter 10, I decide to use the Income Solution for withdrawing money from my 401(k) plan, and I will withdraw only 3 percent per year (see Table 19.1).

Let's look at the analysis in Table 19.2.

TABLE 19.2 Can I Retire Now? Example #1: Results of Analyses, Income Solution

Estimated annual Social Security	$14,400	Estimated using www.ssa.gov, consistent with Table 14.2
I from 401(k) balance	$ 3,000	Use Income Solution, which is 3%, or .03, times $100,000
Defined benefit pension	$ 0	
Part-time work	$ 0	
Total *I*	$17,400	
Total *E*	$30,000	

Answer: My *I* isn't even close to my *E*. It looks like the answer is "no way!"

Then I think, what about the 401(k) Solution? It generates higher *I*. I look at Table 10.2, and see that I might be able to withdraw 4³/₄% of my account balance at age 62, or .0475. In Table 19.3 let's see how this example works now.

TABLE 19.3   Can I Retire Now? Example #1—Continued: Results of Analyses, 401(k) Solution

Estimated annual Social Security	$14,400	Estimated using www.ssa.gov, consistent with Table 14.2
I from 401(k) balance	$ 4,750	Use 401(k) Solution, which is 4³/₄, or .0475, times $100,000
Defined benefit pension	$ 0	
Part-time work	$ 0	
Total *I*	$19,150	
Total *E*	$30,000	

Answer: My *I* still isn't even close to my *E*. The answer is still "no way!"

I'll need to keep working. However, this begs the question (see Table 19.4).

TABLE 19.4   How Much Do I Need in My 401(k) Plan to Be Able to Retire? Example #1—Continued: Results of Analyses, Income Solution

Estimated annual Social Security	$ 14,400	
Total *E*	$ 30,000	
Gap between Social Security and *E*	$ 15,600	
Amount of assets needed to generate $15,600	$520,000	For the Income Solution, divide $15,600 by 3%, or .03

Answer: I need $520,000 to generate *I* of $15,600, using the Income Solution. I have only $100,000!

How about the 401(k) Solution in Table 19.5?

TABLE 19.5   How Much Do I Need in My 401(k) Plan to Be Able to Retire?
Example #1—Continued: Results of Analyses, 401(k) Solution

Estimated annual Social Security	$ 14,400	
Total E	$ 30,000	
Gap between Social Security and E	$ 15,600	
Amount of assets needed to generate $15,600	$328,421	For the 401(k) Solution, divide $15,600 by $4^{3}/_{4}$%, or .0475

Answer: I need $328,421 to generate I of $15,600, using the 401(k) Solution. I have only $100,000!

Either way, that's a lot of money! And even with these amounts, they exactly balance my I and E—there's no margin for safety.

Can I Retire Now? Example #2

Let's assume the same facts as Example #1, only I'm age 65 instead of 62. My 401(k) balance is still $100,000. See Table 19.6.

TABLE 19.6   Example #2: Assumptions

Situation	Single male, age 65
Current salary	$50,000, before taxes
Annual E	$30,000, not including income taxes—about average for a single or retired person
401(k) balance	$100,000—about average for someone my age
Defined benefit pension	None

Let's look at the analysis in Table 19.7.

TABLE 19.7   Can I Retire Now? Example #2: Results of Analyses, Income Solution

Estimated annual Social Security	$19,200	Estimated using www.ssa.gov, consistent with Table 14.2.
I from 401(k) balance	$ 3,000	Use Income Solution, which is 3%, or .03, times $100,000
Defined benefit pension	$ 0	
Part-time work	$ 0	
Total I	$22,200	
Total E	$30,000	

Answer: My I isn't even close to my E. Once again, it looks like the answer is "no."

Once again I think, what about the 401(k) Solution? It generates higher *I*. I look at Table 10.2, and see that I might be able to withdraw 5 percent of my account balance at age 65, or .05. Let's see how this example works now in Table 19.8.

TABLE 19.8   Can I Retire Now? Example #2—Continued: Results of Analyses, 401(k) Solution

Estimated annual Social Security	$19,200	Estimated using www.ssa.gov, consistent with Table 14.2.
I from 401(k) balance	$ 5,000	Use 401(k) Solution, which is 5%, or .05, times $100,000
Defined benefit pension	$ 0	
Part-time work	$ 0	
Total *I*	$24,200	
Total *E*	$30,000	

Answer: I'm getting closer, but my *I* still isn't higher than my *E*. The answer is "not yet."

I'll need to keep working. However, once again I ask the question (see Table 19.9).

TABLE 19.9   How Much Do I Need in My 401(k) Plan to Be Able to Retire? Example #2—Continued: Results of Analyses, Income Solution

Estimated annual Social Security	$ 19,200	
Total *E*	$ 30,000	
Gap between Social Security and *E*	$ 10,800	
Amount of assets needed to generate $10,800	$360,000	For the Income Solution, divide $10,800 by 3%, or .03

Answer: I need $360,000 to generate *I* of $10,800, using the Income Solution. I have only $100,000!

How about the 401(k) Solution? See Table 19.10.

TABLE 19.10 How Much Do I Need in My 401(k) Plan to Be Able to Retire?
Example #2—Continued: Results of Analyses, 401(k) Solution

Estimated annual Social Security	$ 19,200	
Total E	$ 30,000	
Gap between Social Security and E	$ 10,800	
Amount of assets needed to generate $10,800	$216,000	For the 401(k) Solution, divide $10,800 by 5%, or .05

Answer: I need $216,000 to generate I of $10,800, using the 401(k) Solution. I have only $100,000!

This is still a lot of money!

Can I Retire Now? Example #3

For this example, let's keep using the same facts as Example #1, only I'm age 70 instead of 62. I still have $100,000 in my 401(k) plan. See Table 19.11.

TABLE 19.11 Example #3: Assumptions

Situation	Single male, age 70
Current salary	$50,000, before taxes
Annual E	$30,000, not including income taxes—about average for a single or retired person
401(k) balance	$100,000—about average for someone my age
Defined benefit pension	None

Can I retire now? Let's look at the analysis in Table 19.12.

TABLE 19.12 Can I Retire Now? Example #3: Results of Analyses, Income Solution

Estimated annual Social Security	$25,200	Estimated using www.ssa.gov, consistent with Table 14.2.
I from 401(k) balance	$ 3,000	Use Income Solution, which is 3%, or .03, times $100,000
Defined benefit pension	$ 0	
Part-time work	$ 0	
Total I	$28,200	
Total E	$30,000	

Answer: My I is getting very close to my E, but I'm not quite there yet.

What about the 401(k) Solution? I look at Table 10.2, and see that I might be able to withdraw 6 percent of my account balance at age 70, or .06. Let's see how this works in Table 19.13.

TABLE 19.13   Can I Retire Now? Example #3—Continued: Results of Analyses, 401(k) Solution

Estimated annual Social Security	$25,200	Estimated using www.ssa.gov, consistent with Table 14.2
I from 401(k) balance	$ 6,000	Use 401(k) Solution, which is 6%, or .06, times $100,000
Defined benefit pension	$ 0	
Part-time work	$ 0	
Total *I*	$31,200	
Total *E*	$30,000	
Answer: Finally, my *I* is higher than my *E*. Could the answer be "yes"?		

The margin of I over E is close, so I need to think about this a little. What about income taxes? There's an income threshold—$25,000 for a single person—for whether my Social Security benefits are included in my taxable income (see Table 19.14). My web site contains more details on this test.

TABLE 19.14   Example #3: Will My Social Security Benefits Be Taxed?

One-half of Social Security benefits	$12,600
All other taxable income	$ 6,000
Total	$18,600
Threshold for single person	$25,000
Conclusion: My Social Security benefits won't be included in my taxable income.	

Then I look at the federal income tax tables, and I see that my exemption is $5,900. I'll pay federal income taxes on only $100, so my federal income taxes are peanuts.

Even though my I and E are close, I decide to retire anyway. I can always find a little part-time work to give me some breathing room.

Let's go through the same exercise, only for a married couple.

Can We Retire Now? Example #4

Let's make the assumptions in Table 19.15 and then look at the analysis in Table 19.16.

TABLE 19.15   Example #4: Assumptions

Situation	Married couple, both age 62
Current salary	$50,000 each, before taxes (both have worked a full career)
Annual *E*	$42,000, not including income taxes—about average for a married couple
401(k) balance	$100,000 each in our 401(k) plans, somewhat below average for a married couple
Defined benefit pension	None

TABLE 19.16   Can We Retire Now? Example #4—Results of Analyses, Income Solution

Estimated Social Security for both of us combined	$28,800	Estimated using www.ssa.gov, for each of us as a single worker, consistent with Table 14.2
I from 401(k) balance	$ 6,000	Use Income Solution, which is 3%, or 0.3, times $200,000
Defined benefit pension	$ 0	
Part-time work	$ 0	
Total *I*	$34,800	
Total *E*	$42,000	

Answer: Our *I* isn't even close to our *E*. Once again, it looks like the answer is "no."

We think, what about the 401(k) Solution? It generates higher *I*. We look at Table 10.2, and see that we might be able to withdraw 4 percent of our account balances at age 62, or .04. Let's see how this example works now in Table 19.17.

TABLE 19.17 Can We Retire Now? Example #4—Continued: Results of Analyses, 401(k) Solution

Estimated annual Social Security for both of us combined	$28,800	Estimated using www.ssa.gov, consistent with Table 14.2
I from 401(k) balance	$ 8,000	For a married couple, 401(k) Solution shows 4% of $200,000
Defined benefit pension	$ 0	
Part-time work	$ 0	
Total *I*	$36,800	
Total *E*	$42,000	

Answer: We're getting closer, but our *I* still isn't higher than our *E*. The answer is "not yet."

We can't retire on this amount of income, so we'll need to keep working. Once again, we ask the question (see Table 19.18).

TABLE 19.18 How Much Do We Need in Our 401(k) Plans to Be Able to Retire? Example #4—Continued: Results of Analyses, Income Solution

Estimated annual Social Security for both of us combined	$ 28,800	
Total *E*	$ 42,000	
Gap between Social Security and *E*	$ 13,200	
Amount of assets needed to generate $13,200	$440,000	For the Income Solution, divide $13,200 by 3%, or .03

Answer: We need $440,000 to generate *I* of $13,200, using the Income Solution. We have only $200,000!

How about the 401(k) Solution? See Table 19.19.

TABLE 19.19 How Much Do We Need in Our 401(k) Plans to Be Able to Retire? Example #4—Continued: Results of Analyses, 401(k) Solution

Estimated annual Social Security for both of us combined	$ 28,800	
Total *E*	$ 42,000	
Gap between Social Security and *E*	$ 13,200	
Amount of assets needed to generate $13,200	$330,000	For the 401(k) Solution, divide $13,200 by 4%, or .04

Answer: We need $330,000 to generate *I* of $13,200, using the 401(k) Solution. We have only $200,000!

Once again, these examples illustrate that we need a lot of money to retire!

Can We Retire Now? Example #5

For this example, let's assume the same facts as Example #4, only we're both age 65 instead of 62. Our 401(k) balances total $200,000. See Table 19.20.

Let's look at the analysis in Table 19.21.

TABLE 19.20   Example #5: Assumptions

Situation	Married couple, both age 65
Current salary	$50,000 each, before taxes (both have worked a full career)
Annual E	$42,000, not including income taxes—about average for a married couple
401(k) balance	$100,000 each in our 401(k) plans, somewhat below average for a married couple
Defined benefit pension	None

TABLE 19.21   Can We Retire Now? Example #5: Results of Analyses, Income Solution

Estimated annual Social Security for both of us combined	$38,400	Estimated using www.ssa.gov, for each of us as a single worker, consistent with Table 14.2
I from 401(k) balance	$ 6,000	Use Income Solution, which is 3%, or .03, times $200,000
Defined benefit pension	$ 0	
Part-time work	$ 0	
Total I	$44,400	
Total E	$42,000	
Answer: Finally, our I is greater than our E. This looks good!		

We think, what about the 401(k) Solution? It generates higher *I*. We look at Table 10.2, and see that we can withdraw $4\frac{1}{4}$ percent of our account balances at age 65, or .0425. Let's see how this example works now in Table 19.22.

TABLE 19.22   Can We Retire Now? Example #5—Continued: Results of Analyses, 401(k) Solution

Estimated annual Social Security for both of us combined	$38,400	Estimated using www.ssa.gov, consistent with Table 14.2
I from 401(k) balance	$ 8,500	For a couple, 401(k) Solution shows $4\frac{1}{4}$% of $200,000
Defined benefit pension	$ 0	
Part-time work	$ 0	
Total *I*	$46,900	
Total *E*	$42,000	
Answer: So, it appears we can retire at age 65!		

As in Example #3, we wonder about income taxes. The income threshold is $32,000 for a married couple to determine whether our Social Security benefits are included in our taxable income(see Table 19.23). My web site contains more details on these calculations.

TABLE 19.23   Example #5: Will Our Social Security Benefits Be Taxed?

One-half of Social Security benefits	$19,200
All other taxable income	$ 8,500
Total	$27,700
Threshold	$32,000
Conclusion: Our Social Security benefits won't be included in our taxable income.	

Then we look at the federal income tax tables, and we see that our exemption is $11,400. So, we won't pay any income taxes on our 401(k) withdrawals.

We decide to go for it! We can always find a little part-time work to give us some breathing room.

Before we go on to some more complicated examples, I want to make some observations on the first five examples. In examples #3 and #5, we concluded that we could retire because finally our I exceeded our E. In reality, things could be different. We did not set aside any contingency reserve for emergencies; if we did this, we might not feel as comfortable with our situation regarding $I > E$. I'll add this complexity in the next examples.

For the following examples, I use a contingency reserve of $25,000 for a single person and $50,000 for a married couple. This is not an endorsement of these amounts as the appropriate contingency reserve. I used these amounts to show how to reflect them in our calculations. You might have higher or lower reserves. Possible uses for a contingency reserve include car purchase and repair, nursing homes, and unforeseen house repairs. The basic idea is to have an available stash to use for emergencies, so that we don't need to dip into our 401(k) balances, which are generating I that we need for living expenses.

Finally, we might be willing to adjust our E to enable us to retire. This is part of the bargaining that we will do with ourselves when we try to make the finances work for our *rest-of-life*.

Now let's look at some more complex examples.

Can I Retire Now? Example #6

For this example, let's make the assumptions in Table 19.24. Let's look at the analysis in Table 19.25.

TABLE 19.24 Example #6: Assumptions

Situation	Single female, age 70
Current salary	$50,000, before taxes
Annual E	$30,000, not including income taxes—above average for my age. Includes a 25% margin for error. Also, I've paid off the mortgage.
401(k) balance	$325,000—above average for someone my age. I'll set aside $25,000 for an emergency reserve, and base my analysis on $300,000.
Defined benefit pension	None

TABLE 19.25 Can I Retire Now? Example #6: Results of Analyses, Income Solution

Estimated annual Social Security	$24,000	Estimated using www.ssa.gov, consistent with Table 14.2
I from 401(k) balance	$ 9,000	Use Income Solution, which is 3%, or .03, times $300,000
Defined benefit pension	$ 0	
Part-time work	$ 0	
Total *I*	$33,000	
Total *E*	$30,000	
Answer: This looks pretty good.		

However, there is a minor complication. The minimum distribution rules discussed in Chapter 13 will require me to withdraw more than $9,000 per year from my 401(k) plan beginning at age 70$\frac{1}{2}$. I don't need it for living expenses, so I'll just make the minimum withdrawal, and invest the money I don't need in a regular taxable investment account. However, since I'm still withdrawing it from my 401(k) plan, I'll need to pay income taxes on it.

After thinking about it, I realize that my *I* still exceeds my *E* by a few thousand dollars. This is close, but I'm in the ballpark, so I can still retire. If necessary, I can always increase my withdrawals from my 401(k) plan, using the 401(k) Solution. I might do this to pay the additional income taxes, or for additional living expenses. If I used the 401(k) Solution at age 70, using Table 10.2, I see that I could withdraw 5$\frac{1}{4}$ percent of $300,000, or $15,750 per year. This would give me a very comfortable margin of *I* over my *E*. Also, this would comply with the minimum distribution rules.

I decide to go for it! However, I'll look for part-time work anyway, just to keep active and have social contacts. Because of my good financial situation, I can be picky about the type of work and the number of hours. I'll work on my terms!

How Much Should I Save? Example #7

Here's a simple example of estimating how much to save to generate additional *I*. Along the way, I'll introduce some tools we'll need to use.

Let's make the assumptions in Table 19.26.

TABLE 19.26   Example #7: Assumptions

Situation	Single male, age 55
401(k) balance	$125,000
Defined benefit pension	None
Target retirement age	65
Target retirement income in today's dollars	$15,000

I used the *I* > *E* process to determine that at age 65, I'll need to generate $15,000 of annual income to supplement Social Security, expressed in terms of today's dollars. I've already saved $125,000 in my 401(k) plan, which is close to the average 401(k) balance for people my age. I decide to set aside $25,000 for an emergency reserve, and use $100,000 for the basis of my projections.

How much should I save each year so that in 10 years, my total 401(k) balance will generate $15,000 in annual income, expressed in today's dollars? Before I do any math, I need to decide which method I will use to calculate my 401(k) withdrawals. After reading Chapter 10, I decide to use the 401(k) Solution. So, from Table 10.2, I estimate that I can withdraw 5 percent of my 401(k) balance, starting at age 65. For each year thereafter, I'll increase this withdrawal to cover inflation.

Now, here are the steps (see Table 19.27). As I promised, we'll use the new tools. For the moment, just trust me and follow along, and I'll explain them in more detail after the analyses.

TABLE 19.27   How Much Should I Save? Example #7: Results of Analyses

Adjust $15,000 target income for inflation for 10 years.	$ 20,100	Multiply $15,000 by 1.34, which is factor in the Investment and Inflation Rate Adjustor, as shown in Table 19.28. Use 3% as my guess for future inflation.
Project current 401(k) balance of $100,000 for investment earnings for 10 years.	$197,000	Multiply $100,000 by 1.97, which is factor in the Investment and Inflation Rate Adjustor. Use 7% assumption for investment earnings for 10 years.
How much *I* will this generate?	$ 9,850	Multiply $197,000 by my withdrawal percentage factor, 5%, or .05.
What is the gap in *I*?	$ 10,250	$20,100 minus $9,850.
How much extra do I need in my 401(k) to generate $10,250?	$205,000	Divide $10,250 by 5%, or .05.
How much do I need to save for 10 years to accumulate $205,000?	$14,216	Divide $205,000 by 14.42, factor in Savings Accumulator in Table 19.29. Use 7% assumption for investment return.

Answer: I need to save $14,216 per year to accumulate $205,000 in 10 years, assuming I earn 7% per year on my investments. However, my employer will provide a matching contribution of $4,000, so I only need to contribute $10,216 per year.

This is a lot of money, but I decide to increase my savings amount accordingly.

What's the Investment and Inflation Rate Adjustor? This is a technique for estimating the future value of something which grows at a specified rate. For inflation, typical rates that we assume are 2 percent, 3 percent, or 4 percent. In today's environment, I like using 3 percent. To adjust our current E for future inflation, pick an assumed inflation rate, pick the number of years we are projecting, and look up the factor in Table 19.28. Multiply this factor by our current E to get our future E, adjusted for inflation.

I go through the same process if I want to project my current 401(k) balance, using an assumed investment rate of return. My assumption on investment returns should reflect my expectations on my portfolio, given my asset allocation. Here are typical assumptions we might make for different asset allocations:

All bonds	5%
33% stocks, 67% bonds	6%
50% stocks, 50% bonds:	7%
67% stocks, 33% bonds	8%
All stocks:	9%, or 10% if we feel lucky

In the example, I assume an investment rate of 7 percent, which is appropriate for an asset allocation of 50 percent in stocks and 50 percent in bonds.

All right, then what is the Savings Accumulator?

These factors help us estimate the amount of current annual contributions we need to make to hit a target balance in our 401(k) plan. As with the Investment and Inflation Rate Adjustor, I need to make assumptions about my future investment rate of return, based on my asset allocation. I just look up the appropriate factor for this assumed rate of return and the number of years I will be saving.(See Table 19.29.)

The Investment and Inflation Rate Adjustor and the Savings Accumulator are examples of cool tools that we actuaries use every day. (Ain't it exciting? Now you know our secrets!)

FYI, for you actuaries and the financially curious, I assumed that we make contributions monthly. Here's an example of the KISS principle. I wouldn't make adjustments if we make contributions on some other frequency, such as bimonthly. It's just not worth the extra complication.

Now that I've introduced some basic tools, let's look at an example that gets a little more complicated. This will require introducing one more tool.

Table 19.28   Investment and Inflation Rate Adjustor

	Adjustment Factor for Rate of . . .								
Years	2%	3%	4%	5%	6%	7%	8%	9%	10%
1	1.02	1.03	1.04	1.05	1.06	1.07	1.08	1.09	1.10
2	1.04	1.06	1.08	1.10	1.12	1.14	1.17	1.19	1.21
3	1.06	1.09	1.12	1.16	1.19	1.23	1.26	1.30	1.33
4	1.08	1.13	1.17	1.22	1.26	1.31	1.36	1.41	1.46
5	1.10	1.16	1.22	1.28	1.34	1.40	1.47	1.54	1.61
6	1.13	1.19	1.27	1.34	1.42	1.50	1.59	1.68	1.77
7	1.15	1.23	1.32	1.41	1.50	1.61	1.71	1.83	1.95
8	1.17	1.27	1.37	1.48	1.59	1.72	1.85	1.99	2.14
9	1.20	1.30	1.42	1.55	1.69	1.84	2.00	2.17	2.36
10	1.22	1.34	1.48	1.63	1.79	1.97	2.16	2.37	2.59
11	1.24	1.38	1.54	1.71	1.90	2.10	2.33	2.58	2.85
12	1.27	1.43	1.60	1.80	2.01	2.25	2.52	2.81	3.14
13	1.29	1.47	1.67	1.89	2.13	2.41	2.72	3.07	3.45
14	1.32	1.51	1.73	1.98	2.26	2.58	2.94	3.34	3.80
15	1.35	1.56	1.80	2.08	2.40	2.76	3.17	3.64	4.18
16	1.37	1.60	1.87	2.18	2.54	2.95	3.43	3.97	4.59
17	1.40	1.65	1.95	2.29	2.69	3.16	3.70	4.33	5.05
18	1.43	1.70	2.03	2.41	2.85	3.38	4.00	4.72	5.56
19	1.46	1.75	2.11	2.53	3.03	3.62	4.32	5.14	6.12
20	1.49	1.81	2.19	2.65	3.21	3.87	4.66	5.60	6.73
21	1.52	1.86	2.28	2.79	3.40	4.14	5.03	6.11	7.40
22	1.55	1.92	2.37	2.93	3.60	4.43	5.44	6.66	8.14
23	1.58	1.97	2.46	3.07	3.82	4.74	5.87	7.26	8.95
24	1.61	2.03	2.56	3.23	4.05	5.07	6.34	7.91	9.85
25	1.64	2.09	2.67	3.39	4.29	5.43	6.85	8.62	10.83

Table 19.29   The Savings Accumulator

	Factor for Rate of . . .								
Years	2%	3%	4%	5%	6%	7%	8%	9%	10%
1	1.01	1.01	1.02	1.02	1.03	1.03	1.04	1.04	1.05
2	2.04	2.06	2.08	2.10	2.12	2.14	2.16	2.18	2.20
3	3.09	3.13	3.18	3.23	3.28	3.33	3.38	3.43	3.48
4	4.16	4.24	4.33	4.42	4.51	4.60	4.69	4.79	4.89
5	5.25	5.39	5.52	5.66	5.81	5.96	6.12	6.28	6.45
6	6.37	6.56	6.77	6.98	7.20	7.43	7.67	7.91	8.17
7	7.50	7.78	8.06	8.36	8.67	9.00	9.34	9.70	10.08
8	8.66	9.03	9.41	9.81	10.23	10.68	11.15	11.65	12.18
9	9.85	10.31	10.81	11.33	11.89	12.48	13.11	13.78	14.50
10	11.06	11.64	12.27	12.94	13.65	14.42	15.24	16.12	17.06
11	12.29	13.01	13.78	14.62	15.52	16.49	17.54	18.67	19.90
12	13.54	14.42	15.36	16.39	17.51	18.72	20.03	21.47	23.06
13	14.83	15.87	17.01	18.25	19.61	21.10	22.73	24.52	26.49
14	16.13	17.37	18.72	20.21	21.85	23.66	25.66	27.87	30.31
15	17.47	18.91	20.50	22.27	24.23	26.40	28.82	31.52	34.53
16	18.83	20.50	22.35	24.43	26.75	29.34	32.25	35.52	39.19
17	20.22	22.13	24.28	26.70	29.42	32.50	35.97	39.89	44.34
18	21.64	23.82	26.29	29.09	32.27	35.88	39.99	44.68	50.03
19	23.08	25.56	28.38	31.60	35.28	39.51	44.35	49.91	56.31
20	24.56	27.35	30.55	34.24	38.49	43.39	49.07	55.63	63.26
21	26.06	29.19	32.82	37.01	41.89	47.56	54.17	61.90	70.93
22	27.60	31.09	35.17	39.93	45.50	52.03	59.71	68.74	79.40
23	29.16	33.05	37.62	43.00	49.33	58.83	65.70	76.23	88.76
24	30.76	35.07	40.17	46.22	53.40	61.97	72.19	84.43	99.10
25	32.39	37.15	42.83	49.61	57.73	67.48	79.22	93.39	110.53

Can I Retire Now? Example #8

This example introduces a good complication—income from a defined benefit plan. As we shall see, this is well worth the trouble, as these benefits make it possible to retire full-time. For this example, let's suppose the facts in Table 19.30.

TABLE 19.30 Example #8: Assumptions

Situation	Married couple, both age 65, which is also our Social Security normal retirement age (NRA).
Current salary	$90,000 per year before taxes for primary wage earner; the other one of us has worked sporadically until recently.
Annual E	$50,000, not including income taxes—above average for our age. Includes a 25% margin for error. Includes mortgage payment, which will continue for many years.
Combined 401(k) balances	$350,000—above average for people our age. We'll set aside $50,000 for an emergency reserve, and base our analysis on $300,000.
Defined benefit pension	$12,000 per year, using 100% joint and survivor form of payment. Estimated using company's online calculator.

Can we retire now?

After reading Chapter 10, we decide to use the 401(k) Solution for withdrawing money from our 401(k) plans, and we will withdraw $4^1/_4$ percent per year, using Table 10.2. Let's see how the analysis looks in Table 19.31.

TABLE 19.31 Can We Retire Now? Example #8: Results of Analyses, 401(k) Solution

Estimated annual Social Security	$36,000	Use calculator at www.ssa.gov, consistent with Table 14.6. Includes special spouse benefit.
I from 401(k) balance	$12,750	Use 401(k) Solution, which is $4^1/_4$%, or .0425, times $300,000.
Defined benefit pension	$12,000	
Part-time work	$ 0	
Total I	$60,750	
Total E	$50,000	
Answer: This looks pretty good. Can we retire?		

Not so fast. We forgot that the $12,000 pension from our defined benefit plan is fixed, and isn't increased for inflation. We're grateful that Social Security and the 401(k) Solution provide for inflation increases.

This brings us to our next tool, the Inflation Adjustor (Table 19.32). The Inflation Adjustor tells us how much money to set aside so that we can provide inflation increases on a fixed monthly income, either from a defined benefit plan or a fixed life annuity from an insurance company. As with everything else, the result is an estimate.

TABLE 19.32   The Inflation Adjustor

Age	Single Male	Single Female	Married Couple, Same Age
55	4.65	5.57	6.47
56	4.45	5.36	6.25
57	4.25	5.15	6.04
58	4.06	4.94	5.82
59	3.86	4.74	5.60
60	3.68	4.53	5.39
61	3.49	4.33	5.17
62	3.31	4.13	4.96
63	3.13	3.94	4.74
64	2.96	3.75	4.53
65	2.79	3.56	4.32
66	2.63	3.37	4.11
67	2.47	3.19	3.90
68	2.32	3.01	3.70
69	2.17	2.94	3.50
70	2.03	2.67	3.31
71	1.89	2.50	3.11
72	1.76	2.34	2.93
73	1.63	2.18	2.74
74	1.51	2.03	2.56
75	1.39	1.88	2.39

Table 19.33 shows how it works.

TABLE 19.33   Example #8—Continued: Adjust Withdrawal Strategy from 401(k) Plan, to Have Reserve for Providing Increases for Inflation on Fixed Pension

Amount of fixed pension	$ 12,000	
Reserve needed to provide increases for inflation on $12,000	$ 51,840	Multiply $12,000 by 4.32, factor in Table 19.32, the Inflation Adjustor.
Adjusted 401(k) account balance	$250,000	Subtract $51,840 from $300,000, and round to $250,000 to make calculations easy.
I generated from adjusted 401(k) balance	$ 10,625	Multiply $250,000 by .0425, factor for the 401(k) Solution.

Now let's look again at the question (see Table 19.34).

TABLE 19.34   Can We Retire Now? Example #8—Continued: Results of Analyses

Estimated annual Social Security	$36,000	Includes special spouse benefit
I from 401(k) balance	$10,625	As calculated in Table 19.33
Defined benefit pension	$12,000	
Part-time work	$ 0	
Total I	$58,625	
Total E	$50,000	
Answer: This looks pretty good. Can we retire?		

While this result looks like it is greater than our E, we need to consider that we'll pay income taxes on the pension, 401(k) withdrawals, and part of our Social Security benefits.

Let's take a look.

The first step is to see if this extra income will put us over the limit for taxing Social Security benefits. We do the calculation in Table 19.35. My web site contains details on these results.

TABLE 19.35   Example #8: Will Our Social Security Benefits Be Taxed?

One-half of Social Security benefits	$18,000
401(k) withdrawal	$10,625
Pension	$12,000
Total	$40,625
Threshold for married couple	$32,000
Conclusion: I must include $4,313 in my taxable income. This is half of $8,625, which is $40,625 minus the threshold of $32,000.	

Now, what taxes will we pay on our earnings, our 401(k) withdrawals, and part of our Social Security benefits? See Table 19.36.

TABLE 19.36   Example #8: How Much Income Taxes Will We Pay?

Taxable portion of Social Security	$ 4,313
401(k) withdrawal	$10,625
Pension	$12,000
Total	$26,938
Federal income taxes	$ 1,600

Conclusion: We must add $1,600 to our *E*, as well as our estimate for state income taxes, which is $400.

We estimated the $1,600 amount for federal income taxes, using standard deductions for a couple age 65.

Our *E* is now $52,000 ($50,000 plus $2,000 for federal and state income taxes). This is less than our *I* of $58,625. We conclude that we can retire. This is close enough so that we'll look for ways to decrease our *E*, or at least contain increases due to inflation.

There's one more thing to watch out for. Once we turn age $70\frac{1}{2}$, we must start taking minimum distributions from our 401(k) balance. If we needed to do this at age 65, our withdrawal of $10,625 would not be enough. We will be increasing this for inflation, so we might be close to making our minimum distribution at age $70\frac{1}{2}$. If we need to withdraw more from our 401(k) plans than we need for living expenses, we'll simply make the minimum withdrawal, and invest the money that we don't need in a regular taxable savings account.

Whew! Now we're getting complicated. Let's make two observations:

1. Notice that the existence of income from a defined benefit plan made all the difference between being able to retire or not. Thanks to my employer for sponsoring this plan!

2. At higher income levels, we need to start paying attention to income taxes on our Social Security benefits.

Note on the Inflation Adjustor: For those of you who are actuaries, or if you just want to know, I assumed that inflation would average 3 percent per year during our *rest-of-life*. The columns for single males and single females represent the reserve needed for a single life annuity. The column for the married couple represents the reserve needed for a 100 percent joint and survivor annuity.

Can I Retire Now? Example #9

With this example, we explore working for awhile during Stage 1 of *rest-of-life* work, and how to prepare for Stage 2 when we stop working completely. I will introduce a new technique to handle this situation.

Let's assume the facts in Table 19.37.

TABLE 19.37　Example #9: Assumptions

Situation	Single female, age 66, which is my Social Security normal retirement age (NRA).
Current salary	$50,000 per year before taxes.
Annual E	$30,000, not including income taxes—slightly above average for my age. Includes a 25% margin for error. Includes mortgage payment, which will continue for many years.
401(k) balance.	$225,000—above average for my age. I'll set aside $25,000 for an emergency reserve, and base my analysis on $200,000.
Defined benefit pension	None.

I will use the 401(k) Solution for withdrawing money from my 401(k) plan. Using Table 10.2, I decide to withdraw $4^3/_4$ percent from my 401(k) balance. Let's see how the analysis looks in Table 19.38.

TABLE 19.38　Can I Retire Now? Example #9: Results of Analyses, 401(k) Solution

Estimated annual Social Security	$18,000	Estimated using calculator at www.ssa.gov, consistent with Table 14.2
I from 401(k) balance	$ 9,500	Use 401(k) Solution, which is $4^3/_4$%, or .0475, times $200,000
Defined benefit pension	$　0	
Part-time work	$　0	
Total I	$27,500	
Total E	$30,000	

Answer: This doesn't look good. Maybe if I work a little I can make it happen.

I figure I can continue working and make about $12,000 per year, or about $1,000 per month. When added to my previously calculated *I* of $27,500, I'll have a total of $39,500, greater than my *E* of $30,000. Am I okay?

Well, not so fast. There are a few more things to consider. How much will I net from my $12,000 in wages, after considering taxes? The first step is to see if this extra income will put me over the limit for taxing Social Security benefits. I do the calculation in Table 19.39. See my web site for details on these rules.

TABLE 19.39   Example #9: Will My Social Security Benefits Be Taxed?

One-half of Social Security benefits	$ 9,000
401(k) withdrawal	$ 9,500
Wages	$12,000
Total	$30,500
Threshold for single person	$25,000

Conclusion: I must include $2,750 in my taxable income. This is half of $5,500, which is $30,500 minus the threshold of $25,000.

Now, what taxes will I pay on my wages, my 401(k) withdrawals, and part of my Social Security benefits? (See Table 19.40.)

TABLE 19.40   Example #9: How Much Income Taxes Will I Pay?

Taxable portion of Social Security	$ 2,750
401(k) withdrawal	$ 9,500
Wages	$12,000
Total	$24,250
Federal income taxes	$ 2,400

Conclusion: We must add $2,400 to our *E*, as well as our estimate for state income taxes, which is $700.

I estimated the $2,400 amount for federal income taxes, using standard deductions for a single person age 66. (By the way, I'm paying income taxes at a higher rate than the previous example. This illustrates the difference between tax rates for a single person and a married couple.)

I'm not yet done! I still need to pay FICA taxes on my wages of $12,000. I multiply $12,000 by 7.65 percent, or .0765. The result is $918, as my estimate of FICA taxes.

My E is now $34,018 ($30,000 + $2,400 + $700 + $918). This is less than my I of $39,500.

Am I safe now? Not yet; there are two problems.

First, most likely my E will increase with inflation. Therefore, I need to assume that my wages will keep pace. For the moment, I assume that my salary will be increased to keep up with inflation. It not, maybe I'll work extra hours to keep my I from falling below my E, or look for ways to contain inflation increases in my E.

The second problem is that when I get much older, I might not be able to work enough to earn wages equal to $12,000, or its equivalent adjusted for inflation. I figure that I can work until age 75, and then I'll quit working altogether. How do I reflect this in my planning?

I need to calculate the value of my investments to set aside now, such that I can generate an extra $12,000 income at age 75, adjusted for inflation, to replace my wages when I retire full-time. Note that when I did the previous calculations, my I exceeded my E by a good margin, so I didn't need the full $12,000 in wages. So, I might not worry too much about losing these wages if I reduce my E when I stop working. However, let's assume that I will get accustomed to spending the extra $12,000, to illustrate how to use the Wage Replacement Maneuver. Here's how this works:

The Wage Replacement Maneuver

1. Determine the age at which I expect to retire full-time. In this case, it's age 75.

2. Determine the amount of wages that I need to replace, in today's dollars. In this case, it's $12,000.

3. Estimate how much $12,000 will increase for nine years, due to inflation. To do this, I assume inflation will be 3 percent per year. I look up the appropriate factor in Table 19.28 for nine years, which is 1.30. I multiply this by $12,000, for a result of $15,600. This is the amount of income I need at age 75, which will buy the same amount as $12,000 today.

4. Determine my withdrawal percentage using the 401(k) Solution from Table 10.2. In this case, it's $6^1/_4$ percent at age 75.

5. Divide the result of step 3 by the withdrawal percentage. This is $15,600 divided by .0625, and results in $249,600. This is the amount I need to have in my 401(k) plan at age 75 to generate $15,600 in income at that age—*in addition* to the income I am generating from my current 401(k) balance.

This last result, $249,600, is greater than my 401(k) balance! I can't possibly save this amount of money during the next nine years. I conclude that I can't retire yet.

Since I can't yet retire, the next big question is . . .

When Can I Retire? Example #9—Continued

Let's continue with this same example, using the same assumptions.

I decide to see if I can retire at age 70. To make the calculations realistic, I'll need to adjust for inflation between now and age 70.

I'll also need to estimate my 401(k) balance to reflect earnings growth for four years, using the Investment and Inflation Rate Adjustor in Table 19.28. I assume my account will grow at 7 percent per year, since my asset allocation is 50–50 in stocks and bonds. So, the appropriate factor for four years is 1.31. I'll multiply $200,000 by 1.31 for a result of $262,000.

Let's see how the analysis looks in Table 19.41.

TABLE 19.41   Can I Retire at Age 70? Example #9—Continued: Results of Analyses, 401(k) Solution

Estimated annual Social Security	$27,350	Estimated using calculator at www.ssa.gov, using inflation increases of 3% per year until age 70.
I from 401(k) balance	$13,755	From Table 10.2, 401(k) Solution factor at age 70 is $5^{1}/_{4}$%, or .0525. Multiply by $262,000.
Defined benefit pension	$ 0	
Part-time work	$ 0	
Total *I*	$41,105	
Total *E*	$33,900	Adjust for inflation. Multiply $30,000 by 1.13, factor in Table 19.28 assuming 3% inflation for four years.

Answer: What a difference waiting four years makes!

I conclude that I will work until age 70. Also, the analysis assumes that I don't make any more contributions to my 401(k) plan. In reality, I'll make some more contributions, which will add a little more *I* when I retire. I'll also look for ways to reduce my *E* over the next few years. Now I have a plan!

When Can We Retire? Example #10

In previous examples, we didn't make any reductions for possible future cutbacks in Social Security benefits. This example adds this complexity, using a younger couple.

We decide to accelerate our mortgage payments, as discussed in Chapter 18, so we can pay off our mortgage by age 65. This brings our *E* down to $38,000 per year, slightly below average for a married couple.

Let's assume the facts in Table 19.42.

TABLE 19.42   Example #10: Assumptions

Situation	Married couple, both age 55.
Current salary	We each make $60,000 per year before taxes, and have worked full careers.
Annual *E*	$38,000, not including income taxes. Includes a 25% margin for error.
Combined 401(k) balances	$200,000—about average for two people our age. We'll set aside $50,000 for an emergency reserve, and base our analysis on $150,000.
Defined benefit pension	None.

When can we retire? We decide to look at whether we can retire at age 66, our Social Security normal retirement age (NRA).

We use the Investment and Inflation Rate Adjustor to project our 401(k) balances to age 66, which is 11 years away. We assume our account balances will earn 7 percent per year, since our asset allocation is 50–50 in stocks and bonds. The factor from Table 19.28 is 2.10. Multiply this factor by $150,000, and we have a result of $315,000. This reflects the growth in our 401(k) balance at a rate of 7 percent per year.

We decide to reduce our estimated Social Security benefits by 15 percent, to reflect possible future reductions in Social Security. Note that there is no science to the 15 percent reduction for future Social Security benefits—it's just our best guess.

After reading Chapter 10, we decide to use the Income Solution, just to be safe.

Let's take a look at the analysis in Table 19.43.

TABLE 19.43   Can We Retire at Age 66? Example #10: Results of Analyses, Income Solution

Estimated annual Social Security, before adjustment for future reductions	$57,600	Estimated using calculator at www.ssa.gov, as if we were single workers, reflecting that both of us have worked for a whole career. Assume our benefits increase by 3% per year for inflation.
Adjust for possible future benefit reductions	$48,960	Multiply by .85 to reflect 15% reduction.
I from 401(k) balance	$ 9,450	Use Income Solution, which is 3%, or .03, times projected 401(k) balance of $315,000.
Defined benefit pension	$ 0	
Part-time work	$ 0	
Total *I*	$58,410	
Total *E*	$52,440	Increase our estimated *E* for inflation between now and age 66. Assuming a rate of 3% per year, Table 19.28 provides a factor of 1.38. Multiply this factor by $38,000 for a result of $52,440.

Answer: If we add income taxes to $52,440, our *I* and *E* are pretty close.

We conclude that we could retire full-time by age 66, even without making any future contributions to our 401(k) plans. This example shows that if a married couple works all their lives, gets double Social Security benefits at the normal retirement age (NRA), and pays off the mortgage by the time they retire, it doesn't take a lot of additional income provided they manage their *E* carefully.

We're emboldened by this calculation. If we make additional contributions to our 401(k) plan, can we retire earlier, say at age 62? Here are the calculations.

We use the Investment and Inflation Rate Adjustor to project our 401(k) balances to age 62, which is seven years away. The factor from Table 19.28 is 1.61. We multiply this amount by $150,000, and we have a result of $241,500. This reflects the growth in our 401(k) balance, if it earns 7 percent per year.

Once again, we decide to use the Income Solution, just to be safe. See Table 19.44.

TABLE 19.44 Can We Retire at Age 62? Example #10—Continued: Results of Analyses, Income Solution

Estimated annual Social Security, before adjustment for future reductions	$38,400	Estimated using calculator at www.ssa.gov, as if we were single workers, reflecting that both of us have worked for a whole career. Assume our benefits increase by 3% per year for inflation.
Adjust for possible future benefit reductions	$32,640	Multiply by .85 to reflect 15% reduction.
I from 401(k) balance	$ 7,245	Use Income Solution, which is 3%, or .03, times $241,500.
Defined benefit pension	$ 0	
Part-time work	0	
Total *I*	$39,885	
Total *E*	$46,740	Increase our estimated *E* for inflation between now and age 62. Assuming a rate of 3% per year, Table 19.28 provides a factor of 1.23. Multiply this factor by $38,000 for a result of $46,740.

Answer: Our estimated *I* falls short of our estimated *E* by $6,855.

We need to save enough additional money in our 401(k) plan to generate an additional annual *I* of $6,855 at age 62. To make the calculations simple, let's just round this to $7,000. The analyses in Table 19.45 show that we need to save $25,926 per year.

TABLE 19.45   How Much Do We Need to Save to Retire at Age 62?
Example #10—Continued: Results of Analyses

Estimated 401(k) balance needed at age 62 to generate $7,000 of /	$233,333	Divide $7,000 by 3%, or .03. What a difference four years makes!
Annual savings amount needed to accumulate $233,333 in 7 years	$ 25,926	Divide $233,333 by the factor from the Savings Accumulator, from Table 19.29. Assuming our investments will earn 7% per year, the factor is 9.00.

Answer: Between both of us, we need to save a combined $25,926 each year for seven years.

Theoretically, we could each contribute up to $18,000 in 2005 and $20,000 in 2006 and thereafter, if we consider the catch-up contribution limit in our 401(k) plan. If we each save up to these limits, we would exceed the required $25,926 per year. However, we can't afford to save these amounts. We can each afford to save $6,000 per year, and we each get a matching contribution of $3,000 per year from our respective employers. Adding this all up results in a total annual contribution of $18,000 per year.

So, we decide that full-time retirement at age 62 is unrealistic. However, working full-time until age 66 seems like forever. What can we do?

We decide to work full-time until age 60, and then work part-time until age 66. We will defer receiving our Social Security benefits until then, in order to make these benefits as big as possible. We will each save $6,000 per year while we are working full-time, until age 60. Then, we'll stop saving, but we won't withdraw anything from our 401(k) plans until age 66. We remember that our existing 401(k) balances were sufficient at age 66, so the additional contributions we make from age 55 to 60 will only make it better. We decide to work part-time from age 60 to age 66, and work enough to cover our living expenses during that period. However, we won't be adding to or withdrawing from our 401(k) balances during this time.

Now we have a plan!

Making *Rest-of-Life* Work—Example #11

Here, let's demonstrate a technique that I'll call the *Rest-of-Life* Three-Step. We use this when we have a Stage 1 of our *rest-of-life*, where we work part-time while supplementing our wages with our financial resources. During Stage 2, we retire full-time and live entirely on our financial resources.

Our three steps are:

Step 1. Work part-time until age 70 to cover our living expenses, and delay starting our Social Security benefits so that they are maximized. During this period, we won't withdraw anything from our 401(k) balances. This is the first part of our Stage 1 of *rest-of-life*.

Step 2. From age 70 to 75, we'll cut back our working hours further and begin withdrawals from our 401(k) plan to supplement the reduced wages. We will use the Income Solution to calculate how much to withdraw. This is the second part of our Stage 1 of *rest-of-life*.

Step 3. We stop working entirely at age 75. We boost our income from our financial resources by using the 401(k) Solution to calculate how much to withdraw. This is Stage 2 of our *rest-of-life*.

Let's suppose the facts in Table 19.46.

TABLE 19.46   Example #11: Assumptions

Situation	Married couple, both 66, our Social Security NRA.
Current salary	We each make $50,000 per year before taxes, and have worked full careers.
Annual *E*	$50,000, not including income taxes. Includes a 25% margin for error.
Combined 401(k) balances	$250,000—above average for two people our age. We'll set aside $50,000 for an emergency reserve, and base our analysis on $200,000.
Defined benefit pension	None.

We both decide to work just enough between ages 66 and 70 to cover our living expenses of $50,000 per year. This lets our 401(k) balance grow until age 70, when we start our withdrawals. However, we stop making any additional contributions now.

The first question is: Will we have enough to retire part-time at age 70?

We'll use the Income Solution to calculate our withdrawals from our 401(k) plans. First, we need to project our 401(k) balance to age 70, using the Investment and Inflation Rate Adjustor. From Table 19.28, we see the factor for four years is 1.31 if we assume a rate of return of 7 percent per year, which is appropriate for a portfolio invested 50–50 in stocks and bonds. We multiply this factor by $200,000, for a result of $262,000.

Now, we can answer the question (See Table 19.47).

TABLE 19.47   Will We Have Enough to Retire Part-time at Age 70?
Example #11: Results of Analyses, Income Solution

Estimated annual Social Security at age 70	$48,000	Estimated using calculator at www.ssa.gov, as if we were single workers, reflecting that both of us have worked for a whole career. Assume our benefits increase by 3% per year for inflation.
I from 401(k) balance	$ 7,860	Use Income Solution, which is 3%, or .03, times $262,000.
Defined benefit pension	$ 0	
Part-time work	$ 0	
Total *I*	$55,860	
Total *E*, adjusted for inflation at 3% per year.	$56,500	Adjust our *E* of $50,000 for 4 years of inflation. The factor from Table 19.28 is 1.13. Multiply by $50,000 for a result of $56,500.

Answer: We need some wages to make our *I* exceed our *E*.

Can we make it on $12,000 of wages per year? We'll need to estimate our income and FICA taxes, and add this to our *E*.

The first step is to estimate how much of our Social Security benefits are included in taxable income. We add up the amounts in Table 19.48.

TABLE 19.48 Example #11: Will Our Social Security Benefits Be Taxed?

One-half of Social Security benefits	$24,000
401(k) withdrawal	$ 7,860
Wages	$12,000
Total	$43,860
Threshold for a married couple	$32,000

Conclusion: We must include $5,930 in our taxable income. This is half of $11,860, which is $43,860 minus the threshold of $32,000.

Note that the $32,000 threshold does not increase for inflation. This is a sneaky way for the government to increase income taxes, as inflation pushes more and more of our Social Security income over the fixed $32,000 amount.

We add $5,930 to our 401(k) withdrawal of $7,860 and our wages of $12,000, for a total taxable income of $25,790. The federal exemption is currently $11,400 for a couple over age 65. We estimate that our federal and state income taxes will be about $2,000 at age 70.

However, we'll pay FICA taxes of $918 on $12,000 of wages. If we add federal, state and FICA taxes to our E of $56,500, we have a total of $59,418. Our I is $67,860 when we add our $12,000 of wages to the previously calculated amount of $55,860. So, we're okay with $I > E$ from age 70 to 75.

Now, we need to see if we can stop working completely at age 75.

First, we need to project the income from our 401(k) balances at age 75, when we stop working entirely and increase our withdrawals using the 401(k) Solution. This requires a refinement to the Investment and Inflation Rate Adjustor. We are withdrawing 3 percent per year between ages 70 and 75, as our best estimate of the investment income. We're invested in a balanced mutual fund, which earns approximately 3 percent each year in interest and dividend payments. After we turn age 70, we expect to get more conservative with our asset allocation, which we will move to 33 percent stocks and 67 percent bonds. With this allocation, our expected rate of return is 6 percent. However, we must subtract the amount we withdraw under the Income Solution. So, if our expected rate of return is 6 percent per year, then the assets are growing by 3 percent per year after considering our withdrawals (6 percent minus 3 percent). So, we'll need to project our 401(k) balance from age 70 to age 75, using a rate of return of 3 percent from Table 19.28. We see that, for a period of 5 years, this factor is 1.16. Multiplying this factor by $262,000, our estimated balance at age 70, gives us an estimated balance of $303,920 at age 75. So this is the amount we'll use to estimate our income using the 401(k) Solution at age 75.

Using Table 10.2, we see that at age 75 a married couple the same age can safely withdraw $5\frac{1}{2}\%$.

See how the calculations look in Table 19.49.

TABLE 19.49   Will We Have Enough to Retire Full-time at Age 75?
Example #11: Results of Analyses, 401(k) Solution

Estimated annual Social Security at age 75, adjusted for inflation	$55,680	Multiply $48,000 at age 70 by 1.16, the factor for 3% from Table 19.28.
I from 401(k) balance	$16,716	Use 401(k) Solution, which is $5\frac{1}{2}\%$, or .055, times $303,920.
Defined benefit pension	$ 0	
Part-time work	$ 0	
Total *I*	$72,396	
Total *E*, adjusted for inflation at 3% per year to age 75.	$65,000	Adjust $50,000 for 9 years of inflation. The factor from Table 19.28 is 1.30. Multiply by $50,000.
Answer: We can retire full time at age 75!		

We conclude that our plan for phased retirement will work. Still, we'll look for ways to manage our *E*, because the margin is a little close.

Making *Rest-of-Life* Work—Example #12.

So far, we haven't used the Annuity Solution for our 401(k) balances. Let's see how that could work.

Let's suppose the assumptions in Table 19.50.

TABLE 19.50   Example #12: Assumptions

Situation	Single male age 66, which is my Social Security normal retirement age (NRA).
Annual *E*	$24,000, not including income taxes—slightly below average for my age. I have paid off the mortgage on my house.
401(k) balance.	$225,000—above average for my age. I'll set aside $25,000 for an emergency reserve, and base my analysis on $200,000.
Defined benefit pension	None.

I decide to split my 401(k) balance, and use $100,000 to purchase an immediate annuity, and keep the other $100,000 in my 401(k) plan. My $100,000 buys an immediate lifetime annuity of $7,800 per year. I estimate this using the percentages in Table 10.3 in Chapter 10, and I confirm this using the online estimator mentioned in that chapter (www.immediateannuities.com). To be conservative, I used the factor for age 65 in Table 10.3, even though I'm 66. With my remaining 401(k) balance of $100,000, I use the Income Solution.

Let's look at the analysis in Table 19.51.

TABLE 19.51   Can I Retire Now? Example #12: Results of Analyses, Income Solution

Estimated annual Social Security	$18,000	Estimated from www.ssa.gov.
I from 401(k) balance	$ 3,000	Use Income Solution, which is 3%, or .03, times $100,000
Annuity	$ 7,800	
Part-time work	$ 0	
Total *I*	$28,800	
Total *E*	$24,000	
Answer: I have a comfortable margin of *I* over *E*.		

I realize that my annuity income doesn't increase for inflation. However, I don't set aside a reserve for that. I figure that, over time, I can increase my withdrawals from my remaining 401(k) balance, and eventually shift to using the 401(k) Solution.

Making *Rest-of-Life* Work—Example #13

This example shows the value of earning an income from a defined benefit plan. Often, these benefits can make the difference between working or not during our *rest-of-life*.

Let's suppose the assumptions in Table 19.52.

TABLE 19.52 Example #13: Assumptions

Situation	Married couple, both 62.
Annual *E*	$40,000, not including income taxes. Includes a 25% margin for error.
401(k) balance	$250,000—above average for two people our age. Assume we set aside $50,000 for emergencies, and base our analysis on $200,000.
Defined benefit pension	If we retire today, our annual pension is $12,000. The plan reduces benefits if we start them before age 65. Using our company's online benefit calculator, we estimate if we keep working until age 65, lifetime retirement income is $15,000 per year, using the 100% joint and survivor form of payment.

The question is whether we can retire at age 65 (see Table 19.53). For these calculations, we must adjust the $200,000 amount in our 401(k) plan for three years of investment earnings. Assuming we earn 6% per year, the factor from Table 19.28 is 1.19. Multiply this by $200,000 for a projected balance of $238,000 at age 65.

The answer to our question is yes if we decide to budget sufficiently such that our *E* is less than our *I*. We realize that our pension is fixed and won't increase for inflation. We plan to use our

TABLE 19.53 Can We Retire at Age 65? Example #13: Results of Analyses, Income Solution

Estimated annual Social Security at age 65	$30,000	Estimated using calculator at www.ssa.gov, including special spouse's benefits
I from 401(k) balance	$ 7,140	Use Income Solution, which is 3%, or .03, times $238,000
Pension	$15,000	
Part-time work	$ 0	
Total *I*	$52,140	
Total *E*	Less than this!	
Answer: We can retire full-time!		

401(k) balance to make up the difference, and eventually we might shift to using the 401(k) Solution for determining our withdrawals from my 401(k) plan.

I'm very grateful for my defined benefit plan, as this allows me to retire full-time at age 65. Most of my friends aren't so lucky. I still might work part-time after age 65, just to keep active, have social contacts, and add more financial security. However, now I have the freedom to be very choosy about my work.

Making *Rest-of-Life* Work—Example #14

After thinking about housing expenditures in Chapter 18, I can't get this commune thing out of my head.

Let's suppose I'm in my mid-sixties and have nothing but Social Security income. I have four other friends in the same boat. Each of us receives about $1,500 per month from Social Security, or $18,000 per year. We receive this tax-free, since the income for each one of us falls below the limit for taxing Social Security benefits. We decide to band together, pool resources, and live in a big house in an inexpensive area. For all five of us, our income adds up to $90,000 per year.

We try diligently to keep our expenditures close to the average in the United States for five people living in one household, which was about $55,000 in 2002, as we saw in Chapter 18. Our biggest problem? On what do we spend the additional $35,000 each year? One possibility is to hire housecleaners so we don't have to do any dirty work, and chefs to make us tasty, healthy food.

Summary of Tools and Techniques

If we want to project the amount of *I* that a current 401(k) balance will generate in the future, here are the steps:

1. Multiply the Investment and Inflation Rate Adjustor from Table 19.28 by our current 401(k) account, to project the value of this account to a future year. We select an investment rate that reflects our asset allocation.

2. Determine the method we will use for withdrawing from our 401(k) plan—the 401(k) Solution or the Income Solution. This gives us a factor, which we will use to multiply by the result

of the first step. This result is our estimate of our future *I* from our current 401(k) balance. If we decide to use the Annuity Solution, we can go to one of the online annuity estimators and input the projected account balance, to get an estimate of the annuity income we might receive.

We use these steps if we have a one-step withdrawal strategy for withdrawing from our 401(k) plan. By one-step, I mean withdraw nothing until we need the income, and then pick a withdrawal strategy that we use for the rest of our life.

If we have a two-step withdrawal process, where we first use the Income Solution for many years and then use the 401(k) Solution, here are the steps:

1. During our first *rest-of-life* phase, multiply our current balance by the expected rate of dividend and interest payments, to estimate the amount of annual income using the Income Solution. In our examples, this rate has been 3 percent, or .03. We might be able to earn and withdraw more than this rate, depending on our investments. For example, if we invest significantly in bonds, the interest payments will be more than 3 percent. However, these payments won't increase for inflation. If we are invested in a balanced mutual fund, as described in Chapter 12, our estimated income from dividends and interest is about 3 percent. If history repeats itself, this amount will grow roughly with inflation, as dividends increase. This inflation hedge is one important reason to use a balanced mutual fund and only withdraw 3 percent per year.

2. During our second *rest-of-life* phase, we need to project the account from now until the age at which we will use the 401(k) solution. To do this, multiply our current balance by the appropriate factor from Table 19.28. This factor should be based on our expected rate of return, minus our expected withdrawal rate. Then, take this result and multiply by the appropriate factor from Table 10.2 to estimate the amount of annual income using the 401(k) Solution. If we are willing to assume a higher risk of outliving our money, we can use the tables in my web site to determine a higher withdrawal percentage.

Here are more of the techniques we learned:

- If we want to estimate a future 401(k) balance, without adding any future contributions, we multiply the current balance by the appropriate factor from Table 19.28, the Investment and Inflation Rate Adjustor. Once again, our assumed rate of return should reflect our expected asset allocation.

- If we want to estimate the accumulated value of future 401(k) contributions, we multiply our annual contribution amount by the appropriate factor in Table 19.29, the Savings Accumulator.

- If we want to estimate the reserve needed for inflation on a fixed amount of lifetime annuity, we multiply the amount of the fixed annuity by the appropriate factor in Table 19.32, the Inflation Adjustor.

- If we want to figure how to have a few phases of *rest-of-life*, where we work part-time and then retire full-time, we use the Wage Replacement Maneuver or the *Rest-of-Life* Three-Step.

WRAP-UP

We just covered a lot of territory, and it may take awhile for the ideas and methods to sink in. I suggest that you work with the concepts in this chapter, discuss them with a friend or your spouse, and persist until you feel comfortable. I realize this can be easier said than done, but this is part of the hard work to make it happen.

One note: If you have retirement planning software, you may not need some of the tools mentioned in this chapter. However, I still recommend that you understand these concepts, so that you can use the software properly.

The next chapter makes some observations on the examples in this chapter, and discusses some strategies for making the $I > E$ methodology work for our *rest-of-life*. Also, it goes into more detail on the "How much should I save?" question.

Answering the Three Big Questions— Observations and Strategies

Sooner or later I'm going to die, but I'm not going to retire.
—Margaret Mead

f you're reading this chapter with intense interest, you've gone through the other chapters in this section and determined that if you retire now or anytime soon, your *I* is much less than your *E*. You need to save more so that you can eventually retire full-time. Don't feel too bad—we have lots of company!

After getting unpopular answers to the first two big questions, a lot of people ask the third big question—"How much should I save?" First I'll provide five different answers to this question. Then, I'll make some observations on the examples from the previous chapter, and discuss strategies for making our finances work during our *rest-of-life*.

With respect to the "How much should I save?" question, like everything else, there's not a simple answer. Years ago, to answer this question, I used the replacement ratio methodology, described in Chapter 9, to ask a bunch of questions:

- When do you want to retire?

- How much have you saved already?

- What do you think your investments will earn?

- How much do you make, and what kind of raises do you expect in the future?

- What is your target retirement income?

By this point, most people would say "I dunno" and go on to talk about the weather. Eventually, I learned that many people just can't answer these questions, but they *hope* that things will work out okay. Unfortunately, hope is not an effective strategy!

Given this hard-earned experience, my thinking has evolved with respect to the "How much should I save?" question. Now I have a number of answers. Some are simple, and a few require some effort. First, I'll describe the answers, along with the potential consequences. Then I'll go into more detail with one of these strategies. We can pick the method that works best for each of us.

Five Strategies

Here are five different ways to answer the question "How much should I save?"

Savings Strategy #1: Save as Much as We Can Afford

Most people who follow this strategy don't save very much, usually 1 or 2 percent of their pay at most. If we follow this strategy, most likely we will need to work full-time through our late seventies. We really don't have much of a plan, and our main strategy is *hope* that things will be okay. We really don't have a clue when we will be able to retire. So, each year, we should check using the "can I retire now" methodology described in Chapter 9 and illustrated in Chapter 19. If retirement seems too far away, we should try to squeeze in some more savings.

Savings Strategy #2—Contribute the Maximum Matched by Our 401(k) Plan

Congratulations! We're not leaving money on the table. A lot of companies will match at least 50 percent of our contributions up to 6 percent of our pay, for a maximum matching contribution of 3 percent of our pay. Add the matching contribution to our own contributions, and we're investing 9 percent of our pay. However, chances are good that even these saving amounts are not enough to retire full-time soon. Do this for 20 years and we'll probably be able to retire full-time in our early seventies. Some companies have higher matching contributions, which might let us retire earlier. Still, we really don't have a plan for when we will be able to retire full-time. So, each year, we should check using the "can I retire now" methodology described in Chapter 9 and illustrated in Chapter 19. If we don't like the answer, try saving some more.

Savings Strategy #3: Save 10 Percent of Pay

I believe that most people can change their expenditures and find enough room to save this amount. If we have no current retirement savings, and do this for 20 years, we should be able to retire full-time by age 70. If our company matches our contributions, or if we have some current savings, we might retire earlier. Again, we really don't have a plan for when we will be able to retire. So, each year, we should check using the "can I retire now" methodology described in Chapter 9 and illustrated in Chapter 19. If we don't like the answer, try saving some more.

Savings Strategy #4: Use Replacement Ratio Methodology

Again, more congratulations! Now, chances are good we will retire when we want. In spite of my preference for the $I > E$ methodology, this is far better than the first three methods. The only problem is that we might save too much or too little, since this methodology usually ignores changes in our expected spending during retirement, doesn't deal well with inflation after retirement, and doesn't reflect income from working during our later years.

Savings Strategy #5: Use the I > E Methodology

Even more congratulations! Chances are very good we will retire when we want, and we will save just enough to meet our financial needs. We'll be able to consider income from working during our later years, reflect our expected expenses, and devise strategies for protecting against inflation. This is my favorite methodology for determining how much to save, and I've gone into great detail in the last chapter.

While it might appear I'm making fun with some of the answers, I'm really not! A lot of people don't have it in themselves to get very sophisticated with their retirement planning. They do the best they can, given their current situation. In the future, when they want to retire full-time, they adjust their circumstances to fit their resources. I'm not judging if this is right or wrong. However, if you fit this description, I just want you to understand the consequences. None of these is a bad strategy, except maybe the first one if we only save a percent or two of our pay. My goal is to bring awareness to the consequences of these strategies, so we can make informed decisions and adjust our expectations accordingly. Many of us might be willing to live with the consequences, which are that we will work longer than we previously had planned. However, for reasons mentioned earlier in this book, this might not be all that bad.

Unfortunately, life has the habit of getting in the way of finely laid plans. I've seen people go through elaborate analyses, pick the exact age at which they plan to retire, and then calculate how much they must save to hit the target. Then, well before their target retirement age, they get laid off, or get sick, or just plain chuck it all because they are tired of working. Sometimes saving 10 percent of pay works just as well as an elaborate plan.

However, having said that, only the last two strategies give us a good chance of selecting a target retirement age, and putting in place a realistic savings strategy to hit the target. So, let's go into more detail on the replacement ratio methodology. I won't go into detail here on the $I > E$ methodology, since we covered it extensively in the preceding chapter.

Replacement Ratio Methodology

This is the traditional way to determine how much to save, and most retirement planning software that is currently available uses this methodology. This methodology has some drawbacks, and it can be cumbersome or even impossible to reflect our living expenses, inflation after retirement, and part-time work. However, it's much better than guessing, and we'll probably do okay if we stick to our plan.

With the replacement ratio methodology, the basic goal is to maintain the same after-tax income during retirement, compared to just before retirement. We pick a target retirement income, expressed as a percentage of our pay just before retirement. Most financial planners use a target anywhere from 70 percent to 80 percent of our pay. We don't need to replace 100 percent of our pay, because usually our taxes and work-related expenditures go down during retirement, and we don't need to save anymore for retirement. An inherent assumption with the 70 percent to 80 percent targets is that our expenses after retirement roughly equal our expenses before retirement. In reality, we might want to adjust our target up or down, to account for expenses that may change after retirement, such as paying off our mortgage, college tuition, and increased expenses for medical bills or travel.

There's a potential issue with this strategy if we are highly paid, say earning $150,000 per year or more, and have lots of discretionary income. If we mindlessly keep saving to replace our high income because we're trying to duplicate our current standard of living, we're putting blinders on with respect to the alternatives. Chances are good that we can get by on far less income during our *rest-of-life*, so if we want to make changes in our lives, we'll be misled if we use the replacement ratio method.

I won't go into more detail on the replacement ratio methodology here, for a couple of reasons. First, I prefer the $I > E$ methodology. And second, there are several software programs that we can use.

- Check with our 401(k) plan administrator. Many 401(k) vendors, such as Fidelity, Charles Schwab, T. Rowe Price, and Vanguard provide online resources.

- These same mutual fund companies also have online calculators on their web sites for individual investors. (You can see them at www.fidelity.com, www.schwab.com, www.troweprice.com, and www.vanguard.com.)

- AARP has a good calculator on its web site, www.aarp.org.

- For a fee, we can access sophisticated retirement planning software with Financial Engines (www.financialengines.com) and Morningstar (www.morningstar.com). These will also help us develop asset allocation targets and select mutual funds.

With all of these resources, we'll need to provide answers to the questions at the beginning of this chapter, and sometimes many more. These include our target retirement age, our expected rate of return on 401(k) balances, the expected rate of inflation, our expected pay raises, how much we've saved already, and how much we expect to receive from a pension, if any. We'll need to know our target retirement income, expressed as a percentage of pay. A few programs let us input this target retirement income in dollar amounts, expressed in terms of today's dollars or future dollars. Some ask for our federal and state income tax rates, our life expectancy, and the specific investments that we use for our current portfolio.

The results are often highly sensitive to the input, and we can get dramatically different answers just by tweaking our input assumptions a little bit. So, one suggestion is to use different assumptions, to get an idea for the possible variation in the answers.

I highly recommend understanding how the program works, and not blindly using the output. I've used some programs that don't do much checking on the reasonableness of the input assumptions. I also recommend looking at the details and interim steps of the calculations, to make sure they look reasonable.

These programs can be quite useful. If I'm careful about the input and look at different input assumptions, I can put together a pretty good savings strategy. They can get me in the ballpark. I can even use some of these programs if I use the $I > E$ methodology, to project account balances and determine how much to save to reach future targets. For example, T. Rowe Price has a simple calculator that projects expected future I from current account balances, and helps determine how much to save to hit targets for I. The program doesn't use this terminology, but the methodology is quite similar.

I should also point out that some of these resources start blending the replacement ratio methodology with the $I > E$ methodology. Some of the calculators have worksheets on expected expenses, and will adjust these for expected future inflation. Then they calculate our I, to see if it exceeds our E. Again, these programs don't use these terms, but the methodology is very similar. Also, some programs let us input income from part-time work.

Also, T. Rowe Price has a calculator for determining withdrawal amounts from a 401(k) plan, using asset/liability modeling techniques (they call it "Monte Carlo" forecasting). This is similar to the 401(k) Solution, discussed in Chapter 10.

It's a Lot of Juggling!

As we can see from the examples in Chapter 19, it's a challenge to save, invest, and withdraw from our 401(k) balances, and work for a portion of our *rest-of-life*. It's part art, part science, and a lot of juggling. For most of us, we will need to be flexible, resourceful, and resilient.

Here is a summary of some ideas and strategies on how to make our finances work during our *rest-of-life*, based on the examples in the preceding chapter and all the methods presented in this section:

- Several examples show the value of delaying retirement for awhile, sometimes only four or five years. So we'll need to be open and resourceful to make this happen.

- One way to do this is to have a Stage 1 of our *rest-of-life*, where we work part-time during our sixties and seventies. If possible, we let our financial resources grow, so that when we stop working entirely, these resources will be as large as possible. Maybe during Stage 1, we won't save any more and will use all of our wages for living expenses, but at least we won't draw on our financial resources. This means delaying Social Security benefits as long as possible, but no later than age 70. If we have lifetime income from a defined benefit plan, we'll delay that until there is no longer a reduction for early retirement. This is typically age 65, but can be earlier. There are two possible exceptions to this strategy—if we are in poor health, or if there is a small reduction for early retirement, say 3 percent per year or under.

- If we need some income from our financial resources during this Stage 1, we should try to use the Income Solution, where we live just on the income from interest and dividend payments. When we eventually stop working, possibly in our seventies or later, we can increase our withdrawal percentage using the 401(k) Solution, to replace the wages that are no longer there. At this time, we can also use the Annuity Solution, which also provides a higher income than the Income Solution.

- Throughout all of our *rest-of-life*, we should look for ways to decrease our E, or at the very least, contain increases for inflation. In some of the examples, we saw how we need substantial reserves to protect against future inflation. If we don't have that kind of money, when the time comes, we will need to be very resourceful in coping with price increases. For example, if prices go up, we can delay purchases, buy alternative products, wait until they are on sale, and so on. This might work for a lot of things like food and clothing, but it won't work for rent, utilities, and medical expenses. We can cope with these increases by owning our home mortgage-free, looking for investments in our homes that reduce our utility bills, and keeping healthy.

- Example #13 in Chapter 19 shows the value of an income from a defined benefit plan. Often this income is the difference that puts us over the top. So, if possible, we'll look for employment where we participate in such a plan.

- The younger we are, the more likely it is that we might experience some reduction in future Social Security benefits. For planning purposes, I'll reduce my estimates of Social Security benefits by 10 percent to 30 percent, depending on how pessimistic I feel. Also, if I'm at the tail end of the baby boom generation, I'll use a higher reduction; I'll use a lower reduction if I'm at the leading edge. I think it is unrealistic to assume more than a 30 percent reduction, but that's just my opinion!

- When we do our analyses on how much to save, we should look at the results from alternative assumptions. Sometimes small changes in these assumptions, particularly with regard to investment returns and inflation, can result in dramatically different answers. The techniques in Chapter 19 use assumptions on future returns to determine how much to save. If we earn less than these assumptions between now and retirement, we will miss our targets. I could have introduced a stochastic process to determine how much to save, based on asset/liability modeling. My feeling is that this adds unnecessary complexity, and doesn't result in answers that are much different. If we miss our targets, we can always work a little longer if necessary. Also, if we work for awhile and only use the income from interest and dividends, we insulate ourselves somewhat from market downturns just before we retire.

- The same advice applies when we analyze how much to withdraw from our 401(k) plans. We should look at the results from alternative assumptions and methods. Again, small changes in assumptions regarding withdrawal rates, investment returns, and inflation can result in different answers. This just highlights the uncertainty of the future, and how we need to keep our options open as we manage our financial resources. This is another reason to delay drawing down our principal for as long as possible, and just live on the income from interest and dividends.

- Speaking of investment returns, large downturns in the stock market just before retirement can play havoc with our plans if we need to withdraw principal for living expenses. As mentioned earlier, this is less critical if we rely on just the income from interest and dividends. We need to pay attention to our asset allocation and withdrawal strategies as we near the time when we begin withdrawing principal, and at that time reduce our exposure to stock market volatility.

- Buying immediate annuities with part of our resources is one way to protect against outliving our money and from market volatility. Again, we should postpone this as long as possible, to keep our options open and get the best possible price.

- There can be a blending between the Income Solution and the 401(k) Solution. With the examples in Chapter 19, I used 3 percent as the withdrawal rate for the Income Solution. This represents an estimate of the interest and dividend payments from a balanced mutual fund. I like this strategy because it leaves some room for growth in our assets, and hopefully the dividends will grow to help keep pace with inflation. However, if we don't worry too much about inflation and if we are significantly invested in bonds, we could justify withdrawing more than 3 percent. In this case, I would start to get uncomfortable if my withdrawal percentage exceeds the amounts from the 401(k) Solution.

- Speaking of the 401(k) Solution, Table 10.2 in Chapter 10 showed withdrawal percentages with a roughly 1 out of 10 chance of outliving our money. If that feels too scary, we should cut back on our withdrawals, somewhere between the 401(k) Solution and the Income Solution. If we don't mind taking chances, we could increase our withdrawals by up to 1 percent over the 401(k) Solution. This might be okay if we don't expect to live much longer than the averages. It might be spectacularly bad if we take care of ourselves and live longer than the averages. My web site provides additional information on the 401(k) Solution; this will help us if we want to deviate from the withdrawal strategies shown in Table 10.2 of Chapter 10.

Before we wrap up, here's a humorous take on the "How much should I save?" question.

The Retiree Savings Menu

Table 20.1 is courtesy of my friend Charlie Commander at Watson Wyatt. He calls this the retiree savings menu.

TABLE 20.1   Retiree Savings Menu

If We Save This Much as a Percent of Our Pay . . .	Then This Is What We'll Be Eating and Drinking When We Retire
0%	Dog food, rainwater
2%	Spam, tap water
4%	Macaroni and cheese, Kool-Aid
6%	Big Mac and fries, soda
8%	T-bone steak, beer
10%	Seafood, California wine
12%	Roast beef, imported wine
14%	Filet mignon, brandy
16%	Caviar, champagne

I do have one quarrel with Charlie. Given my preference for healthy food, and where I live, I think "seafood, California wine" should match with the highest savings amount!

WRAP-UP

As mentioned at the beginning of Chapter 19, the examples in that chapter provide powerful reinforcement of the themes in this entire book. First, let me point out that the people in these examples didn't have a million bucks, as is frequently cited by articles in the media as the amount we need for a comfortable retirement. So, we don't need to give in to the hopelessness that we will never accumulate that kind of money.

But, I'm not done yet. For these examples, I made assumptions regarding how much these people had saved in their 401(k) plans. I assumed that their 401(k) balances were either close to, equal to, or somewhat higher than average balances for Americans. Remember from Chapter 1 that the average 401(k) balance for people in their fifties and sixties is about $100,000. For my assumptions on E, I used amounts that fell within the range of annual expenditures for Americans, as indicated by the U.S. Department of Labor consumer expenditure survey described in Chapter 18. For most of these examples, people needed to work until their mid to late sixties or beyond, or they needed to work part-time for a lengthy period.

This is why I'm saying we might need to work longer than we had previously thought.

This is why I'm saying that we might need to wait a long time for full-time retirement.

This is why I'm saying we might want to work part-time for an extended period of time.

This is why I'm saying it's so important to keep healthy, so we can continue working.

This is why I'm saying we should carefully manage our *E* and live within our means.

This is why I'm saying we might want to make our lives sustainable now, instead of living deferred lives, waiting for retirement that we now realize is further away than we thought.

This is why I'm saying we should make our work lives meaningful and enjoyable *now*.

This is why you might want to go back and reread the first two sections of this book!

PUTTING IT ALL TOGETHER

Virtue does not come from money, but from virtue comes money and all other good things to man, both to the individual and to the state.

—Socrates

We've gone on a long journey, and we're almost done. Congratulations!

Most of the advice in this book is much easier said than done. It's one thing to know intellectually what we should do, and another to actually make it happen. First, I'll discuss the hardest part of the journey—reaching into our heart, mind, and soul to find the motivation to make important changes in our life. Then, I'll summarize by contrasting the twenty-first-century model of *rest-of-life* with the twentieth-century model of retirement. Finally, for those of you who want to know, I'll wrap up by sharing the next steps in my *rest-of-life* quest.

Ya Gotta Wanna

Courage is being scared to death—but saddling up anyway.
—John Wayne

B y now, you might feel a little overwhelmed. I'm talking about major changes. Exercise, diet, spending habits, transportation, where we live, our outlook on work/life balance, and most importantly, changing our outlook from retirement to *rest-of-life*. For some people, this means a major life overhaul. Altering ingrained, lifelong habits will take more than just reading a book.

Let's conclude by talking about how to make important changes in our lives. Consultants call this "change management." Watson Wyatt is big into "change management," so part of my process was talking with several consultants with experience in this area. I also saw a few therapists, and did some reflecting on how I have made changes in my life.

I don't have a single, magic answer. I do have some thoughts and methods that I will share with you. Some might work for you, and some might not. See what makes sense to you.

However, they all come down to . . . the title of this chapter!

What's Our Picture for Our Future?

A lot of us live day-to-day. We live in the moment, enjoying what's happening now or struggling with the challenges that we're facing now. If we do any planning at all, we plan by looking around. If our parents retired in their late fifties or early sixties, then by golly we should as well. It seemed to work for them, so it should work for us.

We don't spend a lot of time thinking about our *rest-of-life*. Well, that's what I'm suggesting we should do. Fast-forward 20 years, and draw a positive mental picture.

- We're comfortable financially, and we're not living in fear.

- We feel healthy.

- We enjoy what we're doing every day, and we look forward to getting out of bed each morning.

- We have a great network of friends and relatives. We are surrounded by people who love and care for us.

From this position 20 years from now, we look back to today. What did we resolve to do today, so that 20 years later we're in such a good position? How did we get there?

The Story We Tell Ourselves

We all have stories that we tell ourselves about who we are: Our strengths, weaknesses, likes, and dislikes. What is important to us, and what isn't. Who we love, who we dislike, and who we are indifferent to. What turns us on, and what turns us off. Our fears and pleasures. What makes us happy, and what makes us sad. What we need, what we want, what we avoid. What we wish we could change about ourselves, and what we're proud of. The list goes on and on.

For many of us, most of our stories have grown unconsciously, at the mercy of the mind and body that we inherited, our own personal history, and the pervasive culture we live in. Our upbringing formed our initial way of looking at the world, and often this view stays with us for quite awhile on a subconscious level. But some of us want to break out of this old story that no longer works for us, and consciously write our own, more healthy story. This brings me to the technique of affirmations to make important changes.

With affirmations, we write our own stories—stories about ourselves that are positive, supportive, and healthy. Stories that help us make important changes. Examples relating to the subjects in this book could include:

- I am healthy. I eat food that nourishes me. I eat just enough.

- I like to walk, hike, swim, bike, pump weights.

- I am happiest when . . .

- I work best when . . .

- I spend money just on things that I need.

- I invest for the future.

- I'm there for people who need me.

Affirmations work best when they are stated positively and in the present tense. This confirms that they are already true. If we say, "I will do . . ." then it's not true. Write them down. We can take a few minutes each day to settle down, be quiet, and repeat the affirmations to ourselves. One good time might be when we look at ourselves in the mirror each morning.

For more on the power of affirmations, try two books called *The Power of Intention* (Hay House, 2004), by Dr. Wayne W. Dyer, and *The Life We Are Given* (Jeremy P. Tarcher, 1995), by George Leonard and Michael Murphy.

Just Turn Off the TV

Many of the stories we tell ourselves come from advertising on TV, radio, the Internet, newspapers, and magazines. We're happiest when we buy . . . We take care of our families when we buy . . .

Buying is the answer to everything!

Have you ever noticed that much of what TV tells us to buy isn't good for us, either financially or physically?

Most of the good stuff in life isn't advertised on TV. I've never seen a commercial from the tofu producers' association, the broccoli growers' association, the apple growers' association, the love-your-family-and-friends association.

A lot of stuff about the *pleasurable life*, and not much stuff on the *good life* or *meaningful life*.

Commercials are very clever about linking legitimate human needs with buying their products. It is basic human nature to want to be happy, to love our spouses, to take care of our families. Most of us want to feel smart, healthy, slim, handsome, beautiful, secure. There's nothing wrong with that. The problem arises when we link these natural desires to buying stuff that really doesn't do it for us. We're going to the wrong source.

Just turn off the TV. Try it for a week. Use the time to pursue our interests, to take care of ourselves.

I'm proud that I've packed a lot of parenting, learning, exploring, experiencing, and living into my 50 years. People ask me how I find the time to do it all. My answer is, "I don't watch TV."

When my kids were little, they watched a little of Nickelodeon. (Thank goodness they don't watch TV now.) However, I really liked and respected a message that Nickelodeon played frequently. They would urge the viewers to turn off the TV, take a break from virtual reality, and go experience "actual reality."

The Parallel Universe

It might seem to be normal that we watch lots of TV, buy the latest clothes, spend money on cars, work real hard, don't worry too much about weight because it is vain or paranoid, and eat whatever we want because hey, we enjoy life! So-called normal people don't buy organic food or talk back to their doctors. We all want to be normal, to fit in, to be comfortable. The trouble is, a lot of normal people also get heart disease and cancer at an early age, or they may not fully enjoy life.

What happens if we find what makes us happy and healthy, and pursue it? If we stop buying stuff that really doesn't make us happy, spend just what we need that makes us really happy, and save the rest for the future? What happens if we work part-time, while the rest of our colleagues continue on their career ladder? What happens when we buy and eat lots of fresh, organic fruits and vegetables? What happens when we try to have an informed conversation with our doctors? What if this is different from normal people? Will the world as we know it end?

We slip into a parallel universe. Much looks the same and feels familiar. We might see many of the same people, do many of the same things, eat much of the same food. But much might also be very different. At first, it might seem uncomfortable, a little odd and scary. It doesn't have to be a one-way trip—we can move back and forth between the two universes.

We can talk with people on the other side, see how they like it. We meet different people—people who might have seemed a little strange before, but now are interesting. We might do things we never dreamed of before—things that only eccentric people did (but didn't these eccentrics seem to be happy?). We might eat different food, but now we slow down to savor it and find it's really good! We might visit the natural food store, at first a little hesitant, wondering if our friends will see us and think we're weird. But then we find it has a lot of interesting, healthy food, and the people in the store are supportive and friendly.

All this is right alongside the same old world that we used to occupy. And we find lots of company in our new, parallel universe—people who actually do things that normal people don't. We make new friends who share our new interests.

After a few weeks, we're pleasantly surprised to find that our life hasn't gone haywire. In fact, we feel better, more energetic. We look forward to getting up each day. We feel vital, purposeful. We're proud of our diet and exercise, and how it makes us feel. We're glad to be alive. We like this new universe.

We can slip back into our old universe whenever we choose. We can see our old friends, do the same activities, eat the same food. It might seem familiar and nostalgic. But after awhile, some of it might seem foreign, like from a previous life. The same hectic pace of work. The commute. Particularly the food—how could we have ever eaten this greaseburger from the fast-food chain? The sight of it makes us sick.

Eventually our new universe becomes normal. Right alongside the old universe. Now it's very comfortable, but vital and alive. All we did was walk away from the old universe, and into the new.

All we did was change.

Next, let's see what my therapist friends say.

No Pain, No Gain

As this theory goes, we won't make important changes until we are currently feeling lots of pain, or if we vividly anticipate future pain.

If the pain from an unhealthy habit is greater than the pleasure, then we'll make changes. If we eat the wrong foods but get a heart attack, then the pain from eating this food now outweighs (pardon the pun) the pleasure. This also works if we anticipate future pain. Hence one reason for reading other people's stories that are on my web site—we can experience their pain and anticipate future pain if we don't make changes.

Another variation on this theory is "taking the hit," popularized by George Leonard. After we take a physical or emotional hit, we get energized to *do something about it*. Did we just get fired, divorced, heart attacked? Have we lost a close friend or relative to illness? After we settle down, which might take awhile, we feel a surge of energy to . . . you know. Go with this surge of energy, don't let it dissipate. If we visualize a possible future hit, we might get the same burst of energy.

What pain are we currently experiencing? What future pain might we experience from our current behaviors? Will we get ill? Will we work full-time into our seventies? Will we be unhappy and grouchy? Will we miss doing what we really want to do?

Lately, when I've been confronted with a great fear, I live with it, see how it feels, and think about the consequences. Then I take action to address these fears. This gives me great comfort—things don't look so bad after all; everything will turn out okay. This perspective wasn't easy; it took me many years to get to this place!

Don't Let Fear Drive Our Lives

Sometimes I hear people say, "I won't let fear drive my life. I can't waste my time worrying about every piece of food I buy, whether it is organic. I can't worry about my household cleansers. I can't worry about saving for the future, I've got so much on my plate right now."

I agree with the first thought, not to let fear drive my life. But with respect to the remaining fears, I ask these people if they get out of the way of a speeding car that is bearing down on them—or do they stay put because they won't let the fear of speeding cars drive their life?

There's a difference between unhealthy fear and healthy fear. It's just plain old smart to take care of ourselves—we're not being paranoid or fearful in an unhealthy way.

In our business, we call this "risk management." This means we take risks only if the payoff is worth it and we can survive the possible negative consequences. For me, this means that I'll take my chances with skiing, hiking, meeting different people, exploring new cultures, and trying new things. These risks are worth it, and hopefully the payoff will make my life richer. I'll take calculated risk in the stock market—again, most of the time, the risk will be worth the reward, if history repeats itself.

I won't get my thrills from eating food raised with pesticides, putting on deodorant with unhealthy chemicals, using unhealthy cleaners in my house, eating that oversized super-burrito, or spending my money on some worthless gizmo or oversized car. These risks to my physical and financial health aren't worth it!

Now let's see what the consultants have to say.

The Change Model

Consultants use conceptual models for everything, and change is no different. So here's what we call a behavior change model. This comes from the Transtheoretical Model of Behavior Change, and was developed by Dr. James Prochaska, Director of the Cancer Prevention Research Consortium and Professor of Clinical and Health Psychology at the University of Rhode Island. We use it at Watson Wyatt for helping our clients promote healthy behaviors with their employees.

When we make important changes in our lives, we go through five stages. I'll have a little fun with this, to make some points.

1. *Precontemplation.* We're not ready for change. Basically we're clueless. "Gimme that greaseburger with a double serving of fries. And make it quick, because I gotta run to my next appointment."

2. *Contemplation.* We're thinking about making a change. "Maybe I shouldn't eat so many greaseburgers, and slow down a little." Chomp, zoom.

3. *Preparation.* We're ready to change. "I'll look for better foods to eat, and better places to find this food. And I'll find a way to take an hour for lunch each day."

4. *Action.* We make changes. "Can you please give me sauteed vegetables with tofu? No rush, I'll sip my green tea and chat with my friend while I wait."

5. *Maintenance.* We keep on track. "Hey, I've lost 20 pounds, and I feel so much better. My blood pressure has gone down, and my cholesterol level has dropped. I like the new me, and so does my spouse!"

How do we move from one stage to the next? Let's revisit the five stages.

1. *Precontemplation.* We read general information and statistics to raise our awareness and get us thinking about our behaviors. "People who don't save for the future will work full-time until their mid-seventies or beyond."

2. *Contemplation.* We read specific, targeted information to help us translate thinking into doing. "We should save at least 10 percent of our pay for our eventual retirement, and consider investing part of our portfolio in the stock market."

3. *Preparation.* We develop specific strategies to reach our goals. "I want to retire at age 65, with income of at least $50,000 per year from all sources. I'm using an online calculator to determine how much I should save to retire, considering what I've saved so far and what I expect from Social Security. I will probably need to work a few days a week to get to $50,000, and I'm looking into working part-time at my current employer."

4. *Action.* We make change happen. "I've increased the contribution to my 401(k) plan to 10 percent of pay, and I've reallocated my investment portfolio to be invested two-thirds in stocks."

5. *Maintenance.* We reinforce our positive behaviors to sustain our interest and commitment. "I don't miss eating at expensive restaurants frequently, and my five-year-old car gets me where I want to go just fine. The money I'm saving is growing in my 401(k) plan, and I look forward to the future."

Should We Wait for Scientific Proof?

Do we need conclusive, scientific proof before making important lifestyle changes? If this proof isn't available, then why make changes? If scientists later change their recommendations, why bother making changes now?

For example, years ago researchers urged us to reduce our consumption of eggs, due to their high cholesterol content. Now they tell us that eating eggs in moderation isn't bad for us. Why should we listen to them if they can't get it right?

Establishing the link between lifestyle and health is a complicated detective puzzle. It takes a lot of time and patience. The pieces fall into place over many years as researchers complete more studies and new evidence emerges that improves our understanding. I'm comfortable with making decisions using the most current research, even if it isn't 100 percent conclusive. And I'll be open to changing my mind and my lifestyle as new research adds to our understanding.

For years, cigarette industry executives claimed that the scientific evidence hadn't conclusively established the link between smoking and deadly conditions such as lung cancer and heart disease. Unfortunately, most people who decided that they would continue smoking until this proof was conclusive are now dead from the effects of smoking. They paid a dear price for waiting.

The lifestyle changes that I advocate have varying degrees of supporting scientific proof. The most extensive evidence establishes the link between exercise and diet, and our health and longevity. There is no doubt that Americans eat too much and exercise too little, and if we continue this behavior, we'll pay a dear price in our later years—both economically and emotionally. I'm convinced and am changing my diet and exercise appropriately. There is still controversy over how much exercise and which types of food I should eat, but that isn't an excuse to do nothing to change our behavior. I'm constantly open to new evidence and research as it emerges.

We're a little further behind with the link between environmental toxins and cancer, but not by much. Many studies provide evidence for this link (go on Google and search on the words *pesticides* and *cancer* and you'll be surprised at the pervasiveness of this evidence). However, industry supporters still claim that the evidence isn't yet conclusive. They make a number of arguments—animal trials may not carry over to humans, there are many contributing factors to cancer, everybody's got to die of something when they get old, and so on. It seems that the only experiment that they will accept is if we take two groups of humans that are identical in all respects except one—their exposure to environmental toxins—and measure the rates of illness and mortality 20 years later. This isn't going to happen, and even if it did, do I want to wait for this evidence until it's too late? For me, there is enough evidence of the danger caused by pesticides and other environmental toxins that the burden of proof has shifted. Now, the chemical industry needs to show me conclusive proof that pesticides and other toxins are safe; until then, I'm buying organic and green as much as possible, which is a small price to pay for being on the safe side.

We're near the beginning with establishing the link between other lifestyle choices and health and longevity. However, research is emerging that demonstrates the beneficial impact on our health and longevity of social support systems, engagement with life including work, our ability to handle stress, and our intention to live a healthy life.

We constantly make important life decisions with imperfect information, and planning for our *rest-of-life* is no different. Lately I've tinkered with applying scenario planning (a sophisticated consulting technique) to ordinary life decisions. This technique analyzes the possible consequences of alternative behaviors and their costs.

Here is how this analysis might look for deciding whether to eat organic food now, given that evidence isn't 100 percent conclusive about the link between pesticides and cancer.

In 20 years, has science conclusively established a link between pesticides and the incidence of cancer?	Do I eat organic food now, as much as possible?	
	Yes	No
Yes	I've potentially prevented a very costly illness and early death. The cost is paying a little more for my food.	I'm screwed. I've paid a dear price for being wrong.
No	I've paid a little more for my food, compared to eating conventionally grown food—not a bad price to pay for being wrong.	I gambled with my life, and my "winnings" are small amounts of money that I saved by buying conventionally grown food instead of organic food.

To me, the downside of eating organic food is quite small compared with the potential benefits. When I look at the evidence this way, I don't need to think too hard about this.

We can use similar methods for deciding whether to work part-time, and whether building a supportive social network is worth the trouble.

Whenever we make decisions under uncertainty, the best we can do is gather the best readily available evidence, and then make a decision that feels right to us. Eventually we need to formulate our own beliefs and trust our instincts. There's nothing wrong with that!

And here's one more thing to consider: Doing nothing is still a decision. If we don't change our current behavior with respect to overeating and inadequate exercise, we are choosing poor health, high medical bills, a depleted 401(k) balance, and an early death (while broke). Millions of baby boomers are making this choice—aren't we humans interesting creatures?

Next, we can learn from the mystics.

Let Death Be an Adviser

Imagine we're on our deathbed. We're reliving our life—the triumphs, sorrows, boredoms, accomplishments, loves. It's all over now. There's nothing we can do but accept our fate and move on to whatever comes next.

We think about our regrets, what we should have done but didn't. Could have done, would have done, should have done. . . . The excuses that we told ourselves as justification not to do these things—do they now make sense, or not?

What really has value now? Our relationships with spouse, family, and friends? Or that new car we bought 20 years ago? Did all the time and money we spent to impress others pay off? Did we do our best?

I like to live like I'll die tomorrow. This doesn't mean spend all my money, but it is motivation to do what will make me content with my life if I check out tomorrow. I'll get my money's worth out of life.

I like this quote from a brief speech by Oliver Wendell Holmes:

And so I end with a line from a Latin poet who uttered the message more than fifteen hundred years ago, *"Death plucks my ear and says: Live! I am coming!"*

Finally, let's learn from our kids.

Let's Hold Hands

It's a lot easier if we have support when we make important changes. When we do things together, when our friends and family are watching, we have motivation to carry on. We don't want to let them down and slip. We realize how much others love us, and want us to do well. We bring new information and strategies to our partner's attention.

Of course, if we're married or otherwise have a serious relationship, our spouse or partner will need to buy into some, if not all, of our lifestyle changes. Hopefully they will be enthusiastic about it and join us. Find a friend or loved one to share the journey!

You have to want a full, vital, prosperous, long, happy life, and commit to make it happen. Once we set our intent and act on it, it happens!

The Twenty-First-Century Model for Our *Rest-of-Life*

I n the Introduction, we traced the development of the retirement models that our society had in the nineteenth and twentieth centuries.

The model for the nineteenth century was simple:

Retirement = death

The model for the twentieth century wasn't much more complicated:

Retirement = Not working

In this book, I advocate that we replace our outdated twentieth-century model of retirement with a new twenty-first-century model for living the rest of our lives. This new model takes advantage of the latest research in longevity, health, and happiness, and reflects the realities of living and working in this century.

To summarize, in Table 22.1 I compare the twentieth-century model of retirement to the twenty-first-century model for our *rest-of-life*.

The purpose of this comparison is to provoke discussion. I recognize that these models are idealized and represent the extremes—not everybody falls neatly into one column or the other.

TABLE 22.1 Comparing Our Later Years in the Twentieth and Twenty-first Centuries

	Twentieth-Century Model of Retirement	Twenty-first-Century Model for *Rest-of-Life*
Work/life pattern	Work full-time, then retire full-time in our late fifties or early sixties.	Work full-time, then phased retirement for an extended period through our seventies or beyond, then retire full-time.
Income sources	Pensions, Social Security (post–age 62), capital gains from selling investments, and dividend and interest income from investments.	Wages, dividend and interest income from investments, individually purchased annuities, Social Security (post–age 62).
Attitudes toward health	We don't take a very active role in maintaining our health. We assume problems can be fixed through surgery or prescription drugs.	We take an active role in maintaining our health through diet, exercise, and prevention. If we do this right, we might live to our late eighties, nineties, or even 100.
Paying for medical bills	We are covered by employer-sponsored retiree medical benefits and Medicare (post–age 65).	We are covered by medical insurance as an active employee during our phased retirement period, and then we purchase individual insurance (most likely catastrophic coverage). Hopefully Medicare kicks in at age 65 or soon thereafter. We accumulate financial resources using health spending accounts (HSAs).

TABLE 22.1 *(continued)*

	Twentieth-Century Model of Retirement	Twenty-first-Century Model for *Rest-of-Life*
Living arrangements	Live at home with our spouse, if alive.	Live to have daily contact with a variety of people.
Attitude about productivity and career life cycles	We experience one career over most of our working lifetime, which stops somewhere in our late fifties or early sixties. At that time, we become unproductive and washed out, unable to earn any more money or contribute to society.	We recycle through several careers over our working lifetime. We sustain healthy vigor, productivity, and earning power well into our seventies or beyond. We contribute to society for all our lives.
Attitude toward the rest of our lives	Retirement is "not working."	We very consciously pursue a meaningful, purposeful life and the WAI/WSID issues. We engage in several activities, which might include work.

Also, the timing isn't quite precise. In most respects, the twentieth-century model was more prevalent in the early and middle twentieth century, through the 1980s; one notable exception was that retirement well before age 65 wasn't prevalent until the 1960s. We started evolving toward the twenty-first-century model during the 1990s, but we aren't completely there yet in our thinking. That's the reason for this book!

This ends our journey together. It's been fun! I hope I've given you some insights that make a difference in your *rest-of-life*. I wish you well on your journey, and I will be glad to hear from you. I'll enjoy learning from the insights that you gain on your path.

I'll finish with the Epilogue, which shares how I intend to apply what I've learned for my *rest-of-life*, and has my contact information.

EPILOGUE

Researching and writing this book has significantly changed my life for the better. As I learned about taking care of myself physically, emotionally, and financially, I've incorporated many of the findings into my lifestyle. For example, while writing this book, I reduced my regular work schedule to three days per week. I spent the other two days per week writing and researching, which is something I really wanted to do!

Now I plan to take one of these two days per week and speak about the book. Again, this is something I'm passionate about! I love talking with people in a way that helps their lives. I will spend the other free day pursuing my interests—learning, helping others through service, and taking care of my physical and emotional health.

I'm taking George Vaillant's advice, and am cultivating a rich network of family and friends. As a result of researching for this book, I've made many new friends who have given me new perspectives on living a long, healthy, vital, and happy life.

I also make time for my passionate interests—photography, exploring human potential, and exercise, primarily aikido and hiking. Whenever possible, I try to double up. This includes walking as much as possible to work destinations for exercise, and cultivating relationships while working at my job, pursuing my interests, or exercising.

I'll continue my three days per week at Watson Wyatt indefinitely. This gives me a chance to help younger associates in their development and growth. George Vaillant would call this Generativity and Keeper of the Meaning in the workplace. I have many good friends at work; I realize that I may work *for* a company, but I work *with* people. A healthy work life will balance both aspects. And on a practical basis, I will continue my group medical coverage.

I've taken the Dalai Lama's advice and have evolved my attitude about my work. I see the greater good in our work: We help employers reward and motivate their employees through compensation, benefits, and communications programs. We help meet employees' financial needs through benefits plans. And with all of this, we advocate the fair, decent treatment of employees as not only the most *effective way* to achieve business goals, but the *right* thing to do as well.

I've managed my *I* and *E* such that I need to work only three days per week; I've done this mainly through reducing my *E*. As a result, I feel relaxed and free, and very fortunate. This allows me to donate a significant part of the proceeds of this book and my speeches to my favorite charities, which are protecting the environment, exploring human potential, and helping to alleviate pain and suffering in the world.

I'm taking Martin Seligman's advice, and have a good balance between the *pleasurable life*, the *good life*, and the *meaningful life*. I feel like I'm no longer living a deferred life—I can sustain this life indefinitely!

I still have a lot to work on. I still eat too much meat, and I should exercise more. I plan to explore more on proper nutrition and diet, and on the connection between environmental toxins and our health. While I've lost almost 20 pounds since I started on this book, I'm still a few pounds away from my target weight. I don't need to tell myself that I've got dense muscles and bones; instead I lost the density in my brain! I don't miss the extra food, and rich foods are no longer appetizing most of the time. I'm also continually improving management of my *E*, and it's taking awhile to change long-ingrained spending habits. However, now I have the time and motivation to continue working on these goals. I don't need instant progress on all fronts; steady progress will do just fine.

Writing this book has also been very therapeutic for me, at an important time in my life. Just before I started writing, I experienced a great personal loss—without much warning, my wife filed for divorce. I was totally surprised, and it was a shattering experience. Words are inadequate to express the shock, pain, and disappointment that I felt. After I settled down, I knew what to do to heal. I let the tremendous jolt of this event give me the energy to make important changes in my life—to find my true calling. This included writing this book and helping people plan for a healthy, vital *rest-of-life*. Along the way, I heard the case histories of so many other people who faced greater challenges and disappointments, but just kept going on with their lives. I was greatly inspired by their stories, and persisted with the attitude that life goes on. It doesn't end with events that are beyond my control, and there are so many exciting things to do and learn in this world.

Much faster than I ever imagined, I experienced firsthand George Vaillant's wisdom about the value of a supportive network of family and friends. Their love and support helped me recover quite quickly and move on with my life. Also, in a perverse way, I took inspiration from the stock market, as I discussed in Chapter 11. I took a chance in life with the hope to make it richer. I got burned, but more importantly, I *survived* this unfortunate experience and went on to *thrive*. And now, I am in a much better place, just like the others who have inspired me! I have no fear of the future—just a confidence that I will do the best I can to deal with whatever happens, just like so many other people have done.

Now I want to devote a lot of feeling and thinking energy to growing my relationships with my friends and family. I hope to spend much more time giving of myself in service to the community. I'm sure that I will experience more setbacks, disappointments, and tragedies in the future, hopefully to be balanced by good memories and occasional triumphs. But I have no deep fears—this is all part of what it means to "just keep on living"—advice from the centenarians!

I'll keep on learning and seeking on all the topics of this book—what to do with my life, how to stay healthy, and my finances. I'll share what I learn in my web site—www.restoflife.com. Also, I elaborate on some concepts—I couldn't fit it all in one book. Come visit some time!

I feel very fortunate to have embarked on this learning journey. I started focusing just on attaining financial security for my *rest-of-life*. To pursue this goal, we certainly need to do a good job of managing our financial resources. However, I learned that this isn't enough. Life has so much uncertainty that our real security comes from our resilience, our attitudes, our intentions, our relationships, our curiosity, and our ongoing engagement with life. After exploring happiness and health in addition to wealth, I feel confident and optimistic for fully enjoying my *rest-of-life*.

I have been inspired by this quote from the introduction of Roy Walford's book *The Anti-Aging Plan*, in which he describes the reasons for his personal interest in longevity research:

> To me, even a fairly long life seemed far too short to explore the world's outward wonders and humanity's inner realms, to walk all the strange pathways of society's subcultures, to read all the books, hear all the music, climb the mountains and dive the seas, to be present at least at the early stages of the age of space.

However, I've learned that I need even more compelling reasons to keep on living with health and vitality well into my eighties, nineties, and even to 100. Fortunately, I don't need to look far for these reasons. We baby boomers have unfinished business. The challenges and causes that aroused our passions in our twenties still await us—saving the environment, eliminating poverty, improving education, promoting justice and equality—there's plenty to live for!

Now I've expressed how I want to live my *rest-of-life*, and I'm building a financial plan to support it!

I speak passionately about the ideas in this book, and plan to give seminars and workshops. If you think these messages will resonate with a group you are affiliated with, please contact me as follows:

Steve Vernon
Watson Wyatt Worldwide
steve.vernon@restoflife.com

or visit my web site, www.restoflife.com.

I sincerely hope that this book has helped you. I wish you the best for your *rest-of-life*!

Best regards,

INDEX

ABOUT THE AUTHOR

 Steve Vernon is a vice president and consulting actuary with Watson Wyatt Worldwide, the influential human resources consulting firm. For 30 years, he has helped large corporations design, administer, communicate, and fund their retirement, benefits, and rewards programs. Over the years, his clients have included Agilent, Charles Schwab, ChevronTexaco, Dole Food Company, Home Savings of America, Hughes Electronics, Lockheed Martin, City of Los Angeles, Northrop Grumman, Phillips Petroleum (now ConocoPhillips), RAND Corporation, Teledyne Technologies, and Times Mirror (publisher of the Los Angeles Times, now part of Tribune, Inc).

He has published two books with John Wiley & Sons, titled:

- *Employee Benefits: Valuation, Analysis, and Strategies.*

- *Don't Work Forever!: Simple Steps Baby Boomers Must Take to Ever Retire.*

He has published several articles on retirement, benefits, and rewards topics; is quoted frequently in such publications as the *Wall Street Journal, New York Times, BusinessWeek, USAToday, Fortune* magazine, and *Money* magazine; and has appeared on television and radio shows on retirement issues. He is an accomplished speaker, appearing in front of over 150 audiences with his book tour for *Don't Work Forever!*

Steve is a Fellow in the Society of Actuaries and an Enrolled Actuary. He also teaches aikido and holds a second-degree black belt. He graduated summa cum laude from the University of California, Irvine, with a double major in mathematics and social science, and is a member of Phi Beta Kappa.